MAKING MONEY MAKING MUSIC

(NO MATTER WHERE YOU LIVE)

· JAMES W. DEARING ·

Cincinnati, Ohio

Making Money Making Music. Copyright 1982 by James Dearing. Printed and bound in the United States of America. All rights reserved. No part of this book may be reproduced in any form or by any electronic or mechanical means including information storage and retrieval systems without permission in writing from the publisher, except by a reviewer who may quote brief passages in a review. Published by Writer's Digest Books, 9933 Alliance Road, Cincinnati, Ohio 45242. First edition.

Library of Congress Cataloging in Publication Data

Dearing, James
    Making money making music.

    1. Music trade—United States. 2. Music—Economic aspects. I. Title.
ML3790.D36   1982   780'.42'02373   82-17617
ISBN 0-89879-089-1
ISBN 0-89879-101-4 (pbk.)

Design by Barron Krody.

The Permissions Acknowledgments on the following page constitute an extension of the copyright page.

• PERMISSIONS ACKNOWLEDGMENTS •

Quotation from *A Musician's Guide to the Road*, copyright 1981, by Gary Burton, reprinted by permission of Billboard Publications, Inc.

Quotation from *The Music/Record Career Handbook*, copyright 1980, by Joseph Csida, reprinted by permission of Billboard Publications, Inc.

Quotation from *You Can Negotiate Anything*, by Herb Cohen, copyright 1980 by Lyle Stuart Books, Inc. Used by permission.

Quotation from *The Power of Positive Thinking*, by Norman Vincent Peale, copyright 1952 by Prentice-Hall, Inc., renewed 1980. Used by permission.

Quotation from *Music Business Handbook and Career Guide*, 3rd edition, by David Baskerville, copyright 1982 by the Sherwood Company. Used by permission.

Quotation from *Getting Ahead in the Music Business*, copyright 1979 by Ronald Zalkind, reprinted by permission of Schirmer Books, a Division of Macmillan Publishing Co.

Quotation from *Psychology Today* magazine, copyright 1971 by Ziff-Davis Publishing Company. Used by permission.

• ACKNOWLEDGMENTS •

Though a book project begins with robust enthusiasm, it ends somewhere between weariness and satisfaction. Without help from the following people, I'm sure I'd feel wearier and much less satisfied.

First, a gracious thank you to the band I quit to write this book for being understanding, supportive, and cooperative.

To the following people, thanks for your valuable time and advice: Craig Anderton, Nick Angiulo, Martin Ashly, Joe Balardino, Don Barker, Kurt Bischoff, Bruce Bolin, Steve Boutte, Jerry Campbell, Dottie Carpenter, Don Clayson, Brian Cutler, Kim Fowley, Michael Frazin, John Jackman, Barbara Johnson, Dave Knepprath, Stan Lunetta, John Morris, Andy Penn, Bill Perasso, Todd Popple, Greg Saul, Joe Scharfenberger, Lynn Stradley, Gene Thorpe, Rod Toner, Rick Van Horn, Stu Walphall, and Dave Weil.

No less valuable was the expert (and speedy!) assistance of the photographers I worked with: Ellen Forsyth, Ivan T. Hafstrom, Pat Johnson, and Greg Savalin.

Thank you, Carol Cartaino, for recognizing a good idea and making it better, and a very special thank you to Editor Beth Franks, who helped me with all the hard work it takes to bring any good idea to reality.

This book would not have been possible without Bud Gardner's advice on career direction, and Shirley Biagi's further definition of that direction.

Finally—to my parents, for their support and for listening to all that loud music, and to Rebecca, for everything else.

• WHAT THIS BOOK CAN DO FOR YOU •

How many people do you know who have tried, and tried, and tried—and are *still* trying to make consistently good money as musicians?

Unfortunately, there are far too many. "Everyone aims for the top," laughed one musician, "and they totally overlook the middle." So many musicians miss the pot of gold because they're looking in the wrong place!

An enormous amount of "middle money" is there for the taking, right where you live. You can find jobs at churches, nightclubs, high schools, colleges, recording studios, small concerts, weddings, dances, drama productions—almost anywhere! You can even make good money at your own home, in your spare time.

This book will show you how to build your earnings quickly by diversifying your musical talent and building a sound base of business savvy. You'll learn how to plan, audition, select, and present a live performing act; how to promote yourself and your band; how to land recording jobs; how to teach students; and how to uncover many other local markets for your musical skills.

This is not a book about record contracts, record companies, or how to become a millionaire singing star; however, the strategies herein will give you the knowledge you need to "keep afloat" if you do decide to pursue a recording contract. This book explains the newest proven methods for getting a contract (methods no other musician career book even mentions).

I've divided this book into three parts. The first describes my system for making a lot of money locally by carefully examining all the potential markets, diversifying time and talent, and deciding which jobs to pursue. The second part offers detailed instructions for developing a solid financial base by forming, rehearsing, promoting, and leading a live performing act, whether it be a solo act, a duet, or a full-fledged band. The third part concentrates on expanding your income through other musical employment opportunities, including independent studios, TV stations, churches, schools, theaters, working as an "agent-musician," organizing a home recording studio, renting equipment, selling your music and lyrics through the mail.

Whether you're a seasoned local professional or a fresh-out-of-high-school novice, this is the book for you. I've had the same problems you've had making ends meet and hoping for that big break, looking for ways to make what you love best actually pay off. This book is jam packed with answers from my experiences and with advice from other successful musicians. The days of the starving musician are over!

• INTRODUCTION •

In the summer of 1979 I was talking with the guitarist of the most popular band in my town. I had often wondered how this band, which for eight years had been setting and then breaking club attendance records throughout the Sacramento and San Joaquin Valleys, had remained so successful. His answer stunned me.

"We don't care about making it big. When we finally stopped aiming for a recording contract, we became popular. Now there's no anxiety about getting somewhere, because we're already here!"

But where was here? Sacramento? Everyone knows that Sacramento is *not* a musician's haven. There's no big money for musicians in Sacramento! The big money is in Los Angeles, Nashville, New York. Could this group of musicians be doing any better than the rest of the local bands, who dismissed Sacramento as a stepping stone to better money?

"We average about $850 a night," he added, "but sometimes we'll give up three $800 nights for one $2,000 dance."

My band certainly wasn't making that kind of money. He went on to explain that since the group wasn't under any pressure to achieve world fame (like my band was), they could concentrate on enjoying themselves. This feeling of pure joy was transferred to the audience, who danced and drank, and the bar manager, who happily rang up hefty bar tabs. The more I thought about it, the more sense it made: *A musician who shows long-term commitment to a local clientele can command higher wages.* Musicians who only want to establish themselves locally have no uncertainty about the future, and lack of security is the main reason most musicians eventually get scared into premature retirement. By aiming locally, you can concentrate your advertising efforts. Effective advertising builds a loyal following, and since the bands with the largest followings earn the most money, you'll have it made!

Still, this theory surely had flaws. Sometimes bands have difficulty securing consistent employment. Many band musicians don't work during the day, thus a lot of potential money-making time is wasted. The answer was obvious, but someone else had to show it to me.

One afternoon I was in a small recording studio laying down a drum track for a friend. The friend had also hired a singer to add vocals. After I had finished, we began discussing careers, and I happened to ask if this was her first time in a recording studio.

"Oh, no," she replied. "I record every other week on Mondays and Wednesdays." She went on to tell me she also taught vocal lessons, wrote songs, and was leaving soon with a group to try their luck in Nashville.

Now here was a musician making good money recording, teaching, and writing songs, but she was willing to gamble it all on a slim chance in Nashville where she would compete head to head with some of the recording world's best musicians.

All musicians (and I'm no exception) sooner or later want to try their luck at striking it rich. But what lesson did I learn from this woman? Those odd but consistent jobs are the other main requirement for succeeding, and indeed prospering, as a local musician. A musician must *diversify* to maximize income.

These, then, are the two essentials for earning money as a musician, the basic strategies underlying this book. To maximize your income, you must show long-term commitment to local clientele and be willing to diversify your talent.

You *can* prosper as a musician. This book is a logical, step-by-step guide for developing your career. The industry is crowded with musicians; you'll always be competing for the work you get. But staying local in perspective and practicing the skills presented in this book will give you a sharp, definitive edge over the rest of the field.

• TABLE OF CONTENTS •

Part One
Taking the First Step

Chapter One:
Look Before You Leap   2
Why this is the best career you could possibly choose/What's happening to the recording industry?/*Localization* is the key to being discovered/Guess What—the other music books are putting you on!/Staying where you are is the best move you could ever make/Just learning chords? No problem!/Get ready to make big money doing what you really like.

Chapter Two:
Can You Really Freelance as a Full-Time Musician?   12
Hometown is smalltime? The "experts" are nuts!/Why full-time freelancing works/Hold on to your day job until you're musically diversified/Starting slowly just in case/Juggling your schedule and your commitments.

Chapter Three:
Diversification Is the Key   20
Diversify your jobs and your style and you'll never be out of work/The live act that's always in the money/The creativity roller coaster/Think small, deposit big/A large act can sound great, but they don't make much money/Do you have what it takes to be a soloist?

Chapter Four:
The Market Analysis   36
A new, tested approach to finding all the employers you'll ever need/Researching at home and in the library/How to find the jobs that pay the most/Keep your ears open, and write down what you hear/Rating your opportunities/Defining your market.

Part Two
Building a Solid Financial Base

Chapter Five:
Selecting a Group   58
The cornerstone of a large local income/Should you start the group?/Maintaining a power balance in the band/What to ask potential partners/The Musician Personality Test/Decide together on career direction/Do you want to be famous or just rich?

Chapter Six:
Pulling It All Together—
Now What Do You Need?   80
Buying the right equipment for the right price/Whittling down music store prices/Becoming a loyal customer/Why not buy at dealer cost?/Making your own superior equipment and instruments for petty cash/Keeping ownership hassle-free.

Chapter Seven:
Rehearsing the Act   94
Getting serious about playing around/Choose a central location/What's the big difference between practice and rehearsal?/Taping rehearsals to critique your sound/The more exciting you are, the more money you'll get/Stage show tips/Rehearse the show just like the music.

Chapter Eight:
Stack the Deck in Your Favor   110
Define your image/Create a visual association/Ins and outs of the promo package/All about presentation/If you really want to get crazy. . ./Judging and mixing your live sound.

Chapter Nine:
Business Leadership   134

Getting your offstage act together/Give each member a share of the load/ You (or someone else) must be an irrepressible salesperson/Don't underestimate the time involved/Here's what you need to know when booking the band/Band accounting is as easy as one, two, three/Keep the communication lines open.

Chapter Ten:
How to Maximize Performance Earnings   152

How much money are you worth?/Some smaller gigs actually pay better than the bigger jobs/The basics of negotiating—competition or cooperation?/Sample negotiations/Promotion is sometimes better than cash for artists on the rise/The power of a loyal following/Earn a week's salary in one night playing casuals.

Chapter Eleven:
You're a Professional, So Act the Role   174

The unspoken things your employers expect/Always start on time!/On-the-spot management disputes/Silence is golden/When women performers should be extra careful.

Chapter Twelve:
Stayin' Alive   182

The health hazards of performing/Staying in shape/Alcohol, marijuana, and amphetamines: What's their effect on you?/The new anti-drug crusading musicians/To tour or not to tour—that is the question.

Part Three
The Hidden
(and Richly Worth Investigating)
Markets

Chapter Thirteen:
Guess What—You're a Music Teacher!   200

Who says you're not qualified?/Choosing where to teach/That important initial meeting/Homework assignments/Feeling guilty/The foolproof method for making students pay/How about $100 an hour?/Odd jobs at schools, and bona fide public teaching.

Chapter Fourteen:
Layin' Down Tracks 216
Small studios are run differently than the studios you've heard about/ Who's who in the independent studio/What directors look for in studio musicians/Getting yourself hired/Local jingles/Artistic sessions/Bringing business to the studio/Doubling your money/Host your own TV music program.

Chapter Fifteen:
How to Organize a Home Recording Studio 234
A place to diversify from/The investment/Learn as you go/Temporary vs. permanent studios/Create a warm, comfortable atmosphere/Cater to your clients/Recording jingles at home.

Chapter Sixteen:
Why Let All that Equipment Sit Around? 248
Who'll pay to use your equipment?/Renting equipment, not yourself/ Keep the gear in working order/Avoid hassles by mixing the sound yourself/Is this worth your time?

Chapter Seventeen:
The Agent-Musician 256
Turn $50 into $300—in one hour!/The agent option/Success requirements/Be an extrovert/The home business office.

Chapter Eighteen:
Checking Out Churches 264
The changing church/The bigger the church, the bigger the check/Getting the job/Organizing your weekly program/Christian rock.

Chapter Nineteen:
Selling Lyrics and Music—by Mail! 274
The $30,000 question/It's more than inspiration/Disregarding the formula/The test: Do your songs measure up to the hits?/Manipulating the odds/Living by the multiple query/References and the rules/Keeping track of who's got what/Negotiating with publishers.

Chapter Twenty:
Regional, Then National Growth 288
I thought this was a "local" career book/Why the strong record compan-

ies have weakened/How can you grab their attention?/Your launching pad is right in your own hometown/What a company looks for nowadays/Independent production means higher bidding/Why a small label may be better/Long, complex solutions are often the best: Make the album yourself!

Afterword   302

Index   303

• PART ONE •

TAKING THE FIRST STEP

CHAPTER ONE

LOOK BEFORE YOU LEAP

Every year thousands of musicians give up their dreams of making money making music. Why do they put their instruments in storage and start selling insurance? Because they've been disillusioned by the myth that "making it big is the name of the game." Actually, the Big Time isn't the answer to financial success at all. Record royalties from major labels are a painful, bitter joke to most contracted musicians. But more and more musicians are discovering how to make a living—or enhance one—by playing music. C'mon—read this short chapter and decide if music is attractive to you.

Music's Magic

People study and master musical skills for many different reasons. My career began in a typically unceremonious manner. I was raised in a family that had adopted four Hawaiians, so rhythmical Polynesian music featuring an array of percussive instruments was always playing on the phonograph along with an occasional ballet, a musical or two, and the new rock 'n' roll. Soon my older brother began drumming on pots, pans, ironing boards, and finally on a real drum set. It didn't take long for me to follow the beat he laid down.

Other musicians tell similar stories. Many have generations of musicians in their families, and they were simply "expected" to play an instrument or sing. A great many musicians get started in elementary or secondary school by playing in the band. Nowadays guitar inspires thousands of new musicians. And who hasn't heard stories of torturous piano lessons under the keen watch of a strict teacher? But regardless of how you began your career, the reasons why you and thousands of others remain active musicians probably fall into one or more of six categories:

A career in music is exciting—but you don't need to move to L.A., New York, or Nashville to make it big. The best money can be made right in your hometown.

(photo of Bobby Thompson by Greg Savalin)

1. *It's fun.* Of course! This is why music is so popular as a hobby, part, and full-time job. Whether performing live or recording, we have a blast! How many occupations can boast that employees freely choose to attend nonpaying work practice sessions? Although it lowers our per hour wage substantially, the fact that we rehearse our job prior to performing is a sure sign we enjoy this line of work. Nonmusicians envy the fun we have. A conversation between me and a 9-to-5 worker predictably goes like this:

"Hi, Jim, what have you been up to?"

"Well, I just recorded with a church group for a promotion campaign of theirs, I'm organizing a drum line for the high school, and our band is booked solid. How about you?"

"Aw, I'm still working for IBM. It's boring, but it pays all right."

Now, tell me, whose eyes are glowing green with envy? Who's having the most fun in life?

2. *It's exciting.* This is the crux of any musical job. You're the center of attention. If you're teaching students, the students listen attentively to you. If you're in a studio, everything depends on your performance. If you're performing live, colored lights illuminate you as the audience sits in darkness. People go out of their way to meet you, because in their eyes, you're special. It doesn't matter that with a little practice and confidence they, too, could be on stage receiving applause. You're doing it, and they don't need to know you're really hiding behind that guitar!

3. *It's different.* Music is not an everyday occupation. It requires some special skills. You need a little talent (the more the better, but just a little will do), a good business sense, the ability to plan and set goals, a friendly, extroverted personality, a sense of humor, and an adventurous disposition.

Thanks to these special skills (I'll help you with any you're insecure about, don't worry!), you will also be treated differently. People will seek out your services. You'll be in the driver's seat, dictating your own wages. The important thing to remember is that you can do something other people don't consider themselves worthy of doing. This gives you bargaining power.

4. *It's creative.* People enjoy their hobbies, whether cooking, needlepoint, soccer, or music, because these pursuits allow room for creative expression. Everyone loves to forget inflation, crime, and routine everyday worries, and absorption in a creative activity provides a convenient and fascinating escape. Many people are uncomfortable in their jobs because creativity is stifled, so why not make your job a creative endeavor? Those who do, refuse to retire. Musicians, professional athletes, artists, clothing designers, and many self-employed entrepreneurs refuse to quit that which fulfills them and brings them pleasure. As a local musician, you have much more opportunity for creative expression than the average person.

5. *It's instant gratification.* Normal jobs offer little gratification to employees when they perform a task well. Fast-food cooks might get a 10-cent raise every three months, but rare is the direct compliment on a perfectly cooked burger. Gasoline-station attendants never get rave reviews for filling the tank with gas. When was the last time you broke into applause when a cashier accurately rang up your purchase? Yet, as a musician—teacher, songwriter, live performer, or studio musician—you will constantly be reminded of your skill and ability. It's even possible to perform poorly and still be smothered with accolades from listeners. The encouragement we instantly receive from our audience, as well as from other musicians, students, and technicians, makes us feel good. As musicians, we experience instantaneous appreciation few people ever enjoy.

6. *It's adventurous.* Obviously, this is also a disadvantage of being a freelance musician. Our jobs are notoriously short-lived. However, this is exactly why many people choose to make money as a musician.

I hate routine jobs. Predictability breeds dissatisfaction in me, so when a job fails to offer me something new, I start looking for other employment. The life of a freelance musician is neither routine nor boring. You'll meet more people than you have time to keep track of—restaurant owners, waitresses, school band directors, booking agents, tour guides, dancers, musical directors, sound technicians, and of course, other musicians. You'll even become good friends with the nearby late night coffee shop employees. Then suddenly, whooosh! You'll be playing somewhere else—in a new studio, for new clients—and making new contacts. Nothing is predictable in the music business, and in Chapter 10 I'll explain how you can use this to your advantage when negotiating for better money.

I'd like to add that you advance according to your degree of ambition, but sometimes this isn't true. Luck and circumstance play a major role in getting ahead, but a self-employed musician does have more control over what he achieves than the typical 9-to-5 worker. You will make, or share in making, career decisions affecting you. Musicians unanimously agree that perseverance finally pays off. Most musical stars who appear to have become overnight sensations actually have worked long and hard for the breaks.

Exploding the Music Myth

Oh, for the life of a rock star! Long black limos, piles of coke, and cases of Perrier in the dressing room. How could any life be sweeter? Sex, drugs, and rock 'n' roll forever!

Sober up, friend. Because rock album sales are caught in a dizzying downward spiral, record companies can't afford all the luxuries they used to provide for stars. Tour support money has been chiseled away. Groups travel lighter and are forced to economize. The industry has been in shambles for several years. Video games are stealing as much as $1 billion a year from record companies. According to a 1982 survey by Warner Communications, more than $2.85 billion worth of pre-recorded music was taped at home in 1980. Another $400 million is lost annually to counterfeiting. What does all this mean? It means the record industry is hard up. And the cutbacks are coming at your expense. Columbia Records signed 25 new acts in 1979; in 1981 the count was down to 10. Why? Because it costs a quarter of a million dollars to launch a new act. And the acts that do get signed aren't making it.

"The hits still hit very high," Atlantic Records Chairman Ahmet Ertegun told the *Wall Street Journal*. "There are plenty of albums that sell from three to four million copies. Where we're suffering is in the middle range," meaning albums made by new, developing acts.

Walter Yetnikoff, President of CBS Records, agrees: "Albums that might once have sold 250,000 copies now only do 50,000."

This means that artists who are signed aren't making much—if any—money. More than ever before, a contract doesn't mean you're independently wealthy. In fact, most musicians would be better off *turning down contract offers!*

According to Ronald Zalkind, in *Getting Ahead in the Music Business* (Schirmer Books), the expenses an artist incurs for record production often outweigh record royalties:

"Let us now hypothesize an artist with initial record royalties, on the sale of 100,000 units, of $40,600. The artist has a personal manager who gets 20 percent off the top, which reduces the $40,600 figure to $32,480. The average cost of producing an album today (which is what our hypothetical artist ran up at session costs) is $75,000. This means that the artist owes the record company $34,400. Also, the artist receives a $10,000 advance against royalties as bare subsistence income on which federal, state, and local taxes were paid. This raises the artist's outstanding debt, on his first release, to $44,400.

"Now, let us suppose that the artist's second album with the record company sells gold: the initial payout, less container charges, is $203,000. The personal manager gets 20 percent, which brings the artist's take down to $162,400. The artist owes $44,400 from the first album, which further reduces the artist's gold record income to $118,000. Finally, the artist spent $100,000 on the second go-round in the studio and took a $15,000 advance. With a gold record on the wall, the artist after two successful album releases, has only earned $3,000."

Zalkind adds a further sobering touch to the reality of the big time recording musician:

"Our hypothetical artist was also very lucky. Most artists never even approach selling gold. . . . How do they make a living? How do they survive? It can be very rough for a very long time—perhaps the artist's lifetime."

Compare that chilling hypothesis with a local one—let's say a Holiday Inn circuit job. Your band was offered a six-month western states tour by an agent who represents Holiday Inn. These hotels typically book a band for a one-month run—then you pack up and perform at each subsequent Holiday Inn for one month. The agent likes your band and thinks you're good, so he gets you $1,800 a week. The agent takes his cut immediately, which is 10 percent, or $180. The remainder, $1,620, is divided five ways (singer, guitar, keyboards, bass, and drums). This comes out to $324 each. Holiday Inn also provides free rooms for the band, and some throw in a complimentary breakfast. Now multiply your weekly $324 by six months for a tidy sum of $7,776. Who's making more money—the struggling Los Angeles band in debt to a recording company, or your Holiday Inn band, unknown but fat in the pocket?

"Our album cost $180,000," one drummer said whose group had a deal with Epic Records. "We got better promotion in the trade journals and major markets than most bands, and a tour with Pablo Cruise. But still, I personally lost a lot of money. I could have made a hell of a lot more by staying home and playing."

The big-time recording industry is perilous for musicians in general. Why waste your time on a long shot when you can take in thousands of dollars by concentrating in your own locality?

Why Every Other Musician Career Book Is Obsolete

If you're bound and determined to be a star, this still is the book that'll get you there. How can I make such a claim? It's easy. Every band signed nowadays has to be proven locally, or the big boys won't even blink.

The process of sending off demo tapes to record companies has been obsolete for several years. Why authors of music career books haven't recognized this trend, I have no idea. It's inexcusable. Except with publishing companies and small record companies, the demo tape is ineffective. After having demo after demo returned, you begin wondering whether companies are even listening to your tape. Be assured, some don't. Entire artist and repertoire departments have been closed at some companies.

"We sent out countless demos," laments one singer, "until we decided to test whether they were even being listened to. I wound each tape to a certain word on the first song, and when the tapes came back, they were all on that same word! They just took the tape out of our envelope and stuffed it in theirs."

If you really want a record contract, you must take control of your own destiny by *making* the companies notice you. This book shows you how. Then you can let CBS and Warner fight tooth and nail over you!

Why Build a Solid Local Base

You will never be financially secure until you can always play somewhere. The glow of earning $500 in one week tarnishes quickly when you're left jobless for the following two weeks. Strategies for discovering, analyzing, and rating opportunities, along with a system for staying steadily employed, will be discussed in Chapter 4. A money-making musician always has a network of jobs to fall back on. Think of yourself as an octopus, with all eight arms spread out, feeling for new ways to sell your talents to various markets.

An obvious advantage of localizing your talent is that people come to know, trust, and eventually to depend on you. Local television producers will phone if they need a special sound track or advice on a music show; nightclub owners will call to offer schedule openings; high school band directors will turn to you when their load becomes unbearable. Nurture these contacts! As your name becomes familiar, you can charge higher fees for your services.

Talent Is Optional

Anyone who believes that all successful local musicians, or even all international musicians, are incredibly talented is incredibly naive. Of course, there *are* thousands of immensely talented musicians playing professionally, but in this age of advertising and promotion, talent is often an unnecessary ingredient for success. Especially in a local setting, where critical standards of musical skill tend to be modest, studio musicians don't need to be exciting improvisers if they are adept chart readers. The best hiding place of all for unaccomplished musicians is in a local band.

One bandleader I know has an extroverted personality that would embarrass Don Rickles. He handles all the bookings for his band, and seldom does a club owner get the best of him in a deal. Unfortunately, his singing is reminiscent of Jimmy Durante, and his guitar strumming is standard three-chord fare. Yet, he's the band's most valuable member. Why? Because he excels in the non-musical matters, which are just as important to an act as musical talent is.

Here's another example.

There aren't many female drummers around, but I'm fortunate enough to know two. One of them, Diane, has only been drumming for a year and a half as of this writing—a novice.

Four months ago, Diane excitedly told me that she was auditioning for a working band. Tactfully, I urged her to hold off and keep practicing until she was more proficient. After all, I stressed, she was only a beginner. So what did Diane do? Not only did she go to the audition, but she got the job! Diane was smart enough to develop a strategy and stick to it: She knew her musical limits, so she carefully picked out a country band, which didn't require elaborate drumming. She makes good money with that group.

No, you don't need a heap of musical talent to make money locally. It helps if you can sing like Bette Midler or pick like Larry Carlton, but with determination, guile, and ingenuity, almost anyone can make it as a local performer.

Prepare to Start

Are you still determined to pursue the freelance musician's life because:

- **Playing music is fun.**
You'll never be happier.
- **Performing is exciting.**
You'll be the center of attention.
- **You'll be treated differently.**
Musicians are thought to be special. (Ha!)
- **Music is creative.**
You'll actually be paid to do something you love.
- **You'll get instant gratification.**
Unlike virtually all other jobs.
- **The job is unpredictable.**
You won't know what "boring" means.
- **Talent is optional.**
Still don't believe me? Go to some local bars and see for yourself!

And don't forget the money! So:
Go for the local jobs.
The pot of gold is at *this* end of the rainbow.
Establish a solid local base.
Diversify your talents and you'll always have plenty of jobs to fall back on.

Some of you have already discovered the validity of these points through experience. You've recorded, sung in churches, and performed at bars, dinner clubs, and parties, maybe even a bowling alley or two. You know the headaches of rehearsing, auditioning, and landing jobs. I'm going to help you to reorganize, starting at square one, so from now on every move you make will have a definite, career-advancing, money-making motive behind it.

If you have never earned any money as a musician before, you'll learn how to plan a strategy which will advance you quickly into the ranks of well-paid local musicians.

Last, and most important, you'll learn how to minimize expenses while maximizing profits. Too many musicians squander money needlessly.

Chapters 2 and 3—like this one—are "reading" chapters. With Chapter 4 we'll get down to actualizing your goal of making money making music—no matter where you live!

• CHAPTER TWO •

CAN YOU REALLY FREELANCE AS A FULL-TIME MUSICIAN?

Most musicians prefer to work as musicians—why shouldn't they prefer that over routine desk jobs and other mundane livelihoods? Despite their desire to work with music, many musicians still hover somewhere between part-time and full-time musical employment. They dream of getting away from 9-to-5 jobs and concentrating all their efforts on music. But only with good planning does it become reality.

"Can I really freelance as a full-time musician? Is full-time employment more worthwhile than part-time employment? Will I be able to expand my income once I get started? Does starting my career require a lot of time and planning?" The answers to your questions are Yes, Yes, Yes and Yes!

Are the Experts Telling the Truth?

Wage scales for journeymen musicians in cocktail lounges, restaurants, piano bars and other live-performance locations vary but in all cases are rather minimal. How minimal, I will not try to detail. Suffice to say that plumbers, electricians, sanitation department workers and any number of practitioners in other fields not only earn more money than musicians, but also have considerably more work available.

—Joseph Csida
The Music/Record Career Handbook

You probably know that local musicians *can* make poor money, but they don't have to. More to the point, *you* don't have to!

What I'm advocating—working as a full-time local musician—runs directly against the grain of what other music career books urge you to do. They tell you to chase the stars. In their haste they overlook—indeed, dismiss—local possibilities.

But why should musicians behave like cattle being herded together for slaughter? A prerequisite for financial success in a crowded line of work (like music) is distinction. Stand out! You can do this by shifting your emphasis from international stardom to local success. If you value your local job contacts, rather than stepping on them as thousands of cattle (excuse me, musicians) do in their stampede into oblivion, employers will appreciate your down-to-earth, businesslike attitude, and rehire you consistently. Let's face it: Employers need musicians they can count on again and again. By respecting your employers, you'll develop a hell of a local income.

Making the Move—Why Full-Timing It Works

An important advantage of full-time musical employment, especially for live performing acts, is your "down-time." I mean the hours spent formulating, rehearsing, and promoting—everything but the actual job. Unlike working behind a cash register, an incredible amount of time goes into musical preparation. Interestingly, the down-time needed to keep a part-time musical career afloat and advancing can be as much, if not more, than the down-time required for a full-time musical job.

What songs will you learn? Where will you practice? Do you need new equipment? These and many more questions must be answered regardless of how often the band performs. Then, you'll attempt to book the band. It's not easy trying to sell a club owner on a part-time band. His first question is, "Where have you played before?" to which you sputter, "Well, uh, we played downtown a couple of months ago." You know what's going through his head? "Gee, these guys can't be very good if they haven't played in two months . . . They're only part-timers . . . No one will recognize their name, not much of a draw . . . My usual $300 is way too much . . ." And though a full-time band must always be looking for new bookings, the word-of-mouth advertising and references they enjoy make owners easier to persuade. They know they're getting a well-rehearsed, professional act, and they'll pay for it.

The biggest chore a full-time band eliminates is repetitive rehearsals. Whereas a part-time group must regularly review material, full-time musicians consider performance their rehearsal.

I can remember rehearsing long nights with several part-time bands. We all needed to stay up on our chops, that was number one. We also had to go over each song once or twice; after all, we hadn't performed since the weekend before last. With full-time groups I've played in, keeping up the chops was never a problem—we played every night! And most clubs allot bands designated times each day to rehearse or learn new material, thereby eliminating set-up and tear-down time at a separate rehearsal room.

Another problem part-time musicians suffer is a lack of commitment. When no one is giving 100 percent to a band, personal priorities such as vacations and parties tend to outweigh practice or even performance. Because of this lack of commitment members come and go at a rapid rate. Most part-time bands just aren't efficient businesses.

As you pay your bills, and wonder if you could do as well solely on a musician's income, consider that most musicians don't use their time to optimum advantage. Entire days are wasted. Only a few musicians are resourceful enough to organize a teaching schedule, act as agents, present school instrument seminars, rent out P.A. equipment, or operate a studio. I know plenty of local musicians who make a decent living playing in bands, *but very few who earn as much as they could.* Don't underestimate yourself!

Keep a Daytime Job—for Now

Now you know the disadvantages of playing in a part-time band: the pay's lousy, rehearsals are needed, you must self-promote, commitment is lacking, and it's a poor use of time. Now guess what I want you to do. Yep! That's right. I want you to start out in a part-time band. This is particularly important if you currently have a job. Here's why:

1. Part time minimizes risk.

Clearly your objective is to make as much money as possible with local music opportunities, but investigating and critically choosing jobs must come first. By only involving yourself part-time, you can judge prospective jobs more objectively because you're not yet in the position of *needing* the music income. You can still pause, stand back, and decide if the rewards will be worth your efforts.

2. Another job is security and financial flexibility.

I've already mentioned that musicians rarely have the reassurance of job security. Keeping a daytime job equals security. And unless you're already fully equipped, you'll need some money to finance instruments and equipment. Even if you are already equipped, there will be initial band promotional costs to pay. Many musicians take on a day job for the explicit reason of buying new equipment. One month of waiting tables or installing sprinkler systems seems short when the money is put toward a new Mesa Boogie amplifier.

3. Consider it a testing period.

One burning example comes to mind. Two year ago the Sacramento club scene was in a musical lull. Several of the more active, popular groups had disbanded. Suddenly, rumors began to fly that several members, one or two from each group, had formed a new act—kind of a "super group." Their debut was terrific. Rave reviews! Then, suddenly, two weeks later, this "super group" broke up. Why did a group with so much potential disband? Apparently in their haste to stage the act, the musicians overlooked one critical area: They had to rehearse, work, indeed almost live together, but they hardly knew one another. Like oil and water, personalities just didn't blend. A part-time involvement provides time for you to get to know—hopefully, even enjoy—your new business partners, and you won't be as likely to get on each other's nerves.

4. Set your priorities, but don't act yet.

Do you eventually want to try for a recording contract? Would you rather opt for the security of working full-time as a local musician? Are you planning on going to college, and only want to use music to finance your education (while having lots of fun along the way)? These are all valid reasons for being a musician in a part-time band.

No matter what you decide now, intriguing musical opportunities can pop up at any time, making you reconsider career direction. Draw up a mental picture of where you stand, searching for a balance or relation between your normal job and being a part-time musician. Which job do you favor? What's more important? Even if the occupations aren't complementary in some respects, now is not the time to put all your energy behind one career. You're obviously interested in making money with music, and your regular job will help make that goal possible.

5. Hold out until it's unbearable

Playing from 9:00 p.m. to 1:30 a.m. and then working a 9-to-5 job? It's a caffeine junkie's life. It'll also be your life—at least for a little while. For security's sake, plan on keeping your normal job until *after* the band makes the transistion to full-time employment. If you're also going to school, keep it up. The longer you can persevere and stay healthy, the better off you'll be. After the band is reliable and working, you can decide if you want to concentrate on music day and night. Then, and only then, can you quit that dreary daytime job you've hated for months.

Expect Part-Time to Feel Like Full-Time

As I said before, an enormous amount of time and energy are required to put together a working band, and a part-time band can actually involve more "down" or non-paying time than a full-time band. This makes part-time groups rather inefficient; nevertheless, I strongly recommend you start part-time. Trying to climb up too quickly means you might misjudge a step and fall down. Consider your options carefully. Ideally, you'll have a daytime job to help finance the beginning of your musical career. If timing conflicts between work, school, and a part-time band can't be solved, check out your other local musical opportunities to launch your career.

Underestimating involvement in a part-time band ("Oh, I'll have plenty of time. It's only a *part-time* band") is common, and for more reasons than I've mentioned.

Live performances are physically taxing. Expect to be worn out by night's end. Depending on what type of music you'll play, a more accurate description might be "thoroughly exhausted." I've always perspired more than most people, and when I'm drumming I sweat up a storm. Changing shirts four times a night is standard procedure because by the time I'm finished the shirts are all soaking wet. Of course, the physical energy you'll expend on stage depends on what style of music you're performing: high energy rock 'n' roll or jazz, which really burn up the calories; or mellower folk, country, or "lounge" music (in which case I only soak through one or two shirts). But even if your music is soothing and slow, the mental acuity required will tire you out. When you're not concentrating on sounding witty and keeping the audience from dozing off, your brain is directing muscles how to execute dynamics, stops, starts, chord changes, and timing. Singing requires memory, tone control, dynamic balance, breath control, and stamina. Plan on allowing a little extra time for sleeping and recuperating.

The rigors of performing night after night can be both seen and felt, but it's nothing you can't handle with good physical and mental preparation (see Chapter 12, "Physical Conditioning" and "Getting High Without Drugs").

Be Ready for Situational Conflicts

Playing music part-time can conflict with work and school schedules. Usually, the conflict is not direct—you won't have to attend class during performance hours. Rather, you'll be burnt out from staying up late and driving home. From vivid personal experience, here are a few helpful hints:

For the classroom—Most college professors don't care if you miss class. The opinion is that by missing lecture or lab you "cheat yourself." This is true, but it requires stern self-discipline to get off work at 1:30 a.m. and wake at 7:00 a.m. for an 8:00 class. First of all, make sure you never drive home from the gig if you're the one getting up at 7:00 a.m.; that way you can sleep in the car. As for class itself, very few college instructors accept any excuses (remember, they've said they don't even care), so don't bother explaining. Either prearrange with a classmate to photocopy notes so that you can stay in bed, attend a later class, or drag yourself to class with a portable cassette recorder to tape notes. If there's a test, study notes the night before on breaks between sets.

For the office—This is harder to get around than a class; after all, you're getting paid to work. The only approach I've found effective is total, complete communication with your boss. Try to interest and involve her in what you're doing. You'd be surprised at what great advice a businessperson, especially one who's self-employed, can offer you on band decisions.

Make sure your boss sees you perform. This increases her personal commitment and furthers the chance you'll receive some scheduling leeway for group activities. When I worked in a retail record store, I occasionally had to ask the boss for time off because many band auditions were held during the day. I hated asking because I knew he was slightly hesitant. Finally, I figured out how to keep him happy and ease my conscience. I volunteered the band for a "grand opening" he was planning. The band drew a big crowd into the parking lot, and he sold hundreds of albums. He did us a favor, and we returned the favor. From then on he never balked at rearranging my work hours when a timing conflict arose.

Some people ask how I can stand working at night so often. The answer is, I've simply grown accustomed to it. After only a week of performing till one in the morning, you'll be used to it, too. As for disadvantages, I can think of only a couple: Musicians tend to wake a bit late, sometimes missing classic "I Love Lucy" or "Dick Van Dyke Show" reruns; and working as a full-time musician can be hard on relationships. When your girlfriend wants to go out for dinner, you have to work. And when she does get to go out (naturally to the club where you're playing) you watch while she dances with strangers (for the sake of postponing your separation, I won't go into traveling until Chapter 12).

Give Yourself Some Time

Your transition from present situation to full-time musician status shouldn't happen overnight. Good planning is essential.

A friend of mine worked for a tax auditing firm while she pieced together an act. After learning enough songs, they gave a smashing auditions for a Seattle agent. "We were so excited," she recalled. " This guy promised all kinds of work in good clubs. We decided we needed more material, so I quit my job to practice days."

After one week of work they were canned. "They said we weren't 'right' for the hotel," she said. "And we didn't know we had been hired with a one-week option."

Embarrassingly, she was forced to ask the auditing firm for her old job back. Luckily, she got it.

One very good friend of mine suddenly decided to become a musician, so he rushed out and bought a new Fender bass, amplifier, and speaker cabinet. After two weeks of practice, he changed his mind, and lost his shirt selling the equipment.

Starting slowly gives you a chance to try out the lifestyle. Even when you know what you want to do, as the woman did, new groups can have a hard time finding full-time gigs right away. Any self-employed businessperson will tell you that even what appears secure must be carefully thought through. With the right planning, when you at last quit your regular job it'll be for good—with no misgivings.

• CHAPTER THREE •

DIVERSIFICATION IS THE KEY

And not just diversifying your job opportunities, either. Job diversification—the combination of studio, teaching, and live performance skills—is obviously an important part of maximizing potential, but so is *style* diversification—the ability to perform different kinds of music. Pursue both job and style diversification and you'll never be out of work.

Local Bands Earn Fair Money, But Why Not Earn Great Money?

"That's just not our style," Benny the keyboardist said, when I asked if his band booked wedding receptions or banquets. "Weddings are too mellow for our music."

Unfortunately, many musicians adopt this attitude. They're *specializing*, and in the process, limiting their money-making potential. Instead of learning different styles of music, they're turning down jobs that don't suit their own taste.

I hear many excuses why bands don't diversify their repertoires. Most come from rock musicians, since rock is the most popular music today, and many rock musicians are self-taught and limited in musical scope ("Waltz? Who, me? You must be kidding."). Being a rock musician myself, I'm going to pick on rock musicians in general to illustrate the most common excuses why bands don't diversify:

"Rock is the most popular, so it'll pay the most."
Rock sells more records, yes, but at a local gig, a rock band doesn't necessarily make any more money than a good swing band. Since rock is so popular with the public, demand is high, but due to intense competition between rock bands wages are proportionately low.

You can often make much better money as a soloist than as part of a large band. Your initial investment will be much less, too.

(photo of Rebecca Braswell by Ellen Forsyth)

"All the band members enjoy playing rock the most."
This may be true, but I've never been in a single band which didn't combine a variety of musical interests. The bass player digs funk, the lead singer is into jazz, the guitarist likes pop, and the drummer has a reggae sound. Together, they play rock, but separately, they prefer their own favorites. This adds to the musical excitement.

"People will think we're selling out."
This is really false pride. Are jazz, reggae, or bluegrass any less respectable than rock? Hardly. Everybody who works for a living (musicians "play") understands the need to "compromise" what they like to do and what people will pay them to do. There's no shame in making whatever use of your talents will insure you a living wage.

"I was raised on rock. It's all I know."
Quite a common cop-out. This remark clearly reflects a musician who hasn't taken the time or effort to become proficient at other styles. Does this mean you should take lessons? Hey, if that's what you need, do it. It'll pay off (and it's tax deductible!).

"Our rock style wouldn't develop as fast as it has been."
Wrong. Your personal style is a result of all your musical experiences; listening to records, the radio, other groups, and performing music yourself. By diversifying style, your band's "real" sound (your original material) will mature faster since you're broadening your musical appreciation.

Naturally, you're going to want to play the style of music you love, *at least most of the time.* If this happens to be nineteenth-century Polish polkas, you're going to have trouble, but if you really love rock 'n' roll, you'll be able to play rock at 60, 70, or 80 percent of your jobs. It's the same with any popular or semipopular style. If the only music that excites you is jazz, will you be able to book jazz jobs 60 percent of the time, so you won't have to "lower" yourself to R&B? Probably. You might have to book some R&B gigs and a country music dance or two, but jazz still has enough appeal to sell itself, as long as it's sold in the right markets.

Musicians who can adapt to different styles and satisfy different audiences have the best chance of prospering locally. This means you should consider putting in some more hours and becoming a member of two or three bands, and it's not as hard as it sounds. The personnel can be identical in all three acts, just the music and the clothes change. This entails extra rehearsals, but again, this sounds misleading. because your three acts needn't receive equal attention in organizing, rehearsing, and promoting. Here's an example:

Johnny is a hard rocker. He was raised on ZZ Top, Lynyrd Skynyrd, and Ted Nugent, and that's all he really likes to play. From first-hand experience, Johnny knows that his area can't support all its hard rock bands full-time. Several bands play material like Johnny's band plays. The clubs rotate the bands in and out, so that each gets a little work, instead of a few bands getting all the work. But everyone in Johnny's band (called High Voltage) wants to gig full-time to make more money. What do they do? High Voltage becomes *three* bands, each with a separate name, logo, song list, and set of clothes. The emphasis remains on the hard rock band, since that's what these guys like to play, but now they also play country standards under the guise The Hired Hands, and early '60s revival music as Johnny & the Wetheads. The country songs were easy to copy, and all the Wetheads had heard '60s tunes hundreds of times on the radio. Rehearsals were just a quick review of "Your Cheatin' Heart," "Foggy Mountain Breakdown," "Wild Thing," "Wipe Out," and so forth. They could still book High Voltage three nights a week, but now the Hired Hands played Mondays and Tuesdays at a country restaurant, and Johnny & the Wetheads concentrated on booking lucrative special events, company parties, and class reunions. (Wethead gigs were kept to a minimum because of all the Brylcreem.) With a minimal time investment in rehearsals and a few new Western shirts, this group accomplished their goal of working full-time.

Consider this: One friend of mine books his band under two names, but each act plays the same music. The difference is in the method of presentation, not song selection.

"We charge a helluva lot more for our show band," says Rick, "because we put a lot more effort into it. It's totally choreographed and rehearsed—every joke and skit is planned. Pulling it off is physically exhausting." Rick always attempts to book his show act first, and if his asking price scares the potential employer, Rick offers the *other* act—with the same music—at a discounted rate.

"It's surprising how many clubs will pay you for full entertainment rather than just music," he said.

Here's another example of diversification: A very talented saxophonist I knew from playing together in a college jazz band was heavily into jazz-fusion. He auditioned for and immediately began playing with a hot Sacramento fusion band that featured several horn players. "I loved it because we played all the stuff I listened to, like Chicago, Brecker Brothers, Chick Corea. Our problem was that this music wasn't popular enough in town. We were always looking for gigs." Luckily, he had made contacts within the college jazz band, so whenever his fusion band wasn't working he called an old acquaintance and got a temporary job. He's popular because he can read most charts, and is a dynamic soloist.

No matter what new direction you pursue, broadening your repertoire of styles will stimulate your imagination and enhance your creativity as a musician. It can also influence your taste. I never respected country music until I started drumming in a country band. On the surface, drummers don't seem to have much to do in a country format, but what quickly became apparent to me after playing country music was that the *scarcity* of percussion is exactly what's important. It can be very emotional, sensitive music, and overplaying the drums muddles this quality. Now I enjoy country music, because by playing it, I've come to understand and appreciate it.

By playing more styles than just your favorite, you'll also meet many new musicians, with styles quite different from your own. Listening to others play, you'll pick up a guitar riff here or a bass finger-slap there, and gradually your own unique style of music will evolve.

How to Anticipate Industry Trends

When Julie turned 24, she decided she'd had enough of singing music she didn't particularly like. The music she revered—Carole King, Joan Baez, Joni Mitchell—was popular when she was in high school and college. All her girlfriends had counted these singers among their favorites, too, so Julie was convinced a band playing this material would be well received. After the new band repeatedly failed to hold audience attention, Julie was forced to change the band format back to something she didn't really like in order to secure work.

Where had Julie miscalculated? Her favorite music *had* been popular years ago, so she bet that most people still liked what she still liked. She was wrong. Individual taste in music is often formed at a certain point in a person's life, but popular, mass taste moves on.

Musicians often regard the public's taste as poor, but this is really nearsightedness on our part. The mass listening public just doesn't analyze music the way we do, so what we'd consider trash doesn't bother them. That's why the public is so receptive to new trends, and also why you, as a musician, must be aware of these trends in order to offer audiences something that will excite them *and* make them dance. No matter how much it bothers you, the best money available in local clubs is paid to bands that play current, up-to-date, hot-off-the-vinyl-presses material.

Does this sound like a pitch for joining a Top 40 copy band? That's exactly what it is. Wait, don't burn this book yet! I know what you're thinking. You're saying to yourself, "This guy's crazy! He wants me to play all those trashy, simplistic, blatantly commericial sell-outs!" Well, I want you to think about it. Because that giant public out there, that doesn't critique music the way you do, *likes* this music. They hear it every day on the radio, and when they walk into a bar where it's already being copied by a band, they listen, they dance, and they clap, all because the songs are brand new, yet, because of heavy air play, instantly familiar. They haven't gotten tired of the new release from so-and-so, and they won't until a newer release hits the air waves. Then, of course, you'll have to know *that* song!

Most bands I've heard try to strike a happy medium: They pick the best Top 40 or Top 200 songs and mix these current hits with older songs they enjoy performing. This is effective, but a band playing this format finds job-hunting a little harder. A strict Top 40 band seldom lacks work.

The main problem with being a Top 40 band is your time investment. You have to learn about two new songs each week, so rehearsals never slacken. You're always working your tail off rehearsing! Since all your spare time is taken up learning new material for a Top 40 act, style diversity is virtually impossible. There's no time to put together a jazz or rock act for gigs on the side. Of course, you could still diversify your show instead of the music, as my friend Rick did.

There's no denying that constantly trying to guess which songs will become the biggest hits—and, therefore, the songs you should learn—can be a real headache. Luckily, copy musicians can look to other people who must also guess which songs will become hits. The record retailing industry follows several guides which assist in determining song sales, and therefore popularity: *Billboard* and *Cashbox* magazines.

Billboard, publishers of the most relied upon charts, positions fast-selling singles on its Hot 100 chart according to information collected by telephone from record dealers, and from the amount of air play a single receives in certain geographic areas throughout the country. *Billboard* charts indicate how long a single has been in the Top 100, whether it is gaining or losing popularity, and how quickly it is moving up or down. By watching the charts and advertisements in the trade journals, you can accurately predict the bigger hits, which are the songs a Top 40 group should learn.

Many musicians I know rush to a local record store the day *Billboard* arrives each week and ask to look over the magazine and, hopefully, photocopy the lists. Some stores set lists out for the taking, but beware of picking up a list assembled by a distributor or record store: Their lists *usually* follow trade journal charts, but I've known distributors to pad bestselling lists with singles or albums they are simply overstocked with, hoping to move their stale inventory. Make sure you're using a current (to the week), authentic trade journal chart.

Ego Satisfaction Is Pocketbook Starvation

If there is a universal lesson that all local musicians learn at some time, it's how torturously difficult it is to make decent money at performing original music. We all try it at some point. Determined songwriters usually try it over and over again.

Bob's musical career follows a predictable pattern: After saving a tidy sum of money from performing in a copy band, he'll get the urge to start a part-time band on the side, performing his original material. Gradually, the original act takes up more and more of his time, and soon he quits the successful copy band to expand the original music band into a full-time venture. Bob has a blast, but eventually the new band runs out of employers because customers leave early and don't return. They aren't familiar with Bob's music, never having heard it before (bar owners I've talked with all agree that crowds prefer familiar music). The group disbands after several more futile efforts at survival, and Bob joins another copy group until he has some money saved up. Then he organizes a part-time original band again.

Financially, diversification into an original music group is disastrous. Artistically and creatively, it's the only way to go. So where's the happy medium? How do you fulfill yourself without mortgaging the house?

First, determine *why* you want to begin performing original material. The formation of an original band usually follows a succession of jobs with copy bands. How many times do you have to play the Eagles's "Take It Easy," or Led Zepplin's "Stairway to Heaven" before you realize that the lyrics you've been scribbling on binder paper are just as meaningful, just as good? You or someone else in the band will eagerly produce a rough draft of a song at a practice, and after everyone plays around with it for a while, you'll finally decide it sounds ready to perform. After several such songs have been worked into your repertoire, everyone starts wondering when you're going to make the changeover to "all original music." The copy songs become a drag to play. They bore you. Only when you hear the first chords of your *own* music, your *own* songs, do you get excited.

Stop right here!

You're dangerously close to becoming an original music band, and 99 chances out of 100, if you do, your market value will drop to zilch in a matter of months. It's time to answer a question about your future: Are you developing original music in the hopes of landing a recording contract? Of course you are. If not, you're a rare exception (worthy of the title, "Freakish Anomaly"). Everyone wants a recording contract, and it's a perfectly legitimate *dream*. Notice I emphasize the word "dream." If, after rereading Chapter 1, you decide that your desire will outlast everyone else's, concentrate on Chapter 20 to learn how to present your songs in acceptable fashion to the right people, and which books you should read to learn how to market your original material.

And, of course, there's the exception. One of the best groups to come out of Sacramento in recent history struggled for years to amass a following with their original material. Finally, they were recognized as the most popular band in the valley, as evidenced by the crowded bar rooms they appeared in. They had a really unique, polished sound. After another year of performing all originals, they signed a contract with Epic Records, released an album which went nowhere, but now are experiencing mild commercial success with a subsequent release. So you *can* start playing your music now and finally make it to a contract, but for your music to be acclaimed by bar goers—multitudes of them—and accepted by employers, your songs must have a very special chemistry to them. It's wise to base your income on a surer bet.

The Big Money Isn't Where You Think

The lead singer jumps from behind the huge lithographed backdrop—narrowly missing stacks of Marshall amplifiers—and into a mist of artificial fog. The band is already pulsating through the beginning of "Smoke on the Water," when he yells "Hello Sacramento," and bang! the laser show flares up.

But, no, Deep Purple isn't performing their monster hit, it's a copy band, and, well, the guy who declared "Hello Sacramento" was born, raised, and lives here. This is the extent some local bands go to in order to capture a marketplace. In the process, they end up spending all their income on instruments, equipment, and stage accessories. All this equipment is constantly being added to, updated, or repaired, so any leftover money is constantly reinvested. I don't want you to become a fiscal Jack Benny, but I would like to see you save some of your musical income along the way. This requires keeping initial investment down (Chapter 6), limiting operating costs (Chapter 10), and—most important—carefully considering how each personnel addition to your act will affect your share of the paycheck. If you are conscious of all these factors, you'll net a lot more money than the highly outfitted group blazing through "Smoke on the Water."

Almost without exception, the fewer musicians in a band, the more money you'll make. The exceptions are those places that pay a flat rate *per musician*, and they are few and far between. Most employers have an entertainment budget. They'll try to hire you for a price below their limit, but they'll rarely pay you more than their limit or they put their jobs on the line. You are viewed an an entertainment expense (maybe *the* entertainment expense), and if your three-piece group is just as entertaining as the four-piece group before you, the employer will pay you the same $200 a night the larger band received. It's nice making $67 a night rather than $50, isn't it? Sure! But why stop there? Duets can't do a lot of the things trios can, but then again, a softer, mellower, acoustic sound is easier to produce with a duet. The pay certainly rivals what trios earn: $100 to $150 a night, with more and more restaurants hiring mellow acts for luncheon or brunch entertainment.

I'll never forget the time I was on the road with a band, and a few of us stopped in at an espresso shop for coffee. David, a cellist, was playing classical music for the little cafe's morning customers. "I like this arrangement because it's so loose," David said. "I just come in whichever mornings I want, and the owner pays me $25 plus any tips I get in my cello case." I gave David a tip as much for his ingenuity as for his fine playing.

I know one duet who, instead of trying to cover for a lack of musicians on-stage, *emphasize* the point they're short-handed. They claim to be backed up by the Knowone Band whose members are *painted on the backdrop!* A soloist took the same idea one step further. He sits stage center playing keyboards and rhythm sequencer, surrounded by mannequins bent in action poses, guitars hung around their necks. He's even got a mannequin drummer behind a set! The one-sided dialogue is hilarious, and of course, dummies play for free.

Employers find it easy to shell out $50, $100, or $200 for one, two, or three musicians, compared wth the $250, $350, or $450 larger bands need just to make decent wages. Larger clubs, of course, can afford to pay established bands much more, but a full-fledged electric band hides many costs a duo never has to pay.

It never happens this way, but just to simplify a hypothetical financial comparison between a five-piece rock band and an acoustic duo, let's completely outfit each act from the ground up. Usually musicians accumulate equipment over a long period of time and buy some equipment used, but let's assume everything was bought new in one initial purchase:

ACOUSTIC DUO		FIVE-PIECE ROCK BAND	
two acoustic guitars	$ 650	three electric guitars	$ 2,100
two amplifiers	1,200	electric piano, electric string ensemble	2,200
two microphones w/ stands & cords	370	drum set	2,500
two guitar pick-ups	150	four amplifiers	2,400
small mixer w/built in power amp	400	eight microphones w/ stand & cords	1,280
two P.A. speakers	400	mixer, power amp, equalizer	1,500
two P.A. monitors	300	two P.A. speakers	1,200
four sets of clothes	200	four P.A. monitors	600
promo package	300	tuner	100
miscellaneous	75	backdrop	300
		promo package	600
		snake cable	200
		used equipment van	5,000
		light boxes	150
		10 sets of clothes	500
		miscellaneous	200
total	$4,045	total	$20,730
each	$2,022	each	$4,146

If you play in a band with four to six people, that $4,146 probably is realistic, especially if you own a lot of P.A. equipment, play keyboards, or a large drum set. This $4,146 represents initial investment. Now let's list comparative overhead figures, or how much it takes to keep each act afloat. This doesn't figure overhead such as strings and drumsticks:

ACOUSTIC DUO		FIVE-PIECE ROCK BAND	
monthly telephone bills	$30	monthly practice room rental	200
monthly transportation money	50	monthly telephone bills	80
		monthly transportation money	150
		monthly van up-keep fund	25
total	$80	total	$455
each (monthly)	$40	each (monthly)	$ 91

Unfortunately for the rock band, we're not done yet. From my experience, acoustic acts tend to do their own bookings more than rock bands, who may rely on several agents for job offers. Not all gigs will come from agents, but many of the best opportunities will, so let's assume our hypothetical rock band relies more and more on agents for jobs. Luckily, our hypothetical agents are still charging only a 10 percent commission rather than 15 percent. A great many local rock bands also hire a sound technician, who really becomes a "sixth member," but let's give our band the benefit of the doubt and imagine that the guitarist is doubling as technician, saving the band a sixth cut. To recapitulate: Our rock band members are in the hole $4,146 each, must keep up monthly band expenses of $91 each, and are jointly paying a 10 percent fee to agents for jobs.

If our acoustic act is paid $120 a night, four nights a week, each musician will earn $920 a month, and have their inital investment of $2,022 paid off within two and a half months.

If our rock band is paid $350 a night, four nights a week, they'll each earn $917 a month, but it will take each of them *five* months to pay off their initial investments. When our rock musicians are paid the equivalent paid to the acoustic musicians, things look even worse: only $773 a month. With a sound technician, $629 each.

It's not hard to conclude that even musicians in a popular local rock act—commanding $500 or more a night—will have a hard time earning proportionally as much money as a one, two, or three-piece act due to initial investment and overhead.

The Professional Advantages of Small Acts . . .

Rodney is a prime example of a band musician turned soloist:
"I got tired of playing 'Proud Mary.' You know, the same old songs, over and over again. I just decided I'd had enough."

Since he was supporting a family, Rodney wasted no time throwing a solo act together.

"I already knew most of the songs. They were love ballads—the kind of stuff I listened to but never got a chance to play."

After trying out his new act at several spots, Rodney found the military a ready employer.

"I play at dinner time in large air force dining rooms, and they pay very well."

One night, an elementary school principal approached Rodney and asked if he'd be interested in giving an educational performance for school children. That initial offer has now blossomed into a network of 45-minute elementary school seminars throughout Northern California—at $50 to $60 a shot. He has six different presentations, keyed to patriotic, Americana, good citizen, or brotherly love themes. He views expansion of the daytime programs as unlimited.

The best thing about playing alone at both jobs is that there are no hassles. Whatever I want to do, I do it," Rodney says.

Artistically, performing solo allows the greatest freedom of expression. Are there certain messages you want to convey to the audience about your views, feelings, and personality? Soloing allows for this. Solo performers are not expected to play the Top 40 tunes; indeed, I've heard many soloists perform songs I wasn't familiar with at all. A soloist is really expected to transmit a feeling. Whether that feeling is the laid-back country life, a hyped-up hoedown, bittersweet love, getting by in the city, or preservation of the world, doesn't matter as long as your message is clear: "Here I am, enjoy your meal, I'll make your evening pleasant." You are free to pick songs you enjoy which reinforce your theme.

"My show is a nostalgic but sincere look at the '60s," one woman told me. "I sing Beatles songs. A lot of people will stop eating and watch, and you can see they're remembering all the things they used to do."

I heard of one guy who made a solo show out of *one album!* He plays the entire Woodstock soundtrack straight through—from John B. Sebastian to Jimi Hendrix. Despite the wide range of styles, this act still runs on a strong theme: the love, the togetherness, the rebellion of the Woodstock era.

As already hinted, communication is simplified in a smaller group. With fewer partners to confer with, and fewer opinions to consider, all administrative and business matters are simplified. It's easier to write out only *two* paychecks and collect expense receipts from only *two* musicians. Decisions are made quickly, with little wasted time. If you're a soloist, there's no need for band meetings of any sort. Based on an hourly wage scale, a smaller act makes more money because they don't need to bother with time-consuming interpersonal meetings.

Differing degrees of commitment can shake the very foundations of a group, and seriously limit what job offers you can accept. If you're happily married, how many consecutive nights out-of-town will your spouse tolerate? Do you attend classes or have another job? The more members in a group, the more potential conflicts.

If you've made any money as a live performer, you probably know that bands are notoriously short-lived. People come and go at an alarming rate. This personnel turnover means you're often looking for a replacement for someone leaving, or are leaving yourself. This takes a lot of time. It's not uncommon to "take some time off" while rehearsing a new member—and that's money down the drain! The fewer members you start with, the fewer surprise vacancies you'll have to fill.

Rehearsals are much more efficient in a smaller act, simply because you only depend on one or two other musicians (if even that many) to make it to practice. Business gets taken care of faster. Messages and rumors needn't be repeated time and time again, and there are fewer parts to learn. An added bonus is the volume: You won't go deaf from acoustic practices (Chapter 12).

Solo performers also note that audiences seem more attentive. I don't know why, but maybe it's easier for a nonmusician to understand and relate to one person holding an acoustic guitar, or sitting behind an acoustic piano. These instruments are familiar to virtually everyone—not intimidating like synthesizers, giant P.A. mains, 16-channel mixing boards, and racks of electrical gadgetry.

. . . And Why Musicians Shy Away from Them

Okay, you say, if performing alone or with one or two others is the greatest thing since electricity, why don't more musicians do it?

There are some requirements for playing in a small act, most of which reflect on your personality, desire, confidence, and talent.

Personality. Being self-employed in a five-piece band is one thing, but being self-employed as the band is another. First and foremost, you must have a likable personality. Do you make friends easily? Do people seem to want to talk to you? If so, you're probably likable. Conversely, you must like people. Only the best comedians can apparently hate the audience while winning their affection. Get used to meeting people, because as *the* band, you're it, baby!

As in any size band, you must be able to leave personal problems at home (or at least backstage!). This is vital in a small band since there's nowhere to hide, and attention is exponentially focused upon you.

In a solo act, especially, you must be a leader. Be comfortable taking charge and making decisions; in other words, be an extrovert in all band matters, onstage and off. An outgoing personality is especially needed onstage. If your style and the feeling you create is very nonchalant, then you needn't always be outspoken, but when the crowd (or "intimate gathering") is as lively as a sleeping bloodhound, you'd better know how to wake that dog up.

Finally, you shouldn't need the excitement of playing in a full band. A lot of us do—and that's fine—but when soloing or playing in a duet, you must manufacture your own excitement. The audience may appreciate your performance, but don't expect a sea of enthusiastic partiers stomping their feet and raising lit matches, demanding an encore.

Desire. How much do you want to perform alone? Are you willing to give 100 percent every night? In a full-size band, you can occasionally relax and let someone else showcase their talents, but now you're all alone in the spotlight.

One of the major benefits of playing in a full-size band is the support available—there's always a guitarist who will listen to your problems. No such comfort here. Any encouragement or pampering will have to come from somewhere else.

Confidence. Unless a performer is also an actor, his feelings can be detected by the audience as if he were transparent. A lack of confidence is as obvious as a broken guitar string. Musical confidence usually comes with musical talent, but a soloist must also be confident and comfortable talking with people. You should be a good public speaker.

Stage fright is common with all performers. Nervous tension is never conquered, but it can be understood and seen in its proper perspective (Chapter 12).

Confidence consists largely of analyzing and confronting your situation. You're only a local, virtually unknown performer, and you are hired as an entertainment commodity. So what's to be nervous about? At the same time, (believe it or not) you should have a high regard for your position. Sure, you're only making $50 a night in a steakhouse, but then again, no one else in the audience can do what you're doing. Even if they could, they're not! *You're* the one who's pursued it far enough to be up on stage—and get paid for it.

Talent. In Chapter 1, I said "Talent is optional." Well, I've got news for you. Performing alone or in a duet, talent is mandatory! There's plenty of space to hide a beginner in a local rock band, but the spotlight never dims on a solo performer. You've got to be well-rehearsed and competent or you'll never get hired.

While in a hotel lobby waiting for a friend, I noticed a man playing piano in the lounge. He sang very well, but his playing was a disgrace to that beautiful Wurlitzer grand. On studying his technique, I saw he played lightly and very little—only chords. Then I noticed why his lack of talent went mostly unheard: He had a reel-to-reel tape deck at his side, playing soothing rhythm and strings. What a solution! I gave him a "C" for talent, but an "A" for ingenuity.

Talent also manifests itself in the form of endurance, since many jobs are four to five hours long. Can you play this long? Of particular importance: Can your singing voice hold out for hours on end, night after night? In a full band, singing duties are divided up, but a soloist must sing all night long.

As an afterthought, naturally you must play an instrument conducive to solo performance. The audience can't be expected to recognize a melody if you're hammering it out on the tom-toms.

To put the diversification principle to work, you first must locate and list all the possible areas for diversifying in your area. This will help steer your career into profitable, complementary jobs.

Besides investigating employers for live music, you'll also want to note those inconspicuous, "hidden" employers: studios, TV stations, music stores, and churches. A mixture of these, along with private teaching, freelancing to schools and theaters, agency work, setting up a home recording studio, equipment rentals, and selling music and lyrics through the mail, plants your career in solid ground. By receiving income from so many different sources, you protect yourself in case one job opportunity suddenly dries up. All these areas of diversification are explained in Part Three of this book.

• CHAPTER FOUR •
THE MARKET ANALYSIS

The purpose of this market analysis is to find *all possible employment* for your musical talent. If you pass over a musical employer—whether school, agency, or studio—you're limiting your potential to some degree. If you really want to make as much money as possible you must find the most promising areas of diversification, and do a meticulous researching job. *Brainstorm.* Think of everything! Never dismiss an opportunity before thoroughly checking it out.

And one more thing. The first three chapters were *reading* chapters. This one is a *working* chapter; It should take you awhile to get through. Go ahead and speed read it once if you'd like, it's not long or difficult to understand, but later flip back and begin researching.

If you have a musician friend who wouldn't mind making more money, split up the researching and phoning between the two of you. If you research well and really dig around, you'll be rewarded with a comprehensive, up-to-date, accurate listing of places to work. Believe me, it's worth it in the end.

Let Your Fingers Do the Walking

Luckily, the best single source for finding musical markets is already in your home: the telephone book. This reference book hides many of the leads you need to uncover markets. Much of your research time will be spent flipping through it and gathering information via its indispensable partner, the telephone.

Equipped with pen and paper, sit down at a desk with your phone book. Flip to the Yellow Pages Index. Which of these companies hire musicians? Be open-minded and optimistic about all listings A through Z. Many headings won't sound as if they can make you money, but musical

A true gold mine awaiting you in your local library is the phone book collection in the reference room. Yes, believe it or not, the phone book!

(photograph by Ellen Forsyth)

jobs can be found in unlikely places. By scanning the index of my phone book, here's what I came up with:

Yellow Pages

Academies
Accommodations—Vacations
Adult Education Centers
Advertising—Radio
Advertising—Slide, Theatrical
Advertising—Television
Associations
Athletic Organizations
Audio-Visual Production Services
Audio-Visual Programs
Audition Recordings
Auditoriums
Bands—Musical
Banquet Rooms
Bars & Grills
Boarding Schools
Breakfast Nooks & Booths
Broadcasting Stations
Business Films
Business & Trade Organizations
Cabarets
Cafes
Campaign Management
Campaigns—Fund Raising
Caterers
Churches
Clubs
Cocktail Lounges
Community Centers
Community Development
Convention Services & Facilities
Country Clubs
Dance Bands
Dancing—Public
Dinner Theaters
Discotheques
Educational—Audio Visual
Entertainers
Entertainment Bureaus
Entertainment Information
Environmental & Conservation Organizations
Exhibit Rooms
Fairs
Filmstrips
Fraternities & Sororities
Golf Courses
Golf Tournament Booking Service
Guest Homes
Homes for Convalescents
Hotels
Houseboats—Renting
Industrial Exhibits
Instruction—Music
Labor Organizations
Malls
Meetings—Planning & Management
Modeling Agencies
Modeling Schools
Motion Picture Labs
Motion Picture Studios
Motion Picture Sound Services
Motor Clubs
Music—Electronics
Music—Instructional Instrumental
Music—Instructional Vocal
Music Producers
Music Publishers
Musical Organizations
Musicians
Nudist Clubs
Nursery Schools
Nursing Homes

Organizations
Party Facilities
Party Planning Service
Playgrounds & Parks
Private Dining Rooms
Private Schools
Professional Talent Management
Public Schools
Recording Service—Sound & Video
Religious Schools
Restaurants
Sales Promotion & Counseling Service
Schools—Music—Instrumental
Singing Telegrams
Slides & Filmstrips
Social Service Organizations
Sound Recording Service
Talent Management
Taverns
Television Film Sound Recording
Tennis Clubs—Private
Trade Unions
Universities
Wedding Consultants
Wedding Receptions
Yacht Clubs
Yachting Associations
Youth Organizations & Centers
Youth Services

Do some of these entries sound strange? Admittedly, some, like "Breakfast Nooks & Booths," "Industrial Exhibits," and "Sales Promotion & Counseling Service," are a little off the beaten path of musical employment, but they all hire musicians.

Nursery schools, for instance, will hire you to come perform for their children, as long as your presentation includes an explanation of your instrument and how it produces sound. Cafes and breakfast nooks are interested in providing a comfortable atmosphere for their diners (remember my friend David the cellist?), so they're willing to pay a harpist or folk singer to relax customers. What about modeling schools? Periodically, modeling schools will sponsor a fashion show at a banquet room or a restaurant to give their models on-the-job experience. Clothing stores do the same thing—trying to sell restaurant customers clothes or just advertise their stores. In either case, musicians are hired to play music that befits the style of clothes being modeled.

I've been to industrial and manufacturing exhibits where dance bands played during cocktail parties. I've known businesses in shopping centers to collectively hire a sales promotion service for grand openings or sales, and a live band invariably performs out in the parking lot. Rest homes occasionally solicit acoustic performers to entertain residents, trade unions schedule annual parties, and customers frequently ask caterers about reliable bands for wedding receptions. How can you find work through adult education centers? By applying and being approved to teach community center classes (all you need is knowledge of the instrument and good communication techniques). For example, in "Percussion for Beginners," you can teach many students at once, substantially multiplying your hourly wage. How about houseboats? Occasionally, houseboat rental companies receive requests for entertainers from vacationing floaters.

Does this seem like an abundance of businesses, associations, and organizations that need musicians? It is! And this is only a partial list of opportunities.

Many of these entries are cross-referenced to each other, but don't make the mistake of assuming that "Academies" can be found under "Adult Education Centers," or that "Boarding Schools" can be found under "Private Schools," or that "Public Schools" can be found under "Universities." Take the time to scan the entire index, and write down all promising entries with their corresponding page numbers.

Then look up each entry and try to determine its worth to you. Might they realistically hire musicians, even if only once a year for a New Year's Party? Mark all pages listing potential employers, putting a check beside each likely prospect.

Now you've got a wide variety of potential employers, and you're on your way to developing a career. But since most job opportunities are live performances, we'll now get specific in our research. You might have uncovered all the live-music employers in the Yellow Pages, but not all businesses are listed there (or even in the White Pages). You need a more comprehensive list of places to perform that will round out the names and numbers you've marked in the phone book.

Find a List of Live-Music Employers

Information is your key to exploring all possible markets for your talents. Almost without exception, whatever information you want is already counted, collected, and categorized *somewhere*. Someone has done a tremendous amount of work, and the fruit of their labors is waiting for you.

But often you must hunt for it, because the paper you want is invariably collecting dust in either a library, county building, or office. Where should you begin? First of all, define what you need, for without knowing *exactly* what you want, valuable time will be lost nagging clerks for useless information.

Ideally, you should have a list of all employers who consistently or occasionally hire musicians. This list is valuable because with it, you instantly know all your performing options, and can more easily discover the best paying jobs in town.

I'm consistently amazed by the wages some inconspicuous, nonadvertising clubs pay. One lounge in particular comes to mind, since I drive by it two or three times a week. From the outside it looks like a dumpy place without much to offer musicians, but when I got the opportunity to fill in for a drummer and play there (my band never even considered checking the place out) I was shocked. Not only were the stage and club designed perfectly for live music, but the pay was nearly double what my "classy" band was receiving. Here's another example showing the value of a comprehensive list of employers:

The owner of a restaurant 80 miles from Sacramento was passing through and stopped at a club where my band was playing. He immediately offered us a job, complete with travel expenses, rooms, and meals. He paid us more per night than we received at the club where he discovered us!

If I had been equipped with a comprehensive list of employers and had researched each possibility, I would have long ago realized the importance of these two clubs. Without the list I was blind, overlooking good opportunities for my band.

Depending on what state you live in, lists can be found in different places. Restaurant owners associations might have lists which would prove helpful. Also try your local government. Some states require a "registration for live music," "carbaret license," or "dancing permit." My county, because of fire department regulations, requires a dancing permit, but nowhere is there a "list" of those establishments with permits. I located the information at my local county building, but it wasn't filed on computer. So I would have to go through the files myself, find the information, and compile my own list, which could take weeks. And this would only include places with dance floors, but I've played in many clubs which were either too small to dance or were arranged in "concert seating," so my list wouldn't be comprehensive. For states that require a cabaret or live music license (call your local county building, licensing center, or restaurateur's association), a comprehensive file will be available, and if you're lucky, it might be "on call" in a computer.

I had no such option, so I took a different route to get my list. Since live music is nearly synonymous with the serving of alcoholic beverages, I went to the Alcohol Beverage Control Board (ABC), which requires that all businesses or organizations serving alcohol hold a liquor license. Success at last! Not only did ABC have a comprehensive list, but the information was stored in a computer. Every year, an additional state or two computerizes their ABC departments, so check with yours. The information (in my case, 1,004 different license holders) comes complete with price tag: It cost me four cents per license, or $40.36 for the enormous printout. Of course, many of the names and addresses on this list were not in the market for a live band. How do you sift out the potential employers?

This is where the work begins.

Narrowing Your Listings

After your telephone directory is bulging with book markers and you've managed to get your hands on a list of live music employers, you're ready to eliminate some of these listings. The object is to cross out all the studios, organizations, etc., that don't hire musicians. Then you'll be left with an accurate list of live-music employers, at which point you can begin to collect specific information on each employer and categorize it.

To start, scan the phone book names you've marked. Are you familiar with any of these listings? Under "Country Clubs," for example, you might recognize the Loomis Racquet Club, but since you know they lack any facilities for live music, you can cross out that listing. Or, while scanning "Hotels" you might see the Cozy Room and Tight Quarters hotels, which you know are too small ever to hire musicians. Under "Discotheques" you might recognize D Jay Palace, a nice club, but one that spins records exclusively. You might see 12 McDonalds and seven Burger Kings listed under "Restaurants," but you cross them off since you've eaten there for 10 years without noticing any employees but cooks and servers. Under "Youth Services," you note the Draft Registration Referral Office, a small non-profit group that hands out pamphlets, and has little or no interest in musicians. They should be crossed off too.

This is the quick way to eliminate inappropriate listings—personally knowing that they don't hire musicians. Most listings, however, you won't recognize, so you'll have to find out if they offer work by the next quickest means: telephoning.

Simply asking, "Do you feature live music?" is enough when phoning nightclubs, bars, cocktail lounges, restaurants, cafes, and churches. But for banquet rooms, country clubs, or caterers, for example, you'll have to ask, "Do you ever *refer* entertainment to customers?" Inquiries must be tailored so that whoever you're talking to will correctly understand what you want to know. For occasional music employers, like business organizations, campaign management, or nudist clubs, you'll need to ask if they *ever* hire live entertainment. When calling advertising agencies, visual production services, filmstrip companies, or recording studios, you'll want to know if they ever rely on musicians for recordings, as opposed to using pre-recorded music exclusively.

This is the time-consuming part of your market research. It's not hard, but it takes a long time. If you know one, two, or three other musicians who would like to share the rewards of a comprehensive file of markets, divide up all this phoning between you.

After you've systematically eliminated listings that don't hire or refer entertainment, you can still increase the list of prospects if you'd like. If you're considering traveling to surrounding counties or states to perform, you local library should have a collection of telephone books from which listings can be noted. Proceed to look up subjects just as you did at home—through the Yellow Pages Index. Librarians won't want you to mark up their books, so photocopy promising listings.

Finding the Best-Paying Gigs in Town

Most local acts protectively cling to the one or two extravagant, high-paying annual parties they manage to book each year, kind of like hungry dogs guarding their favorite bones. Casuals. The word is music to a musician's ears. A casual job, as opposed to a steady, running engagement in a nightclub, is highly prized because a whole week's wage can be earned in one evening. That's why bands scrounge for every casual they can get.

Yet some groups work year-round playing nothing but big parties. What's their secret? Information—knowing who throws the parties, who's in charge, when the annual dates are, and which sponsors pay the most money.

Usually casuals are sponsored by private individuals (wedding receptions), businesses and organizations with enough employees to warrant hiring a band, or associations. The best-paying casuals are those sponsored by large businesses, organizations, and associations. But while looking up "banks," "chemical manufacturers," or "insurance companies" will give you their names and numbers, it won't disclose which of these sponsors employ the most people, and hence will allot the largest party entertainment budgets.

How do you discover the largest sponsors? Go to the reference department of your library. Ask for your librarian's assistance—that's what she's there for. The directories most helpful in locating information are two chamber of commerce publications, the *Manufacturers & Processors Directory* and the local *Business Directory*. Both references list how many people are employed by each company. Jot down the companies with at least 50 employees. Companies this size schedule Fourth of July picnics, Christmas parties, and/or New Year's celebrations, all of which are great opportunities for you! Larger companies stage more—and bigger—celebrations. The *Business Directory* also lists names, officers, and addresses for all associations and labor organizations in town—more outstanding prospects for booking casuals.

Other sources for finding out about local upcoming parties and conventions are large hotels. Go meet the reservation clerk and tell him you're interested in booking their banquet facilities for a wedding reception, but you're not sure of the date yet. Ask to see his reservation calendar, which, at a good hotel, will be chock full of party dates. If you're lucky, phone numbers will be listed with the sponsor's name. If they're not, you'll have to look them up later. In either case, act inconspicuous!

Concentrate on dates at least three months in advance. The further the party date is away, the better the chance that the sponsors haven't yet found a band.

Many reservations might be from out of town organizations (visiting conventions), so you'll be calling long distance. Nevertheless, these sponsors will appreciate your interest in helping them find local entertainment, and you'll be in an enviable negotiating position.

This is a devious trick, but it can work again and again because often large hotels have as many as four reservation clerks working different shifts. And of course each member of the band can decide to get married!

Negotiating for casual gigs (Chapter 10) can be an especially rewarding experience. One of the best aspects of booking casuals is that once you play for businesses, they're more than likely to call you for annual parties in the years ahead.

If your repertoire of songs is *really* extensive—you know everything from Brahms to Basie to Beatles to Bacharach—you may be qualified to work as an agent-musician (Chapter 17). Agent-musicians book casuals as a rule, but their wages make what other musicians get for casual gigs look like small change.

Word of Mouth Advice Is Invaluable

Certain things you can only learn about an employer by hearing it from someone else, and more often than not, "someone" is a musician who has enjoyed a harmonious working relationship with the boss or been thoroughly screwed over by way of up-tight management, inhibitive rules, or bad checks. This "second-hand" information from friends is often more valuable than the standard job information—wages, hours, etc.—the employer will recite to you.

One singer new to the Sacramento area was anxious to get some gigs, so she agreed to sing three nights a week at a cozy European-style club. She was excited about getting on as a regular at the place, since it looked like an ideal showcase for her talent. Any local performer familiar with the club would have warned her: The room acoustics are simply terrible—feedback is always a problem. When the manager asked her to stay on a weekly basis, she balked. "I wanted to work on my singing and build up my stage presence," she remembered bitterly, "not hassle with some damn P.A. all night long."

Have you ever known anyone who is really easy to get along with—until you try working together? A studio director can be the nicest person you've ever met, but when the pressure's on to produce a tape, all hell breaks loose. Suddenly tempers flare and your coffee breaks are kept track of with a stopwatch.

A nightclub or hotel which is failing at the bar is a classic example. "It was intense," a guitarist told me. "Right when we started he laid all this stuff on us about dress, 'dead' air (silence between songs), and no drinking while working. Then he started complaining about our music! He knew *in advance* what he was hiring."

If he had inquired at the local music store the guitarist would have learned that this bar had been struggling for a steady clientele. The manager was under the gun to do *something* to increase the bar tab, so he dumped all his frustration on the bands he hired. No one who knew him wanted to work there.

Gather all the notes and bits of information possible about music employers in your area. Carry a note pad, and make it a habit whenever you meet musicians to ask them these questions:

1. What's the best place you've worked in town?
2. What kind of music went over best?
3. How about the worst place?
4. Have any places where you play changed in format or management lately?

Next ask follow-up questions to each answer: "How was the atmosphere? Were any songs especially popular? Who made you uncomfortable? Do the new owners pay better wages?" Meeting a fellow musician is a time to exchange information, and remember that the one who talks the least learns the most!

Another reliable source of information on employers are other, non-musical employees. Whereas hearing rumors "through the grapevine" via musicians can be a slow, muddling process, by questioning technicians, students, mix engineers, waitresses, and other co-workers you can learn first-hand what's happening. Usually just asking, "Confidentially, how do you like working for so-and-so?" will yield a fairly truthful response. Be aware, however, that regular employees may hold an unfair grudge against an employer for a petty reason. If the bartender complains to you, "Just because I occasionally forgot to put detergent in the sink and 98 people have gotten food poisoning so far this year, she's always reminding me to clean everything," maybe this guy *needs* to be reminded to pour detergent in the sink. As a last resort before passing up the job, confront the boss with the anonymous complaint in an off-hand way to hear both sides of the story.

How to Organize All Those Notes, Names, and Numbers

Now it's time to sort out all the information you've gathered and file it. The best way to have this information instantly retrievable without wasting time searching through hastily scribbled messages and torn papers, is to type up "Market Research Sheets." This is the most effective method I've found for keeping abreast of ownership, management, and policy changes of the various clubs, schools, studios, agents, and others who hire musicians. On page 48 is the market research sheet I use to record my notes on nightclubs, agents and studios, and on page 51 is my sheet for casual employers.

Ever since I began keeping a file full of these forms, I've felt much more in command when negotiating. With a personal file folder on each business you'll become more aware of your options, and can tell at a glance which job pays the most.

Type up one sheet of each kind and have them photocopied enough times to cover all your markets.

Here is a breakdown of all the information that goes on the sheets, and why:

1. *Type of Business*—This distinction helps when rating markets, since markets can be easily grouped together.

2. *Market Rating*—Money will mostly determine your preferences when booking jobs, although there are other considerations (see next section).

3. *Sent Promo Package*—Keeping track of who has received what information is important—sending two tapes to the same place is expensive.

4. *Last Update*—Businesses which depend on music change personnel and format rapidly, so knowing when the sheet was last updated is imperative.

5. *Name of Business or Organization*—The business address is needed for mailing notices, promotion packages, follow-up letters and bills.

6. *Owner's Home Address*—A precautionary measure, so that a court summons can be served if needed. In the reference room of your library, ask the librarian for the *R.L. Polk & Company Directory*. In the Polk directory's white pages, look up a business from your list, and the owner or manager's names along with their home addresses will be listed.

7. *Person To Contact*—Usually a manager. This, along with "Style of Music/General Information" number 9, must be periodically updated.

8. *Directions*—Having a van full of equipment, running late, and not knowing where a club is, can contribute to a nervous performance. Before leaving, make sure all drivers have a copy of the directions.

9. *Style of Music/General Information*—What musical preferences does this business have? Rock standards? Rhythm & blues? Do they draw well? How old is the clientele?

10. *Word of Mouth*—As I said earlier, this advice can be very helpful when deciding which markets to pursue. Write any additional comments on the back of the page.

```
                          MARKET RESEARCH SHEET

Nightclub         Agent             Studio            Other (specify)

Market Rating _____   Sent Promo Package _____
Last Update _____
Name of Business or Organization _____
  (and address)                  _____
                                 _____
                          ph#    _____
Owner's Home Address             _____
                                 _____
                                 _____
                          ph#    _____
Person to Contact _____
Directions _____
_____
Style of Music/General Information _____
_____
Word of Mouth _____
_____

Agent Information: Representation _____ Percentage _____
References _____
_____

Nightclub Information:
Agents Dealt With _____
(address) _____
Exclusive Agent _____
Exclusive Union Club _____
Days of Employment _____
Hours _____  Dinners Served _____
Pay Scale _____  Type of Payment _____
Full Liquor License _____  Tax Forms _____
Regulations _____
Advance Booking Time Required _____
Stage Size _____  Lighting _____
Room Capacity _____  Sound System _____
Special Arrangements _____
```

Agent Information

11. *Percentage*—How much is this agent charging? 10 percent, 15 percent, or even 20 percent?

12. *Representation*—Many clubs, to save time and trouble, book primarily through an agent. What places does this agent book?
13. *References*—Ask for the names and numbers of at least two other acts this agent handles. Are they satisfied with her? Does she hustle and aggressively find them work?

Nightclub Information

14. *Agents Dealt With*—Find out who (if anyone) books this room, then jot down name and address here.
15. *Exclusive Agent*—Will the club circumvent the agent? Doing this can save the owner money while making you more money, but don't expect to get further jobs through that agent.
16. *Exclusive Union Club*—Most clubs don't hire union bands, but some banquet halls or large nightclubs hire union bands exclusively. Some clubs hire both, even though they're not supposed to. Ask if they hire union or non-union bands.
17. *Days of Employment*—This is very important information. I've played in many five-night-a-week clubs which pay as well as six-night-a-week clubs. That's a whole night of studio work or teaching music lessons.
18. *Hours*—Just as important as how many days per week they book is how many hours per night they want you to perform. Only in nightclubs that hire union bands will you be paid for additional hours automatically.
19. *Dinners Served*—Dual purpose information: Premises serving dinners usually can afford to pay musicians more, and you might want to bargain for free meals.
20. *Pay Scale*—Knowing how much and how little a club pays is incredibly valuable infomation when negotiating. Watch which acts play at each club, and either approach them in person at the club or over the phone through an agent. Ask them what they're receiving, and what they've heard that other bands have earned there.
21. *Type of Payment*—Before you play any job, always know what type of payment you'll be receiving, whether cash, check, or another arrangement. Almost anything is fine besides a personal check. If you haven't dealt with the employer before, insist on cash or a check that can be cashed immediately at the bar, right after the performance. As a general rule, chain companies can be trusted more than small bars. Usually, if a check is issued, it will be for the lump sum of your agreement. Most businesses consider writing out individual checks for every member in the band a bother, but large chain hotels or restaurants usually require that

individual W-2 forms be filled out, and issue individual checks matter-of-factly.

22. *Full Liquor License*—Premises with a license to sell hard liquor are more profitable than those holding only a beer and wine license. A percentage reflecting this difference should be passed on to you.

23. *Tax Forms*—Some managers expect musicians to be businesspeople, too, and arrive with completed tax forms.

24. *Regulations*—Know in advance what will be expected of you, so you won't get in trouble with management the first night. I remember one night very clearly. My group was dressed in loosely matching clothes, with half of the band wearing blue jeans. The owner came in, didn't like our appearance, and phoned the agent in Texas. Within minutes the agent phoned us, wanting to know what the hell we thought we were doing. "You're wearing matching outfits in your promo picture," he said, "so that's what you've got to wear on the job!" Well, that's one way to learn the rules.

25. *Advance Booking Time Required*—You've got to know how far in advance each club books, so that you can plan your schedule around the clubs. Some bars book only a month in advance, but others have filled up their calendar six months in advance (and these are usually the best paying spots!).

26. *Stage Size*—If the stage doesn't have room for a 16-piece drum set, there's no sense in bringing the extra drums, and maybe you'll be able to take one less vehicle.

27. *Lighting*—Does the club have permanent stage lights, or must you bring your own?

28. *Room Capacity*—This is dual purpose information. The "maximum occupancy" number can give you an idea of room size, thus telling you how much sound equipment is necessary. Knowledge of bar capacity can also help you when negotiating, since a bar that holds more customers makes more money, and can pay you more.

29. *Sound System*—Does the club have a built-in sound system? Is your P.A. equipment (or even the sound technician) necessary?

30. *Special Arrangements*—Knowing a little about the business you're dealing with opens up new negotiating options which frequently benefit both employer and employee: Is the bar part of a restaurant or hotel? Providing food and lodging costs a business less than paying out cash, and not having to pay full price for these services saves you money, too.

The following are of particular importance when collecting information on casuals:

MARKET RESEARCH SHEET FOR CASUALS

Business   Organization   Association   School   Referral

Market Rating _____   Sent Promo Package _____
Last Update _____
Name of Business or Organization _____
   (and address)   _____
                         ph#   _____
Owner's Home Address   _____
                                _____
                         ph#   _____
Person to Contact _____
Past Locations of Parties _____
_____
Style of Music/General Information _____
_____
Word of Mouth _____
Age of Partygoers _____
Annual Parties _____
Payment Range _____
Type of Payment _____
Usual Size of Parties _____
Regulations _____
Special Arrangments _____
_____
Music Listening Level:
     very soft   soft   normal   loud
Advance Booking Time Required _____
Exclusive Union Band _____

- **Style of Music/General Information**—The crowds at casuals are generally adamant about what they want to hear. This ties in closely with the age of the party-goers. The Lions Club isn't going to enjoy hard rock, no matter how softly you play it.
- **Payment Range**—Sometimes the person in charge of hiring entertainment will divulge this information, but more likely than not, you'll have to ask who they hired last year, and then get in touch with that band to find out what they can afford. Of course, this doesn't mean you know their *entire* payment range, but rather you know one price they were willing to pay. You should be able to push them up (see Chapter 10).
- **Type of Payment**—The sponsors of casuals are not necessarily as stable or financially solvent as a nightclub. A casual sponsor doesn't have to

"exist" anywhere; they might just get together for parties. Because of this, demand cash, a money order, or a cashier's check. I also request full payment halfway through the show. You never know if the person with the cash might drink too much and go home early.

- **Music Listening Level**—Some casuals (wedding receptions are the classic example) employ musicians as background music. There's something more important going on than the music. That's fine as long as the band realizes it, is comfortable just kicking back, and plays *very softly*. At other parties the bands is where it's at. Query the person in charge ahead of time so that the band will be mentally prepared for the type of event you'll be playing.

To complete the research for your marketing analysis, fill out the sheets as completely as possible. Do this by phoning each business and organization, which is faster, cheaper, and *more appropriate* than scheduling a person-to-person meeting. You are *not* representing a band, merely gathering information. Most managers, owners, and agents are busy and wouldn't consider a meeting with you worth their while unless you were selling something—namely, a band. Identifying yourself as a person "researching area opportunities for musicians" will likely catch the employer off guard, and you'll probably get more accurate information than if you thrust the employer into a defensive, competitive situation by insinuating the information will be used to your advantage in negotiation (which it will!). Your official position when talking on the phone to employers should be that of a "third party." I've found that most employers are impressed when I explain my marketing system to them. As experienced businesspeople, they appreciate a musician who takes a businesslike approach to landing jobs.

After a proper introduction, (ask that all names be spelled out), explain why you're calling. With a market research sheet in front of you, systematically ask each question. Sound alert and businesslike, and keep the discussion as short as possible. Since you did preliminary research in phone books, government offices, and library references, you should already know one person's name (owner or manager), the business address, and, for clubs, the owner's home address. It's a good practice, immediately after the introduction, to recite the business address to the employer (say it's for verification purposes) because most people appreciate it if you show you have already gone to the trouble of learning a little about their business.

Never ask for anyone's home address. This would be inappropriate—even rude—to request. You should already have gotten this information from *Polk's*.

Phone calls beat driving to each business, but they still take time. To boast a full file of job information, you've got plenty of phone calls to make (again, hopefully with the help of friends). Get to it!

It's Time to Play the Rating Game

To make as much money as possible, you can't be caught playing for $300 a night if a $400 job is available. Rating markets enables you to investigate the top-paying jobs before accepting middle or low-paying jobs.

First, divide up your file folders into the following categories: part-time club work (including restaurants, bars, nightclubs, live discos, hotels and motels); full-time club work (again, restaurants, bars, nightclubs, live discos, hotels and motels); nighttime casuals (including associations, unions, organizations, schools, concert promoters); daytime casuals (including schools, retirement homes, fairs, shopping centers, churches, and other miscellaneous occasional employers); studios (including private, radio, TV, and motion picture); and agents.

For each category, you need to decide what constitutes a top market, or "A" rating. Here is a listing of important criteria:

Clubs

1. *The Money.* This is the top consideration for most jobs. However, musicians often overemphasize money in negotiations with employers.

2. *Additional Fees.* Does this club book through an agent? If so, take the agent cut off the top. This shrinks many "A" markets to "B" status. Also, if a friend tipped you off on the job, or made phone calls to the agent, that person is due a "finder's fee," (2 percent or so), usually privately negotiable.

3. *Travel Costs.* If your Baltimore-based band is offered $1,500 for a week in Philadelphia, but you must commute the 98 miles daily in an old pickup that gets 10 miles to the gallon, travel suddenly becomes the big factor. All out-of-town jobs must have transportation costs taken into account.

4. *The Working Hours.* After fees and travel costs have been deducted from an offer, you can divide what's left by the total number of hours you'll work during the week. This will give you a comparable hourly wage for each job. The higher the hourly wage, the higher rating the job should receive.

5. *Rooms and Meals.* When traveling any distance, these considerations, like gasoline, loom large. If neither rooms nor meals are included, will the gig provide enough to pay expenses *and* turn a reasonable profit?

6. *Advertising.* A bar that advertises your name on the radio, takes out a newspaper ad for you, or prints and distributes flyers (saving you that chore) with your name on them is helping sell your band. Give a few plus points here. This increases in importance if you're

trying to promote a local hit song.

7. *Potential Opportunities.* It's not at all uncommon for bands to agree to play a gig with the understanding that, "If we do well, they'll hire us full-time." If the club really offers you something, money or otherwise, and the manager seems sincere, give that club a slightly higher grade.

8. *Complimentary Drinks.* Do you plan to drink while working? If so, a bar that refuses to serve complimentary drinks should get a slightly lower rating.

9. *Likability Factor.* It won't get you rich, but it can't be ignored. Playing for appreciative employers in a comfortable place, where all your friends will come out to see you, sure beats being paid a little extra to play in a smoke-choked bar room where the boss gripes about everything you do.

Studios

1. *Potential Opportunities.* Certain local advertising clients pay better than others, and they rely on regular stables of proven musicians for sound tracks (Chapter 14). Does this studio have better clients than the other studio? The only way you'll find this out is to talk with musicians currently recording in the local studios.

2. *Money.* Studio work, when contracted through the studio and not an advertiser, generally follows standard pay scales, so any variance is minimal.

Agents

One of the goals of this book is to help you with the practical business skills you'll need to book your band yourself. Not relying on agents for work increases your share of the money live-music employers are willing to pay. In some areas or in certain clubs, however, working directly with employers is next to impossible because agents have firmly established themselves as reliable sources for finding musicians. This is especially true in big cities. In such an instance, you'll have to go through an agent to get into a club. An important question to ask an agent is, "What other acts do you book?" You'll want to choose agents who book well-known area groups, so you can benefit from that agent's success with certain clubs. Ask the agent for phone numbers of some of these acts, so you can call them and learn how effective that agent *really* is. While you're on the phone with the agent, ask about these other two criteria:

1. *Percentage.* A five-percent difference may not sound like much, but it can easily translate into hundreds of dollars. If you can find agents advertising services for 10 percent, give them some extra credit points.

2. *Representation.* Once you decide on your musical direction,

certain agents will have better contacts in that field than others. Also, some agents book more rooms or better paying rooms (See Chapter 12, "Finding a Reliable Agency").

The easiest method of rating jobs is to base your rating on money as primary (A—highest paying), secondary (B—good paying), or tertiary (C—average or low paying) markets. Many of the aforementioned criteria can substantially cut into a wage, so consider all expenses associated with each job, especially out-of-town gigs. Your final ratings should reflect net income that the act can take home.

Who Purchases Your Style of Music?

Finding, investigating, and pursuing those employers who seem to be most receptive to the style of music you'll play is your next concern. This should be detailed under "Style of Music/General Information" on each research sheet. Add up the various markets for jazz, rock, pop, or funk and decide where the live-music emphasis is in your area. Will the type of band you have been planning have a long list of employers? Ideally, yes. Many performers of obscure music are forced by economics to play popular music in one band in order to play what they really love in another band.

After each market is rated, your interest will naturally fall on the primary ("A") markets. After all, they pay the most money. But plan carefully. To approach a manager of a primary market club about hiring your band without being totally prepared is suicide. Since many primary market clubs are one link in a chain corporation, or book through influential agents only, the word on your band—good or bad—will precede you wherever the band auditions. One pet peeve by an agent or hotel representative can "black ball" the band, so don't rush into these markets until you've mastered the information in Chapters 6 through 11. A good policy after rating markets is to send a personally addressed follow-up letter to each primary market, thanking them for their answers to your questions. Keep it short, and mention you will notify them when ready to present your group for an audition. It helps if managers at least become aware of your existence.

In your haste to court the best paying jobs, don't completely dismiss secondary and tertiary markets as worthless. They are valuable both as testing grounds for your material and as reliable jobs to fill in sudden lapses in scheduling (don't worry, it'll happen!). If you take the time to prepare thoroughly now, however, your act will fly straight to the primary markets, and land in some lucrative jobs.

• PART TWO •

BUILDING A SOLID FINANCIAL BASE

• CHAPTER FIVE •

SELECTING A GROUP

The cornerstone of your freelance musical career should be a live performing act. Why? That's where most of the money is! It's also where most of the job opportunities are. If you decide to work only as a music teacher or by renting out your home recording studio, you'll be ignoring the biggest market for your talent.

But no matter how big your band is, or what style of music you play, you'll want the finished product to be great. Set your sights on playing in a red-hot band: Instead of believing "we'll get better as we go along," plan on busting out of the chute at full speed, ready to take your area by storm. There will be a warm-up period, of course, but by taking care of as many details as possible before your first performance, you'll quickly show black ink in the band ledger.

What determines a great act? As a musician, you'll listen for the music: Does the act sound clean and tight? Does everyone groove together on stage? The bottom line for you will be musical quality.

Club managers will judge you by the bar tab. Was the bar busy? Was tobacco smoke so thick that visibility was only five feet? Were there long lines at the rest rooms? The bottom line for your employer will be cash.

Members of the audience will judge you by entertainment value. Was the group exciting to watch? Was the music danceable and the volume at a comfortable listening level? Was it a fun evening? The bottom line for the audience is having a good time.

In order to be great, your act should satisfy the musicians, the manager, and the audience by playing well, selling a lot of drinks, and creating an exciting atmosphere. Just as important, your group should also be judged by how much money you're making, your negotiating skills, and the businesslike manner you project offstage.

In order to satisfy everyone and accomplish these goals, you've got to

An array of keyboards and the right person playing them can change your R&B group into a country swing band, and then into a Top 40 act—all in the same night.

(photograph by Greg Savalin)

find the right business partners. This chapter deals with successfully choosing people to work with.

Should You Start the Group?

You'll be the obvious (and only) boss if you decide to start a solo act, but like most musicians, you'll probably choose to form a band with several others. Now is a good time to consider an important question: Should you start the group, or join someone else's group? This clear-cut question often has an ambiguous answer. Whose band is it if you and a friend join up with two other musicians? What if you join a duo that has already rehearsed and knows a complete show, but rehearsals are held at your house and you own a beautiful new P.A. system the trio plans to use? How about if you and a friend answer an ad for a singer, bassist, drummer, and saxophonist? What then? Who holds the aces and makes the decisions?

At most initial meetings where no one is clearly in charge, everyone sits down and talks things over. Then each musician has a chance either to take the initiative in band matters, or to adopt a passive, neutral position. The leaders will distinguish themselves from the followers. In this situation, you can rise to whatever interpersonal prominence you desire.

If you want to start the band yourself, you should:
1. Have a good deal of free time to devote to the group.
2. Be outspoken.
3. Have confidence in yourself and your ability to work with people.
4. Know what style of music the band will play and have an idea of what instrumentation is ideal for that style.
5. Own some P.A. equipment (a full P.A. could consist of mixing board, amplifier, equalizer, microphones, stands, main speakers, and monitors), besides whatever instruments and amplifiers you personally need.
6. Have some money to invest, or know an individual willing to do so.

If you start a band, you are assuming a leadership role. Most groups work this way. Rarely does a keyboardist, for example, invest time, money, and effort in starting a band and then relinquish this position of power. Instead, when the keyboardist *decides* to start a band, with all the obstacles to overcome, that person has also decided to see the business through to the end.

The most crucial consideration when putting a group together is *time*. How much time will you have? It takes even experienced musicians months to plan, find complementary people, and rehearse an act. If you're wavering in your decision of whether to start a group or not, make *time* your main consideration.

Being confident, outspoken, and knowing how to work with others are valuable leadership qualities. You need to be both assertive and tactful when resolving differences between band members, or kicking someone out of the band.

Before going any further, figure out ideal instrumentation for the band you want to start. It's impossible to advertise unless you can clearly state what you want. Having specific material in mind is another prerequisite. Usually, the first question prospective partners will ask you is, "What kind of stuff do you play?" Answering "I don't really know," or "I haven't given it much thought," doesn't say much for your planning and organizational abilities.

If you're not sure how much time you can devote to the band, or don't feel comfortable with the responsibilities involved, then join up with other musicians who are starting a group, or are looking for a replacement (you!) in their established band. Later you can expand your influence by doing the things nobody else wants to do, such as arranging printing and promotions, lining up gigs, offering your vehicle as band transportation, or writing songs.

Whether you decide to start a band, or join a forming or an established band, now is the time to advertise yourself. The most common, and probably most successful way of getting into a group is by word-of-mouth.

After a group I was in disbanded, I sat down one evening and tried to think of how I could quickly get into another band. I was young, and the group that had just broken up hadn't attained any degree of recognition. I didn't know too many musicians, but I called everyone I knew and told them I was looking for a new band. Then I plastered the local music stores with cards announcing my availability. Nothing happened. Finally, two weeks later, a bass player knocked on my door, and said that my neighbor had called him. "I guess she's tired of listening to you practice by yourself," he said. That evolved immediately into another group.

If you are a member of the American Federation of Musicians (AFM), check with your local to see if they keep a list of musicians available for work. Some areas have musician referral services operated by radio stations, songwriters' showcases, or talent agencies.

Newspaper classified ads are an increasingly popular way for musicians to contact one another. The ads for musicians I've seen are run in the "Help Wanted" column under "M" for musicians. Since you are charged by the word or by the number of lines in the ad, keep the message short. Here are two examples:

>MUSICIANS—C&W Band being formed. Need hardworking singing pros, keys, steel, drums, trumpet, reeds. (Phone #)

> MUSICIANS—Bass player needed for working rock band. Eves. (Phone #)

The second example is the better since it's shorter. In a newspaper ad limit the information to the kind of musician you're looking for, what style of music you're playing (or prefer to play), and the telephone number where you can be reached. Including adjectives such as "hardworking," "serious," or "professional," doesn't help, since they are interpreted to mean different things.

Music stores usually provide a bulletin board for messages, which are avidly read by just the people you want to meet. Posted advertisements should never be scrawled on a half-sheet of binder paper—you want to appear professional. Remember, the person reading your ad begins forming a mental picture of you immediately.

When one of my bands was looking for a bassist, I found one ad in a music store written in pencil on the ripped off top of a Styrofoam Big Mac carton! Needless to say, I passed over that one. A sloppy image doesn't help your chances of contacting worthwhile musicians.

A typed, dated card (3x5 or 5x7 inches works well) can contain more information about you than a newspaper ad, since you're not paying for space.

> GUITARIST AVAILABLE
>
> 8 years experience playing clubs, concerts. 22 years old.
>
> Will travel or stay local. Have transportation and full equipment.
>
> Prefer jazz/rock to pop/rock. (Jean-Luc Ponty to Hall & Oates in style.) Also have played jazz and hard rock.
>
> Ready for immediate work--Call Ryan at [phone #] after 5:00 p.m.

Play up your positive attributes while ignoring the negative aspects of your playing or your personality. Don't lie, but putting yourself down won't get results. So what if you've never been in a band before. Don't mention that unless asked. Are you a natural showperson? Do you have a large van that could be used to haul equipment? List the things about yourself that will get you an audition—a foot in the door—and then take it from there.

Card advertisements also receive good exposure on school or college bulletin boards (particularly in the music department). Supermarkets and bookstores are worth posting cards at, too. Does all this mean you need to type more than one card? You bet! Go into mass production.

The Band as a Unit Must Be Stronger Than Any One Member

If your band is to survive for a long time, it must be evenly weighted and not wholly dependent on one person. Consider a predicament I encountered several years ago:

I answered an advertisement which read, "Experienced rock drummer needed for working local band." I called and arranged an audition, in the meantime learning the songs I was to drum. I arrived on time for the audition, and everything was working out fine until suddenly the lead vocalist, Rick, abruptly stopped singing and glared at me. Everyone became strangely silent. Had my pants fallen down? What crime was I guilty of?

"Didn't you learn that last drum part?" asked Rick.

I replied that yes, I had, but I didn't like the original drum part so I had changed it.

"Well, change it back!" he insisted.

When I declined, he flicked off the P.A. and marched out of the practice room, microphone in hand.

The other musicians offered their condolences, said they enjoyed my drumming, but sheepishly admitted they had no power to change Rick's mind.

Why did Rick wield such great power? Simple. He owned the P.A. equipment, this was his house, and he handled all the bookings for the band. Quite accurately, without Rick, there was no band. He had a stranglehold on the other musicians.

Avoid dictatorship bands like Rick's. Some bandleaders who finance, select, and handle bands are great people to work with (or *for*), and openly consider others' viewpoints. They realize that abusing power is dangerous, since power is often imagined, and can change hands quickly. When a bandleader tries to control everything, animosity between band members is usually the result. Staging, booking, rehearsing, financing and promoting all need attention and direction, but if one member directs all these areas, that person controls you. Besides, who wants to be responsible for *all* those chores? Instead, divide the power in your band by distributing ownership, duties, and responsibilities as evenly as possible. If you think you're the only one capable of handling band responsibilities, you're probably being narrow-minded. Look objectively at your time and personal qualifications. Much of the success of small businesses results from one person *not* trying to do everything, and learning how to delegate authority.

Mixing the Sexes Opens Doors, But . . .

Probably the biggest single step your group can take toward gaining acceptance at a variety of jobs is to feature both sexes on stage. For all-male groups, hiring a woman—usually as lead singer—automatically increases income and gains access into a whole new genre of clubs they couldn't get booked into before. Many large hotel and restaurant chains require that groups have a woman in the act. Some tour agents I've talked to won't even listen to a demo unless there's a female vocalist in the group.

A woman adds another musical dimension to an all-male band, singing high harmonies men can't reach, or singing songs made popular by female recording artists. Many songs, particularly ballads, just sound better sung by women.

The vocal ranges of current popular songs must be considered when choosing group members. Today, medium to high register vocal arrangements predominate in the Top 100. Just listen to the radio. Night after night of straining to reach high notes will take its toll on a male singer, either through hoarseness, or in more serious cases, swelling of and developing nodes on the vocal cords. Women are more comfortable singing those higher parts. But the main reason many clubs want a woman in the band is entertainment value. Most bargoers—and an even higher percentage of the people *paying* for drinks—are men. There's no question that a female performer can hold a predominantly male audience's attention better than a male performer, especially when the crowd is imbibing alcoholic beverages. Managers reason that the best way to keep men—the spenders—in the audience is to have a woman coaxing them from the stage to drink up and have a good time. Since most bands are predominantly male, managers don't worry about keeping women in the audience. They've got plenty of men to watch.

For an all-female band, hiring a man typically increases band credibility as a tight musical act. This is unfair, but it's true. Men are generally considered better musicians. A woman's musical ability is questioned by audiences—again, who are mostly male—until she demonstrates she can perform. Because of this bias, a man in an all-female act makes booking into exclusive nightclubs easier to accomplish. However, all-female groups, by capitalizing on that fact in their promotion, can usually stir up enough interest to counter this prejudice, and get bookings. Some popular songs do call for a low, masculine voice, which an all-female band will be hard-pressed to duplicate.

The musical and visual variety created by mixing the sexes is obvious and well proven. Unfortunately, the drawback of performing with both men and women is even more obvious. Close male-female relationships, particularly sexual interactions, can end with the kind of bitter animosity that destroys the very ties binding bands together. Without going into a course on human sexual behavior, let me ask you to review your own close relationships past and present, and look at how volatile, fragile, and intense they can become. Is it reasonable to assume you can work and play—indeed, practically *live*—with attractive men and women without yearning for more than a handshake? Can you control your desires and emotions, or will you even want to?

I know of several tight-knit groups that broke up due to sexual conflicts—one band barely escaped a lawsuit! When they left northern California on a six-week tour, the female lead singer/guitarist was going to bed with the lead guitarist. By Arizona she was sleeping with the drummer. They reneged on their contract and came back home within three weeks, the lead guitarist and drummer not speaking and the lead singer quitting the group to avoid more hassles. Luckily, the agent didn't sue them for breach of contract.

I've seen three arrangements work well for male-female groups. The first, and probably best, is a strict "hands-off" policy, openly decided upon by everyone connected with the band, including managers, sound technicians, and road crews (they're human too, so I'm told). A second arrangement is a close, openly acknowledged undisputable relationship between two people. I've seen married or stable couples never have any problems with this, as long as the rest of the band and crew understood and repected the relationship. The third arrangement I've known to work is a "no-holds-barred, anything goes" policy. Personal inhibitions can be a problem in this sexually open arrangement, but it can work, as long as everyone knows that no permanent or selfish stakes can be claimed. Whatever your mutual agreement, make absolutely certain that everyone understands the possible consequences of a breach of faith, because it takes only two individuals to jeopardize the security of the entire organization.

A Versatile Keyboardist Means Money

Due to design and electronic advances in keyboards during the past five years, a pianist or keyboardist is potentially the most versatile-sounding instrumentalist in any band. Instrument companies like Roland, Moog, Korg, and Linn are producing keyboards that can mimic guitar, bass, drums, acoustic pianos, and string ensembles, and are also capable of producing a wide array of new sounds, distinctly different from existing instruments. Although many older musicians refuse to acknowledge the newest crop of electronic wizardry as legitimate instruments, younger players are eagerly discovering the possibilities of the latest hardware. The testing ground is the recording industry, where a new and unique sound can gain mass popularity in a hit song.

Bands such as Toto and Devo rely on synthesizers to simulate horns, flutes, and keyboard instruments. Classical arranger Isao Tomita uses synthesizers exclusively to recreate compositions by Strauss, Debussy, and Stravinsky. And movie producers are choosing to use synthesizers instead of live musicians to save money and create unearthly sound tracks, such as those heard in *Star Trek II* and *Chariots of Fire*.

A good keyboardist who is quick on a swivel chair can eliminate the need for one or two other musicians, while "creating" horn sections, drummers, and string sections to fill out the group's sound.

There's a double standard here—while you may be the talented keyboardist, or have one in your group, you could also be the musician no longer needed because of a piece of machinery. Though I hate to see the number of musicians employed drop, I must side with technology, innovative musicians, and the right of bands to cut costs and make more money. If you are aggressive and smart (talent helps too), you won't have anything to worry about. The fittest musicians will find work.

The newest synthesizers are barely short of amazing. While the '70s were dominated with "analog" synthesizers capable of reproducing sounds or creating their own, the '80s are springing forward with "digital synthesis machines"—synthesizers which consist of a keyboard and a computer. The computer performs any number of functions, such as committing a melody to its "memory," to be recalled and played with a live solo or with other memorized parts.

A top-of-the-line digital machine, like the Synclavier II 32-voice, allows the programmer keyboardist to program his own software on a minicomputer viewing screen. It sells in the $30,000 price range. Emulator makes a full-function digital machine capable of recording sounds for about $8,000. For $5,000 you can buy a Synergy synthesizer that uses small cartridges with pre-recorded information to direct its computer on what sounds to create.

The introduction of these new synthesizers has resulted in price wars between manufacturers of analog keyboards. A small, conventional synthesizer can be purchased new for under $500, and prices for used equipment have dropped dramatically.

Not only are instrument manufacturers coming out with increasingly versatile keyboards, they're also packaging these instruments in smaller, more convenient cases. It's possible to buy one unit that will sound like an electric piano, bass keyboard, organ, conventional synthesizer, and also contain a rhythm sequencer.

It's difficult to copy a full night's worth of current hits without a keyboardist. In the '60s or early '70s, a four-piece local group consisting of two guitarists, a bassist, and a drummer could reasonably copy new hit songs. Nowadays, popular music relies heavily on keyboards, so a four-piece guitar band runs into trouble. How do you play a delicate acoustic piano part or a synthesizer solo on a Stratocaster? A keyboard-based band, with two keyboardists, a bassist, and a drummer, can recreate virtually all the new music, while adding horns and strings.

The variety of unusual keyboards on the market has spawned a new phenomenon: the keyboard musician who can't play piano! Some of the electronic units resemble computer programming boards, and place greater emphasis on twisting knobs and balancing levels than on piano-playing technique. The same goes for pianists. They can't automatically play all the new keyboards because many of the new electronic gadgets don't even resemble a piano keyboard. When you're auditioning keyboardists, find out where their strengths—and preferences—lie. The guy might have all the latest synthesizers, but not be able to play any of them well.

The major factor keeping keyboardists from owning all the latest equipment is the cost of the units. I've seen local musicians with $12,000 invested in *just* keyboards. This is much more than anyone else will have invested in personal equipment, so buying a string ensemble keyboard or electric grand piano as a *band* expense might be worth considering. Of course, you can avoid this expense by finding a keyboardist who already has a van full of equipment (but if you do, give me a call).

Auditions

Now you're ready to make some choices based on what you've decided so far. You've scouted your area, and the possibilities for live employment look good. As a matter of fact, some of the local bands playing around are so bad, and some of the organizations you've talked with on the phone can afford so much, that you're itching for a chance to prove what a hot act you can stage.

You're going to start the band. You've decided on the style of music you want to play (or at least, the style you'll stage *first!*). You sat down and listened to a few of the songs you plan to play, and figured out what instrumentation and vocal ranges you'll need. Then you placed ads around town. You've been conspiring with a couple of musician friends, and the three of you have learned 10 songs, but damn it, it gets boring keeping time without a drummer and having to imagine all the lead solos! Now the phone starts to ring with interested musicians. How do you sort out which ones are also interesting to you? On the phone discuss these topics and jot down their responses:

1. First, explain what you're trying to do. State your goals and degree of commitment. Outline your plans. Is the person still interested? If so, continue.
2. Ask the person's musical preferences, with examples of specific artists. Expect to give the same information about yourself.
3. Find out how long the caller has played, with whom, what different styles, and how things worked out. (If you have never been in a band, you might want to limit your questions, because she'll then ask the same questions of you.)
4. Find out the prospect's commitment to music. Is music a side occupation?

5. How much time could they he or she devote to rehearsing?
6. Has the caller handled business matters or bookings for any previous bands?
7. Ask age, marital status, and where the person lives. Musicians close in age tend to enjoy the same things and communicate easily. Marital status is important because a newlywed may not want to travel.
8. Ask about personal transportation and equipment.
9. Get a phone number, say you appreciated the call, and you'll call back about an audition.

As soon as you hang up, ask yourself some questions. Did you like the person? Did you believe what the person said? Are you interested in meeting and listening to that person play?

If you're excited about the possibilities, you should call back after figuring out a way to get the person a tape of several songs to learn. Jam session auditions rarely tell you what you need to know about playing style. Maybe she can play like lightning, but does she know when *not* to play? Does she have enough incentive to really learn songs, or does she feel she doesn't need to practice? Asking someone to learn specific material will answer these questions.

Set up short auditions (30 minutes is plenty of time; many times it only takes half a song to discover the guy's an idiot or a musical genius). Make the atmosphere as comfortable as possible. Terrible cases of nervousness are common at auditions, and if this is the situation, string out the audition to see if they'll loosen up enough to play well. Listen closely to the last song or two. Did she get bolder and more self-assured as she played? If not, she may be too inexperienced to help your act grow.

Choosing complementary vocalists is extremely important. Initially, after talking with vocalists on the phone, you'll have to get them tapes of songs that feature vocal parts in their singing ranges. Make sure the audition songs will allow you to hear their voices clearly over the instrumentation. If you're starting a progressive jazz band or hard rock act, you'll want to hear them sing really hot, fast songs to judge energy and stage presence, but assign one or two ballads so you can hear their tone quality. If they're back-up singers, you'll have to assign them specific harmonies to learn so you can judge how well they pick their part out and perform it while singing with other members of the group.

You'll want to cover the broadest possible vocal spectrum, due to the diversity of popular music. Pay particular attention to the higher register if you'll be copying hits, since more and more songs feature ear-piercing high harmonies. If you want to stage a four-piece band, you can cover the whole spectrum by having a soprano-range female, a tenor-range female or male, a baritone-range male, and a bass-range male. A few experienced singers capable of a four- or five-octave range cover most of this spectrum themselves, but the majority of professional singers only have a two- to three-octave range. This is still better than most people, who are limited to a one-and-a-half-octave range.

Be professional. All auditions are two-way streets: The person you're auditioning is likewise auditioning you. If you're overly casual and fumble through the songs, your hot prospect may well shine you on.

Discuss Commitments Beforehand

Immediately after auditioning an exciting player, gather everyone around to talk. How are the vibes? Relieve any tension the audition might have caused. Reiterate the group's basic direction, artistic likes and dislikes, and any other pertinent information. Gradually get across the point—without scaring the person away—that this band is serious about making consistent money. Describe your personal position—daytime job, college classes—and show the degree of commitment going into this project.

By laying yourself on the line, revealing your time and financial investment, and the extent of your interest in the band, you're showing sincerity. By giving away information, you make it emotionally comfortable for this new person to do likewise. Then, hopefully, you'll understand where he's coming from, why he's interested in joining your band, and what he hopes to get out of it.

In short, you hope to better understand his commitment to the group, without blurting "How committed are you to playing with us?" This is a scary question, coming from some bassist he's only known for 45 minutes. He's likely to become frightened and state indifferently, "I'm not sure I even *want* to play in this band!" Then everyone loses.

Once when my band was auditioning a keyboardist, the bassist and I looked at each other and said with our eyes, "This guy's fantastic! He's a monster. Just what we've been looking for!" We played through two songs, stopped, and immediately asked him if he wanted the job. He seemed happy with the offer and accepted. We all said a hurried goodbye and left. Two weeks later, after missing several rehearsals, he quit. Why? After the initial audition, we put a lot of heat on him to learn the tunes and make the rehearsals. We pushed too hard. We failed to ask him at the audition what *he* wanted out of the band, why *he* was interested, and where *he* was coming from. We had no real idea of his degree of commitment.

It's not fair to ask for a promise of lifelong commitment, but you should reach a consensus on rehearsal hours and time availability. Listen for genuine interest, excitement, and sincerity in someone's voice. Asking for a minimum two weeks' notice when quitting is acceptable, but a two-year, no-cut contract will scare off any worthwhile musician.

The Musician Personality Test

Now you have a representative idea of each person's instrumental and/or vocal strengths. Maybe one or two stood out as better musicians. You want the most talented musicians you can get, but having the fastest lead guitarist in the world won't help a bit unless that person is also easy to get along with and, indeed, easy to *live* with. Fortunately, you've talked with each musician after hearing them, so you have an idea of who you like the most. A few seemed very friendly—really nice people. To help you narrow the field, here's a list of questions to ask yourself about musicians vying for the same position:

Were they naturally friendly? This should be quickly apparent. First impressions often reveal true dispositions. Ask yourself, "Does she smile and laugh easily? Does she have a sense of humor?"

Who seemed the most secure? Partners should be able to cope with their own private lives, and not drag you into personal problems. Did he seem worried about something or complain continually?

Were any of them stubborn or hot-tempered people? Nothing ruins a feeling of goodwill like someone storming out of a practice, or, worse yet, a gig. Stubborn or hot-tempered players make communication difficult by putting up mental barriers to suggestions and opposing viewpoints. Did she really listen to what you said, or dismiss it and adamantly endorse her own opinion?

Which players adapted easily to special conditions? Ideally, members should be open-minded and able to adapt to sudden changes in plans. In this freewheeling, freelancing lifestyle, little is for certain until it happens. Will this guy be able to take sudden news in stride, without getting all worked up?

Who was the most positive person? Having a pessimistic person around is like dragging a ball and chain everywhere you go. They usually disagree with the majority of the group and slow progress, advocate taking no chances, and complain about trivial things. Did she counter your every statement with a pessimistic view? Look for optimistic people.

Who had the most energy? Some entertainers can turn their energy on and off like a light switch, but most performers who bounce around and are witty and bright onstage are that way offstage, too. Offstage band work requires stamina. Moving equipment is hard work! Was he lethargic and uninspired, or peppy and enthusiastic?

Who learned the material and came prepared? Many times the best prepared musician gets the job because he *sounds* good. If this person doesn't have it together at an audition, what promise do you have she'll be any different at a gig? Did she start apologizing and giving excuses as soon as you met?

If you've scribbled one musician's name nine out of ten times, you've got a good idea of the personality most likely to fortify your long-range goals.

These personality preferences don't apply only to musicians you audition or members of bands you audition for. They also apply to you! Expecting professional behavior from others while acting unprofessional yourself is unrealistic. Set a good example.

Selecting Members (the Moment of Truth)

Deciding on your business partners is a time of high expectations, so consider everyone's "application" carefully to have a good chance of attaining those expectations. You've heard several people play and sing at auditions, and you have a pretty good idea of who the most dedicated musicians are. You've talked with everybody about where they stand, and you've run them through the "Musician Personality Test" to determine who will contribute most to the band's growth. Now is the moment of truth. Who will it be? Hopefully, the ones you want haven't joined another band since you last talked with them. This occasionally happens, since talented and likable musicians are always in demand.

Set up a meeting with other members of the band (if there are any!) and solicit opinions. Seemingly trivial questions such as "Did he arrive on time?" and "Did she come prepared?" can come back to haunt you if not given some consideration. If you've been able to get any tips from musicians who have previously worked with a person you're considering, judge that information's accuracy by what you think of the musician from the audition, and by the credibility of the source: Grudges are not unheard of. Air everything before your partners and then decide, by vote, if necessary, who is the best all-around choice.

How do you choose between a good musician who has a new Maxi-Van and a complete P.A. system, and a great musician who drives a '59 Bug and uses mediocre equipment, when they're both nice people? It's tough. Musically, the band will always be limited by the weakest link in the chain, and discriminating judges of talent will hear that weak link. But is she committed to practicing or taking lessons? Will she improve with rehearsals and initial performances? Does she *want* to get better? If you use a moped for transportation and only own one microphone, her van and P.A. will look very inviting. Decide on individuals who will help the group *the most*, musically or otherwise.

Decide Together on Goals

After working in bands for many years, I've found that career direction is often ignored. It's just never discussed. The group never formally comes to a consensus as to what this business hopes to accomplish. It's always sad to see an act break up just because the singer expected something different from what the conga player did.

Once your personnel are finalized, set up a career-direction meeting. The purpose of the meeting is to agree on band direction and goals, and to draw up band time tables detailing how you will pursue those goals.

The major decision the group must make is *what type of act are you forming?* The choice is *very* clear: You either aim to quickly make money as a local band, or aim for a recording contract in hope of striking it rich. You could do both, but each requires a uniquely different process. This is the biggest stumbling block for most beginning bands. Half the group wants to open for The Who in two months, while the other half just wants to pay the rent and buy groceries.

Up until 1980, you could realistically accomplish both in one band. You could play the Hilton Inn circuit and record demo tapes to send off with the idea of landing a recording contract. But demo tapes carry very little influence now, and indeed may never even get listened to. The possibility of sending out a tape to a record company and getting a deal used to be remote. Now, thanks to the economic hardship felling the record industry, it's impossible. Artist and repertoire departments have been cut, and in some cases, closed. *They're not listening to demos!*

Obviously, a few acts are still being signed. How are they getting contracts? By taking the bull by the horns! Informed groups serious about signing with a major label no longer pin their hopes on a postage stamp. Smart bands realize record companies won't risk $250,000 on an unknown, unproven act. So what do they do? They prove themselves!

Here's one way of doing it: First, they agree that almost all profits will be plowed back into the act, financing vehicles, lighting systems, sound equipment, and a road crew. They concentrate on developing their local reputation and drawing-power until they are the premier band in their area, then press a single or album for local release, and attract the interest of music trade journals. Soon, the phone is ringing off the hook with record company executives, anxious to sign the band (for details on getting yourself a contract, see Chapter 20).

What's wrong with this approach? It's an all or nothing shot. You won't make *any* money until the record companies notice you, if in fact they do. And even after signing the contract, your chance of making any money off the album is slight (Chapter 1). But it's a dream we all share, so go ahead and give it a try.

To really give it your best shot, you'll need to have money saved up to compensate for not being paid. This is the perfect reason for first forming a group with *only* local aspirations. Then when you've saved up enough money, you can start a new band or redirect the old one, with the goal of regional, then national stardom.

To recapitulate: At your career direction meeting the group must agree either to form a band that will quickly yield a net return, or form a band that will plow all profits back into itself in hopes of a bigger payoff in the end.

Here's a chart detailing the steps required for each type of act (the steps required for becoming a bona fide recording band can vary somewhat within a local perspective; see Chapter 20 for alternate routes):

Recording Band
1. Form band (with songwriters).
2. Initial investment.
3. Book gigs with radio spots included.
4. Keep non-band related job.
5. Constantly reinvest vast majority of profits in audio, visual, transportation, and road crew improvement.
6. Record & release a single (45).
7. Sell off-stage, in local record stores, and send to radio stations.
8. Remind following to phone in radio requests.
9. Get on local Top 40 charts; send charts to national trade journals.
10. Acknowledge record company interest.
11. Contact investors & raise money.
12. Hire independent producer & attorney; record album master tape.
13. Sell pressing, promotion, & distribution right to record company.
14. Realize net income.

Local band
1. Form band.
2. Initial investment.
3. Book gigs.
4. Pay off initial investment.
5. Realize net income.

Make Band Timetables

Planning is the essence of any career. How thoroughly, how realistically, and how progressively you plan will determine your chances of attaining your goals. Successful people—especially successful musicians—repeatedly stress the importance of plotting a course and taking one sure-footed step at a time. Foresight, the ability to see many things in relation to each other, is a necessary partner to limited goal-setting, the ability to plan a detailed process of goal attainment. It is rare when one individual possesses both visualization skills. More often than not, two people with opposite, complementary abilities will plan together, each providing a natural check and balance system for the other.

Outline two band timetables now, listing both long-range and short-range goals in chronological order. You should also make an appointment calendar to keep track of specific dates. Don't expect to draw the final charts right away. They will be periodically rearranged when new circumstances create new goals. And when I say "long-range," I don't mean 40 years from now. That's too distant—too easy to lose sight of. Consider long-range one or two years from now.

Long-Range Time Table
1. Complete market research.
2. Form local band.
3. Learn five hours' worth of material.
4. Begin playing part-time.
5. Apply at music stores for daytime job.
6. Advance to full-time band employment.
7. Begin recruiting students.
8. Start depositing money in savings account.
9. Purchase equipment, sound-proof basement, build control room.
10. Advertise equipment for rent.
11. Continue purchasing equipment.
12. Advertise studio facilities for rent.

This timetable is much more general than the Short-Range Timetable or the Appointments Calendar. It will help to reaffirm your career direction when short-range goals clutter your vision. Whereas a change in the Short-Range Timetable or the Appointments Calendar might not have any lasting effect, a change in your Long-Range Timetable probably signals a major change in career direction, or in the method you plan to obtain your goals.

As for short-range, detail all the definite advances you can see within a month's time. What significant goals should be accomplished? Less important steps toward your monthly goals can be detailed on the appointments calendar. (See pages 78-79 for examples of these calendars.)

The importance of frequent goal attainments has been proven again and again—it's the old "reward system." When a dog receives a pat or a cookie, its eyes gleam with satisfaction. It has *achieved* something, just as you breathe a sigh of accomplishment when the group rips through a difficult number in rehearsal, or the hottest bassist in town agrees to join the act. Goal attainment must be frequent so that the glow of success can be felt over and over again.

Always allot a little more time than you really believe it will take to complete a goal. Then you'll also feel the exhilaration of being ahead of schedule.

Follow the short-range timetable as if it were the gospel. Distant goals can look tantalizing and deceptively easy to attain, but unless the groundwork has been laid down well, the footing can get shaky.

One last note: Congratulate yourself and everyone concerned on reaching each and every goal, but move right on. Don't gloat over a goal achievement, because after all, it is a very small step when viewed wth long-range vision. Begin tackling the next goal!

Notice these goals are relatively modest accomplishments. If the only goal on the chart had been the "first band rehearsal" entry on the 25th, the group might not have completed each small goal before that. The first rehearsal probably would have been delayed because the previous goals had been allowed to slide.

A timetable shouldn't be confused with an ordinary appointments calendar, which goes into further detail by listing each specific move helping to achieve each timetable goal.

Both timetables and calendars should be large, and hung on the wall in a highly visible spot. To achieve your goals on or ahead of schedule you must be constantly aware of them.

Should You Join the Union?

No. Certainly not yet. You'll know from your market research sheets whether joining the American Federation of Musicians (AFM), or, if you're a singer, the American Federation of Television and Radio Artists (AFTRA), will make more work available to you. Chances are, it won't.

Why is the AFM, a labor union that regulates wages and working conditions for its 330,000 members, largely ineffective in most communities? Independent studios provide a vivid example: "I don't bother calling the union for session players because they don't have any," says the director of a 24-track studio. "All the professional studio musicians in this city, and almost all cities, are non-union."

Union wages do deter many small nightclub and small studio owners from hiring union bands, but a greater problem is the unavailability of hot, young union musicians and groups: "I call the union and get a list of swing bands," said a club owner. "That's fine, but *my* customers want rock music."

Why hasn't the union attracted or pursued young recruits with better success? The union newsletter, *International Musician*, is filled with news on union policy, and bills that the union is lobbying for or against, and it's saturated with news of interest to symphonic and jazz musicians; there's little to interest a young player. Moreover, sales from classical and jazz records account for only 8-12 percent of total record sales. The union is catering to older musicians, not today's trend-setting performers.

A body that will guarantee musicians a minimum wage is desperately needed, because many inexperienced non-union musicians agree to perform for shamefully low wages—the same $10 a night the club paid to musicians 15 years ago. If the older, wiser union musicians in locals across the nation can become more responsive to the needs of today's young musicians, the union could reverse the current trend of "not joining until I absolutely have to."

The AFM could revitalize its ranks with new blood. Until that time, however, only join your local when it is clearly advantageous for you to do so.

The Band that Plays Together Stays Together

One local group I know well has remained intact for 10 years. This is no easy accomplishment, and it speaks for their close friendship. "We were lucky because we grew up together," the keyboardist says. We've known each other since we were 14 years old. I've never seen a closer team than this one."

Another group, an acoustic trio, has been together two years, but they felt the need to get to know each other as friends. "We were always together because of gigs," says the leader, "and pretty soon everything was business, business, business. It got kinda hairy. These week-long vacations we take together every five or six months are a great way to revive our friendship *away* from the music thing."

The individuals in performing acts are closer than people in other types of small businesses. Every time you step onstage you're risking your reputation and all that you've worked for. You depend heavily on your partners. This necessitates a tight "family" relationship where everyone gets along well together. Because we get so close, tensions and frustrations develop. To let off some of this steam—and keep it from building in the first place—band members should participate together in non-musical activities. Play together!

It's a sure sign of stalled progress and limited interest when members punch in and out of performances with time-clock accuracy. When music is all work and no play, the group is in serious danger of splitting up. By enjoying each other and becoming acquainted with each other's family and friends, individual loyalty and excitement about the act will remain high.

SHORT-RANGE BAND TIMETABLE

Sunday	Monday	Tuesday	Wednesday	Thursday	Friday	Saturday
	1	2 Auditions through 2/7	3	4	5	6
7 Decide on keys, bass & sax	8 Comprehensive equipment inventory; discuss transportation	9	10 song selection	11 Gather tapes & records	12 Taping through 2/14	13
14 Distribute tapes	15	16	17	18	19	20 First vocal & rhythm section rehearsals
21	22	23	24	25 First full band rehearsal songs 1-10	26	27
28						

APPOINTMENTS CALENDAR

Sunday	Monday	Tuesday	Wednesday	Thursday	Friday	Saturday
	1	2 Jil (keys) 2:00 pm Bruce (keys) 3:00 pm	3 check back w/ Skip's	4 Jim (bass) 2:30 pm Ryan (bass) 3:30 pm	5 research phone calls call Lou	6 Phil (sax) 1:00 pm Rod (keys) 2:00 pm Julie (sax) 3:88 pm
7 meeting at Lou's 7:00 pm	8 meeting here at 6:30 pm call Skip's	9	10 meeting here at 6:30 pm	11 call Lou early	12	13 Go with Ryan to store
14	15	16 shopping at 2:00 pm w/ Ryan	17	18 Go with Lou for amplifier	19 Band party at Lou's 8:00 pm	20 practice at 1:00 pm
21 Band picnic at Discovery Park	22 practice w/ Ryan 7:00pm	23 practice w/ Ryan at 7:00 pm	24 practice w/ Ryan at 7:00 pm	25 practice at 2:00 pm	26 get new tapes from Lou	27 Band equipment shopping day - Skip's
28						

• CHAPTER SIX •

PULLING IT ALL TOGETHER— NOW WHAT DO YOU NEED?

Outfitting yourself or your group with equipment isn't easy. Buying instruments *sounds* fun, but making the right choice demands careful consideration of your needs.

A lead singer and I once auditioned a guitarist for a band we were starting. When he unpacked his Anvil cases we whistled our approval: A gleaming Gibson Les Paul with a new Ampeg amplifier! This guy must be serious! With the first song our excitement soured to hidden embarrassment. He was tone deaf. He sounded like he was tuning up throughout the whole number.

A woman I know had the opposite problem: She is an accomplished instrumentalist thanks to twelve years of piano lessons, but when she finally decided to buy a piano she only spent $250. After two months and six professional tunings (at $35 a visit) she traded it in on a quality piano, losing $360 in tunings and trade-in cost.

Group purchases are miscalculated almost as often as individual purchases. Often groups buy P.A. speakers that are perfectly adequate for indoor perfomances, but are too small for outdoor wedding receptions, for instance. And most bands trade up in mixing boards or power amps sooner or later.

This chapter will help you to buy equipment with foresight so that you won't wind up over-equipped or under-equipped. Both mistakes cost you money.

How to Choose the Right Equipment

When I bought my first set of drums, I was in love with them. I don't know why, but those were the most beautiful drums I'd ever seen. I'd draw pictures of them in class during lectures, mastering every detail

82 Making Money Making Music

Making your own electronic equipment is easier than you think, and the results will be high quality for a low price. A switch, like this musician is building, costs up to $90 in stores, but you can build it for $15.

(photo by Ellen Forsyth)

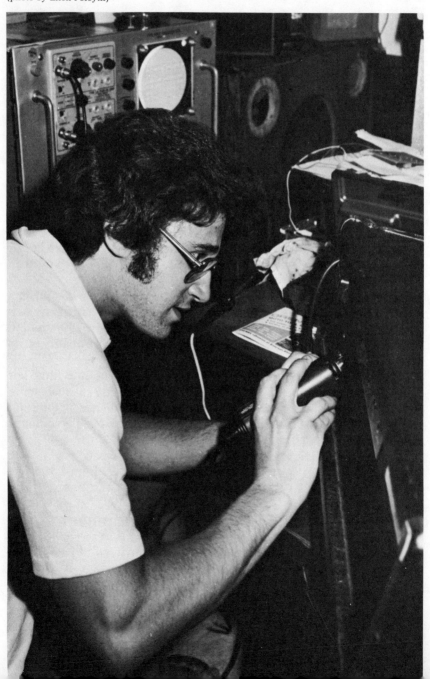

from the cymbal wing-nuts to the brand logo on the bass drum head. Needless to say, I favored that company's drums over all others.

But soon after purchasing that first set, when I ordered parts and delivery took eight weeks, when the company discontinued my style of hardware in favor of a newer style, and when I found out that there indeed were better drums available than mine, my criteria for choosing instruments changed just the tiniest little bit. Rather than falling in love with an instrument for no reason other than image, I found that instruments must be judged in terms of price, quality, service, and company history.

One of the easiest marketing ploys to get caught up in is buying instruments and equipment because of whose endorsement accompanies the advertisement. You know. Remember when you were 10 years old and you bought the "Mickey Mantle" softball glove instead of the plain "genuine leather" glove? How did you know Mickey thought the endorsed glove was better than the plain glove? You didn't. It's the same with instruments and equipment. Product endorsements can be bought (would you turn down all the free equipment you could ruin?), so separating sincere endorsements from "strictly business" deals is impossible. Choosing a Gibson over a Fender because your favorite guitarist poses with a Gibson isn't a good criterion for shelling out the money.

Music store personnel will be up on the different brands. Retailers I talked with emphasized that heavily advertised equipment is not necessarily any better than lesser-known products. They stressed the importance of considering all brands. One good way of comparing brands is to watch for product tests in music magazines.

Price will be your first consideration, unless you've already put out a double-platinum record. Once you've decided how much you can afford, you can investigate all the components within your price range.

Quality is the natural partner to price, the two supposedly going hand in hand. Again, try not to let old established brand loyalty influence your comparison between equipment. Be wary comparing something carried by the store and something not carried by the store. The sales people might be working on a commission basis. Instead, always ask for comparisons of two products they don't carry or two products they do carry, keeping in mind that in the latter case, a commissioned salesperson will tend to push the more expensive of the two, since commission is proportional to the sale price.

One of the best questions to ask a salesperson is, "How long have you stocked this brand of merchandise?" Most store owners drop brands requiring frequent service or replacement. If she proudly states, "We've handled this company's line for 20 years," you can be reasonably certain the company has a good track record for needing few repairs.

Service is often overlooked in the face of a 50 percent clearance sale, but as manufacturers place more emphasis on mass production rather than quality, finding a service-oriented retailer is increasingly important. Ask questions like, "Do you do in-store repair work, or does the unit have to be shipped back to the manufacturer? Who pays for shipping costs? Will you give me a replacement until my unit is repaired? Are this manufacturer's parts expensive or inexpensive? How long does it take to get parts?" I've found that although foreign manufacturers often sell at a lower initial price than American companies, foreign companies charge more for service and parts, and are generally slower in processing shipments.

Inquire about parts availability before buying anything. It's important to find out how quickly the manufacturer abandons models in favor of newer "competitive" models. It's not uncommon for manufacturers to strive to offer the latest designs, and in the process discontinue parts for the equipment you bought last year. A full-service retailer should have a stock of parts that wear out fast—ask to see his parts inventory.

Carefully consider how you intend to use the equipment before buying it. If you're aiming to play in smaller rooms, or might mike your amp through the P.A., why buy the larger, more powerful amplifier? Will you be playing dances and parties? If so, you'd better buy the more powerful equipment now, rather than buying the less powerful equipment and taking a beating at trade-in time. If you plan to play country music, why buy a drum set with eight tom-toms? Try to predict what you'll need by asking other working musicians who are gigging in places you want to gig. Musicians habitually trade up in equipment, so why not suffer another month until you can afford the more expensive unit? It's hard to be creative if you're worrying about your instrument or your equipment.

Bigger isn't necessarily better, either. Technology enables units to be built smaller without sacrificing quality or volume. "Hot Spots" and similar tiny but powerful monitors prove this point. Choosing equipment with size in mind also saves space when packing the van—and may eliminate the need for an extra vehicle.

Getting What You Need for Less

Since price will determine which equipment you'll consider, let's look at some ways to get the most for your money. These techniques will save you a little by themselves, but used together they can really cut into a dealer's asking price.

Checking around at all the local stores is a good start. I've driven hundreds of miles to buy equipment at cut rates, but then servicing was a major problem. You don't want to drive two hours every time something breaks down, so try to stay local. Besides getting a price quote (you can *always* beat a full list price!), ask the questions about service listed in the previous section, and write the answers down on a note pad. It's also a good idea to award a little favoritism to the stores with the friendliest personnel. A nasty sales clerk can hold up an order indefinitely.

Managers will grudgingly participate in price quoting and inter-store competition with you. When you self-righteously state that "Johnson's Music has the same bass for $30 less *with* a case," the manager will usually contort his face and run his fingers through his hair while secretly fiddling with a pocket calculator. They don't like to be on the receiving end of it, but managers use your same cross-referencing bargaining leverage against distributors when they're buying stock. Most equipment in music stores is marked up 30 to 50 percent, so they have room to deal. You'll probably get the case and $40 off!

Just as store cross-referencing is useful, if overdone it can cause the manager to throw his hands up in despair and ask you to leave. When he offers you the case and $40 off and you say you'll have to come back after talking to the other store manager again, his patience will be wearing thin. If you don't play fair, he won't take your money on a gold platter! Why should he? Profit has been beaten down and, more important, there's no satisfaction left in the deal for him. Nobody likes losing.

Group purchases can often save you another 10 percent. Wait until you and a couple of other musicians are all ready to buy equipment. After separately getting price quotes, ask each store manager for a "group discount" on top of the normal discount. A $6,000 sale is harder for a manager to pass up than several $1,500 sales.

The real value of cross-referencing price quotes is in service deals. A manager often finds it easier to give up something other than a cash discount, such as a year-long service agreement or a free rental guarantee in case your unit needs servicing. He figures you might be touring in Alaska or traveling through Texas when your amp gives out, so you won't be around to collect. He might be right.

Plan on spending a little time in each store. Rarely will a salesperson feel content with offering a substantial discount unless you've heard the sales pitch, tried the thing out, sat around for a while, and demanded a lot of attention. By increasing a salesperson's time investment in you, you increase his need to get some satisfaction out of you.

Avoid letting the salesperson know you love the product and will do anything for it. This strengthens her bargaining position, since it's obvious you're going to buy the thing sooner or later. Make it known that although you're prepared to spend the money; you're not in any big hurry. Make her *sell* it to you. Nonchalantly mention that you can't decide between this new piano or a pool table. Act unconcerned, but make it clear that you'll go with the best deal since you don't appreciate being taken advantage of. As Herb Cohen says in *You Can Negotiate Anything*, "Regard youself as someone who wants to sell money. *Money* is the product that's up for sale."

The Band Equipment Checklist

Figuring the size and power of equipment you'll need for your act is not easy, but by reviewing the Nightclub Information box on your individual Market Research Sheets (Chapter 4), you can make an educated guess. Which clubs will you most likely play at? Of particular importance are stage size, room capacity, lighting, and sound system information. If all the clubs in town have installed stage lighting, why should you buy or build your own? They wouldn't be used unless you plan to play casuals or the band hits the road. If most of the clubs seat fewer than 75 people, why do you need Community Light and Sound P.A. mains? They're too big! You'd be better off renting for those occasional dances and outdoor concerts.

Inventory everything—instruments and equipment—to make sure some component isn't being purchased needlessly. Sometimes keyboardists have two or three amps on stage. Are they being used simultaneously, or could a rhythm guitar be run through one that isn't always in use? If one guitarist has an amplifier with enough power to blow the roof off the practice room, how about running another instrument through channel B on that amp? It'll save stage space and $600. If you plan on making all the instruments through the P.A., why not go with small amps on stage? That'll save space, money, and your hearing! What about running some instrument direct through the P.A., and filtering the sound back through the monitors? That could save an amp or two.

Also, you can greatly reduce costs by purchasing used equipment. Check classified ads, bulletin boards and any local papers specializing in second-hand goods. Sometimes music stores sell used equipment (trade-ins) at discount prices.

Compare your inventory with this list, checking off those things the group already has:

Band Equipment Checklist

INSTRUMENTS:
Total keyboard instruments: _____

Total guitar instruments: _____

Total percussion instruments: _____

Total reed & horn instruments: _____

Total other instruments: _____

Electronic instrument accessories (volume pedals, effects boxes, switches, etc.): _____

P.A. EQUIPMENT:
- ____ low impedance microphones
- ____ mike cords
- ____ mike stands
- ____ mixing board
- ____ equalizer
- ____ power amp(s)
- ____ digital delay/echo unit
- ____ other effects
- ____ main speakers
- ____ monitors
- ____ tuner
- ____ speaker/monitor/snake cords
- ____ direct boxes for amps
- ____ console rack for P.A. units
- ____ backup cords
- ____ road cases for equipment
- ____ extension cords
- ____ tool kit/spare fuses
- ____ duct tape
- ____ CLOTHING:
- ____ outfits (at least two each)
- ____ STAGING:
- ____ drum riser
- ____ light boxes
- ____ connectors & extensions
- ____ special props
- ____ TRANSPORTATION:
- ____ van
- ____ other

After filling in this checklist, you should have a clearer idea of exactly what the group still needs to buy, individually or together. With what you know about choosing the right equipment and bargaining techniques get ready to . . .

Shop Regularly at One or Two Music Stores

Different retailers emphasize different things. Some sell at "cut rates," but they cut as much off customer service as they do off the price tag. You might have to grab the handtruck and wheel the boxes out of the storeroom yourself. Some stores sell at full retail prices, but they shine your shoes and hand you a cup of coffee as soon as you walk in. Still other stores offer reasonable discounts and are designated "factory-authorized service centers." Unless you're really hard up for cash or have money to burn, this is the best type of operation to deal with.

No matter how a store is run, owners all hope for the same thing: a steady, reliable clientele. They want your repeat business. Well-known customers can be acknowledged and then left alone in the store. They don't need to pamper you because they know you're there to buy something. New customers require the most help and persuasion, so a return customer is a minimum time investment and a valuable word-of-mouth reference.

All of these advantages are double-edged. Familiarity breeds friendship, and as friends they'll give you purchase incentives and preferential treatment—service you wouldn't receive if you shopped at several stores. When you desperately need a part, they'll phone in your order immediately and request priority shipping. If they don't carry something you want, they'll call around to other stores until they find it for you.

Why Not Work at a Music Store?

Think about it. Instead of working at Safeway (making $12 per hour), you could be working at a music store (making $6 per hour). That's discouraging, but now consider the benefits. You'll be surrounded by music, meeting all kinds of musicians, trying out all the new equipment, and buying at employee discounts. You'll get first pick at all the sales. For a musician, a music store is a great part-time job!

I know plenty of musicians who worked in music stores for the express reason of buying instruments and equipment. One woman abruptly gave notice after three months, but not before she had bought a Stratocaster, two Peavey amps, and a Rhoades piano. I know one drummer who bought a $6,000 custom-built set at an embarrassingly low $2,400 just because he knew about a scarcely publicized company promotional sale by working at the store. The savings make it worthwhile, and the atmosphere is stimulating. Owners usually set no limits on how much equipment employees buy, since moving stock looks good to distributors and manufacturers. It's not uncommon for employees to buy a whole P.A. or even outfit a whole band at a discount. You can save thousands of dollars.

Another beneficial place to have a part-time job is a record store. Employees are generally allowed to take home any records they want to tape, and since musicians usually learn new material from albums or tapes, this works out nicely. The opened albums are then returned to the record store and resealed in a "shrink wrapper." If a band member works at the store, this means free taping, employee discounts on blank tapes, and access to trade journals mailed to the store. Whether band members work in music stores, record stores, or both, the fringe benefits more than make up for the low to moderate wages.

Building Your Own Equipment Is Realistic

The answer to your wildest dreams may be on that music store display floor, but your realistic means may be your own two hands. If you know a little about electronics, would like to, or know someone who does, you can drastically cut initial investment by building your own equipment. Hey, why overlook your own ingenuity?

"Many people who didn't know which end of a soldering iron to hold have successfully built projects," says Craig Anderton, author of *Elec-*

tronic Projects for Musicians. "I have many letters attesting to that!" Because components are easy to build and designs are becoming simpler, interest is increasing in do-it-yourself electronics.

"Any basic knowledge of electronics, even just wiring, is adequate," one technician told me.

Another reason is quality. "The ability to customize equipment, and the fact that performance is often superior to commercial equipment of the same price, are powerful incentives to build your own stuff," Anderton says.

Theoretically, if you have your amplifier schematic, which is a diagram of how the unit is assembled, you can build a duplicate of your amp. Parts availability can be an obstacle, although comparable parts—for a lesser price—can often be found. Said one keyboardist: "My foot switch cost $5 to make, and my preamp was less than $15. A comparable preamp would cost over $100."

"You can design in more expensive parts that manufacturers won't touch," adds Anderton, "and still have a price-competitive unit."

Using a schematic will save time as well as money. As one musician said, "It's hard to find the time to design your own equipment and make it if you're playing six nights a week. But if you've got a schematic, building doesn't take long."

Good sources of designs are *Popular Electronics, Radio Electronics, Guitar Player, Modern Recording & Music, Contemporary Keyboard,* and *Polyphony.* Several manufacturers, including Randall, Mesa Boogie, and DOD, include schematics with new units or will mail you the plans. Some offer electronic project kits, including Southwest Technical Products Corporation, PAIA, and Heathkit. Books on building equipment are listed at the end of this chapter.

Because of the differing complexity of components, a natural progression from switches, matching transformers, preamps, and tone controls, to filters, compressors, and power supplies, and finally on to delays and synthesized modules is possible. You actually learn as you go! Probably the best way to learn basic electrical principles is to enroll in a college electronics class. Classes such as "Elements of Electronics," "Electronic Amplifier Circuit Applications," and "Integrated Circuits," all are instantly applicable for the home enthusiast.

Get to Know an Electronics Expert

A friend of mine recently had some pick-ups and wiring repaired on his electric piano. It was still under warranty, so the $8.68 parts bill was covered. That's nice. Unfortunately, the warranty didn't cover labor charges of $57.50. That's not so nice.

Obviously, it would be convenient and save money if someone in the band had the expertise and tools to repair equipment, but usually broken down equipment gets dropped off at a music store, where qualified technicians charge whatever the market will tolerate. Store's repair departments are often backlogged with broken amps, so a routine part replacement might put you through weeks of agony.

Here's what I've seen several groups do: Walk into a music store and quietly ask the technician if he's interested in freelancing his talents. He can charge much less than the store because he has no overhead, and still make more per hour than the store pays him. The arrangement can take several forms. You can call only when something breaks down, when routine check-ups are due, or pay him a fixed rate to keep all the equipment healthy.

Getting to know a technician who has "hands on" experience fixing audio equipment presents another great possibility: Would he be interested in designing and/or building equipment? If they have the spare time, most technicians enjoy tinkerng with home projects. Making electronic components from loose parts is to an electronics technician what performing original music is to a musician. Irresistible!

Whose Van Do You Use?

Probably whoever has one. Any large capacity-vehicle, from a small truck, station wagon, or pickup, to a van or trailer, is valuable to a group. When five musicians take five small cars to a gig, transportation money adds up to more than the group can afford. Vans and larger, converted delivery trucks are the most convenient, since equipment can be walked or wheeled right into the vehicle.

Providing equipment transportation seems to fall naturally to the bandleader, or the musician who formed the group, although there's no reason why a lesser member can't provide the equipment vehicle. Whoever ends up donating his vehicle should be known for promptness. (That prerequisite, of course, eliminates most musicians right now.)

If no one owns a van or no one is willing to use their van for hauling speakers and amplifiers, a vehicle can be jointly bought by all the members.

However you get a vehicle, the band should pay for mileage and upkeep out of an expense account. At income tax time (Chapter 9) van deductions are 20 cents a mile or actual vehicle expenses, whichever is greater.

Stop! Now, Who Owns What?

Jerry was moping around his house. "Yeah, the band's breaking up, and it's too bad. I've seen it coming for several months."

"You seem pretty depressed for knowing ahead of time that it was going to happen," I said. He looked surprised.

"Oh, it's not *that* that I'm worried about. It's how we're going to divide all this stuff up!"

Jerry had a problem common to most groups—ownership. Instruments are usually individually owned, but after things begin to click, most acts decide they need to invest further in sound, staging, and transportation. Rarely does one person flat out own *all* the equipment (nor is this advisable). Two guitarists might go in on a tuner. Microphones might be paid for with one week's total income. Pretty soon ownership gets vague and confusing. You own one-half of this, but five-eighths of that.

The best way to keep clear records of investment is to set up a separate group expense account fed by depositing 10 to 15 percent of net income from gigs. This way each member has an equal stake in all equipment. If someone wants to quit (or is fired), that person's contributions to equipment are added up and paid off, or in other words, his share is bought by the group.

If you're jointly borrowing money from people to get the band off the ground, repay the loan in full before paying yourselves. Find a willing financier when launching the act (possibly among yourselves?), repay the loan quickly, and set up an expense account. This plan provides for immediate needs and long-range growth. More on financiers in Chapter 20.

When everything is divided up and accounted for, consider insuring your equipment. Normal homeowner's coverage, without a separate attachment, won't cover band equipment for professional use. Check with insurance companies for full coverage at group rates. I've known several bands who had all their equipment stolen from vans or destroyed in nightclub fires. The AFM offers insurance to members at reasonable rates. For instance, an AFM band can fully insure $25,000 worth of equipment for $550 a year. You'll rest much easier if your prized instrument is not only locked in the van, but also insured to replacement value.

For Further Information . . .

If you'll be playing acoustic instruments, *Country Instruments: Makin' Your Own*, by Andy De Paule, will show you how to make them. Written in a flowing conversational style, the book is well-diagrammed and shows you how to make a $500 guitar for $30. Write Van Nostrand Reinhold, Ltd., 1410 Birchmount Rd., Scarborough, Ontario, Canada M1P-2E7.

Irving Sloane has written several books that include histories, construction theory, and supply sources, entitled *Classic Guitar Construc-*

tion, *Guitar Repair,* and *Steel-String Guitar Construction,* all available from E.P. Dutton, 2 Park Ave., New York NY 10016.

If you would like to save money by building your own percussion odds and ends, *Sound Designs: A Handbook of Musical Instrument Building,* by Reinhold Banek and Jon Scoville, Ten Speed Press, P.O. Box 7123, Berkeley CA 94707, contains easy step-by-step instructions.

The Hayden Book Company, 50 Essex Street, Rochelle Park NY 07662, publishes a whole series of "cookbooks" for building your own electronic equipment. Craig Anderton, author of *Electronic Projects for Musicians,* describes 27 projects you can build. This book is available from Polymart, P.O. Box 20305, Oklahoma City OK 73156.

For electronic kits only needing assembly, write Southwest Technical Products Corp., 219 W. Rhapsody, San Antonio TX 78216; PAIA Electronics, Box 14359, Oklahoma City OK 73114; or Heathkit, Benton Harbor MI 49022.

• CHAPTER SEVEN •

REHEARSING THE ACT

Rehearsal is the dark side of performance. It's the side no one sees, yet it can encompass more of your time than the performance itself. But the reward of rehearsing is preparedness in performance—certainly nothing to be scoffed at.

The problem is, most musicians regard rehearsals lightly, as a time to laugh and mess around. In fact, rehearsal is time to coordinate parts, critique sound, and improve your musical skills and visual projection.

Maybe the best reason for getting serious about rehearsing is that the pay isn't very good. Something like $00 an hour, minus transportation expenses. You need to make everyone conscious of time so they'll regard rehearsals as a time to get things done.

Finalizing Song Selection

Once you've decided what style of music you're going to concentrate on, and what emphasis popularity will have in song selection, here are some additional criteria:

1. *Choose songs from a number of groups.* Playing more than four or five songs a night from one band is tacky—the audience may get the impression you're playing only for yourself or lack variety. Featuring songs by a number of artists increases the chance listeners will recognize the material. Besides, reeling off a long list of groups you include music from is expected when talking with agents and employers.
2. *Maintain an identifiable theme.* For listeners to return again and again, the music should focus on a central theme. If the musicians all wear Hawaiian shirts and play hits by Jimmy Messina, Dave Mason, and Pablo Cruise, back-to-back numbers by Foreigner

Many places can be made into ideal rehearsal sites—basements, garages, warehouses, or just a large room in someone's house. This band rehearses in a downtown loft, where the bassist happens to live.

(photo by Lynn Seaton)

and REO Speedwagon might create confusion. The songs are recognizable, but now your direction is hazy. Just who are you trying to appeal to? "Everyone" is too broad an answer. You'll probably fall just short of recruiting any loyal listeners. The songs should sound good together.

3. *Pick danceable songs.* Employers want return customers, so they appreciate a group that keeps the audience working up a sweat on the dance floor, or at least entices patrons to have a good, uninhibited time. Choose songs that are catchy and easy to step to. The last thing you want to do is change from $4/4$ time to $5/8$ time in the middle of a number—watch everyone leave the dance floor as they trip over their feet. Embarrassing people guarantees they won't take any more chances by dancing. People don't go out for the evening to listen to your incredible musical execution. They go out to have fun.

4. *Select songs your instrumentation can handle.* In this age of constantly evolving electronic instruments, it's increasingly hard to duplicate the sounds recording groups create. The equipment is usually available, but the price is prohibitive. A guitar band just can't sound as "produced" without the string, horn, and bizarre synthesizer sounds of a keyboard band. Likewise, a keyboard band usually comes up short when playing straightforward guitar-based rock songs. Live by your limitations. Lots of parts can be faked or ignored without drastically altering a song's sound, but without horns or a suitable keyboard, how much Earth, Wind & Fire can you realistically play?

5. *Stay within the group's vocal ranges.* Hearing a singer straining to hit notes is not pleasant, nor does straining enhance vocal health. Recording artists frequently sing very high parts, made possible by many years of experience and elaborate studio production. Most local bands lack both the talent and equipment to duplicate the vocals of Styx or Rush. If you can't match the vocals, why advertise it? Choose songs that feature your group's vocal ranges.

6. *Pick artists your singers sound like.* If the organist sounds just like Rick Springfield, take advantage of it! People appreciate uncanny style likeness, so having a singer sound identical to a recording artist is a big plus in your favor.

7. *Pay attention to tempo.* The ratio of fast songs to slow songs varies with most jobs, but by knowing where you'll be playing you can organize a song list to include the proper tempo mixture. A group playing in an afternoon or dinner restaurant may saturate its repertoire with slower, "easy to digest by" material. A hot jazz or rock club may require only one or two slow songs per 10-song set, if that many. Go listen to some groups and note their ratio. Estab-

lishing and holding a mood is a critical part of your image projection.

8. *Tally up a complete list of songs.* Figure out how many songs the group needs to know in order to play the places you want to play. Five 45-minute sets are most common. This is anywhere between 9 and 12 songs per set, so you'll want to learn 45-60 songs before seeking regular gigs. Ideally, you'll eventually have about 70 to choose from to vary the show and keep your interest up, but for starters, just jockeying song position is adequate.

9. *Try to satisfy everyone in the band.* No one should assume complete responsibility for song selection. All tunes still need to satisfy the basic criteria, but everyone's preferences should be included, unless there's a stylistic clash. The group must project a clear image. This is one reason it's so important to find musicians with similar preferences. If it's a choice between Helen Reddy or the Rolling Stones, you'll have to choose. You can't play both.

Whenever the band learns a new song, write down the date in a song logbook. It's easy to get caught in a rut playing songs for a long time. This way you can tell if you've played the tune too long. If it's a year old, dump it!

Find a Rehearsal Site and Insulate It

A guitarist drove me over to her group's practice room to show me their set-up. It was in a row of abandoned storage rental buildings, now doubling as a junk yard. "Gee, nice neighborhood," I said, glancing over my shoulder every five seconds. After she kicked a pipe out of the way and unlocked the door, I was amazed. What a practice set-up! Carpeting on all four walls with two sound-control booths overlooking the main room through glass. And it was spacious enough for *two* bands. What looked like a dump from the outside was actually a well-designed rehearsal room/studio.

What is the ideal rehearsal site? After seeing the interior of that rundown warehouse-turned-junkyard, I realized many places could be made ideal. Warehouse or industrial zoned areas are good because there is no one to disturb. The rent is usually high, but not as high as renting a house to rehearse in. A musician favorite is a garage or basement converted into a rehearsal room. Rent is usually minimal or free, depending upon how much the landlord enjoys the music. A large room in someone's house works well if the group isn't too large and the people living there don't mind sidestepping music stands and guitar cases. Try to find a place that's centrally located between all band members, so gas money and transportation time are equable.

Nothing is a bigger asset to a group rehearsing in a residential area than friendly, understanding neighbors. If one neighbor considers you a major disturbance, you'll spend more time worrying about when the police are coming than you'll spend rehearsing.

Wherever you rehearse, insulate the room. Not only will this lessen the chance of complaining neighbors, but it'll also improve the room acoustics. Low-cost insulating materials are everywhere. Blankets or quilts hung on walls and ceiling work well when coupled with a carpeted floor. Old carpeting nailed to the walls is fine, too. Egg cartons are a standard. (You don't have to eat 2,000 eggs. Just call an egg distributor.) Cork and acoustic tiling are also widely used, though a bit more expensive.

Call your police or sheriff's office and find out permissible noise levels for your area, and curfew time. Have the band crank up a loud number with a dBa sound-level meter (available for about $50 at music stores), stand outside and measure how much noise is still seeping through your insulation. Buy more old blankets from the Salvation Army if necessary.

If you're using someone's garage or house, pay a portion of the telephone and electricity bills, plus any rent agreed upon. Good locks should be installed so that equipment can be left at the rehearsal room. Eventually, you should own some cheap equipment and instruments that can be left there while you move the good equipment from job to job.

Minimize Rehearsal Time (Remember, You're Not Getting Paid!)

A developing act has a way of stealing all your time. It's exciting to predict how great you'll look and sound, and pretty soon you're totally preoccupied with band matters. Every waking moment is spent thinking about the new group.

But this excitement must be kept to a simmer if you or the other members expect to reserve any time for non-band-related matters (you know, little things like families or jobs). Rehearsals must be streamlined for maximum time efficiency.

Taping is the most popular way of learning songs, because it's fast, effective, and can be done alone any time. One person collects albums, singles, and tapes of the songs you've chosen to learn, records them onto tapes (usually cassette), and distributes one to each musician. When rehearsals begin, each person is responsible for knowing 10 songs, or whatever everybody's capable of learning. Next week you learn 10 more, and so on.

Avoid buying new records just to record from. Either borrow them from friends, or approach a record-store owner and offer a free band performance in the parking lot, coinciding with a store "Giant Summer Sale." In exchange, you'll be allowed to borrow (and tape) any albums, singles, or pre-recorded tapes. The owner will keep a regular account of what you've borrowed and what you've brought back (debits and credits). You should also ask for a discount on buying new blank tapes to use for the recordings. This arrangement saves you a lot of money.

Plan a regular weekly rehearsal schedule, and make sure everyone is familiar with it. This eliminates redundant phone calls and a lot of uncertainty. It also helps with individual schedule planning.

Arrive at rehearsal ready to perform, both by knowing your parts and by having all the necessary equipment, cords, and endless paraphernalia (which can delay rehearsal while someone drives back home to get a foot pedal or something).

Travel to and from rehearsal should be arranged to save time. Unless all of you live on the same street, don't pick everyone up in one vehicle, or the driver and first person picked up will spend an hour in the car going from house to house. Arrive in groups of twos or threes.

Think of rehearsal as work—pretend a boss is staring down at you. This will make you conscious of your time, and maybe a bit more responsible. If rehearsal is scheduled for 1:00 p.m., arrive in time to allow yourself to set up and be ready to *play* by 1:00. Treat it like a job.

Respect your fellow bandmembers' time by realizing that your commitment to the group probably differs from theirs. What's important to you may not matter at all to them, so don't phone every member to spread the latest rumor of employment. Mention it at a business meeting or at the beginning of rehearsal, but don't impose yourself or go out of your way to share band-related information.

Leave the Beer at Home

Not only is efficiency important when preparing for and traveling to reheasal, it's also the key to getting work accomplished *at* the rehearsal. How many rehearsals have you been to where everyone casually sets up, talks and tunes instruments for an hour, then warms up with a 15-minute jam session? Often rehearsals only become time-efficient after years of experience with agonizingly slow musicians. Here are a few tips to circumvent the headaches:

1. Designate one person to write out the songs to be rehearsed, in a specific order. This eliminates any indecision about what's next. That person must know which songs are easy to warm up on, and which songs require retuning or a change of instruments. This way, no one will strain a voice, and time between songs will be minimized.

2. Even though you are ready to play by 1:00 p.m., don't do it. After everything is set up, take a 10-15 minute break to talk, laugh, and gossip. I've never known a group of musicians to be short on

things to say. Relax, and ease into a rehearsal after shooting the breeze. This way, any urge to talk is taken care of, and all the instruments are tuned and ready to go.

3. Listening to your partners when they've got something to say saves time. As soon as someone begins talking, immediately stop playing lead licks or drumming paradiddles and wait, or people end up yelling over the noise of one or two musicians. If you must go over a part alone, turn your volume completely off; then finger your way through it. Drummers can be particularly bothersome if they don't know when to be silent. Warm up on your drum seat—not the snare!

4. The beer run shouldn't be the highlight of the rehearsal. If you want to drink, do it *after* rehearsal. Alcohol alters perception and relaxes the mind (Chapter 12), so you won't even realize when you're wasting time.

5. Limit rehearsals to three hours per day with one 15-minute break, or attention span wavers and efficiency drops. Those marathon rehearsals really don't accomplish much more than tiring everyone out. Why not just call it quits and start fresh the next day? While you're learning the show before advertising yourself for hire, four or five three-hour rehearsals per week can be arranged without becoming boring since all the songs are still new to everyone. After you've learned a complete show, two rehearsals per week are adequate to learn new material and smooth out rough parts. When the group is performing regularly, there's no need to rehearse old material at all unless it sounds bad.

Rehearsals and Practices—Together and Alone

I'll never forget the day John picked me up for rehearsal with a new group. We arrived early, set up our instruments, and were ready to play. Everyone else was ready, too. When John announced the first tune, the three vocalists said okay, pulled up chairs, and began discussing who should sing what parts. I just sat there, behind my drums, sticks in hand, trying to figure out what was going on. Evidently, they didn't know the song yet. I asked if we could move on to a number they'd learned. "We haven't figured any of them out," said one indignantly. "Isn't that what rehearsals are for?"

Sure. Don't call me, I'll call you.

Everything needn't be done together. No one should ever be left sitting around twiddling thumbs. Remember, you're not being paid.

Practice *is not* rehearsal. Practice is time for you to better yourself musically by polishing individual skills—doing scales, exercises, or just free-form playing—*alone*. Rehearsal is sometimes done alone, but the material you rehearse is what you will eventually perform. It's prearranged. Songs and specific parts are rehearsed, not practiced. If you learn by tape and/or sheet music, first rehearse alone to get the feel of the music. You can probably master all your parts just by solo rehearsal. This is very efficient since you can rehearse any time you like, at home. If it only takes half an hour to learn, that's great! If it takes ten days, then you're not wasting anyone else's time.

After everyone feels comfortable with their parts, a full group rehearsal is held. If all the members are good musicians, the songs will fall together after three or four attempts. If the song is difficult, some members are having trouble, or parts could intertwine more precisely, the next rehearsal time should be designated a "sectional" rehearsal. Do the harmonies need to be clearer? Is a double-lead not quite truly "doubled?" Could the bass and drum parts fit together more tightly? These, by themselves, are not problems that concern the whole band, so half the band shouldn't have to sit around (like John and I did) while the other half learns to coordinate parts. Instead, schedule a vocal, guitar, or rhythm sectional to clear up the specific problem. A sectional can be held wherever is convenient for the members in question. Usually, they can also be held without any amplification or drums.

Sit Down and Listen to Yourselves

Chances are, if your five-piece act goes and listens to a band, you'll end up with five different critiques. The guitarist wasn't very good. The drummer dragged a little. The bassist was imitating Jaco Pastorious. Each of us listens for something different, and usually it's the instrument we play. Besides this bias, everyone also hears and perceives a little differently. The result is an inaccurate, individual perspective of sound. What the organist thinks should be played subtly, the saxophonist thinks should be played forcefully.

How do you come to agreement? Tape yourselves. I remember performing with an original music band, and really feeling good about the parts I had integrated into the music. Then I heard a tape of our show. Oh, my god! I was badly overplaying several songs. What sounded good to me as a musician in a rehearsal and performance sounded terrible to me as a listener.

You can record right in the garage. A common method is to connect one channel of a stereo tape deck through the mixer input to pick up vocals, and place a microphone plugged into the other channel somewhere in the room to pick up instruments.

What to Listen for . . .

1. Not clarity! Don't worry about achieving a masterful recording. The

parts should all be played as they normally are and as long as you can hear what each musician is doing, taping quality doesn't really matter.
2. Pay attention to tempo. Live versions of studio-recorded songs tend to be fast, due to the excitement of performing live, but they shouldn't be so fast as to ruin whatever mood the song originally created. Also, listen for variations in tempo between songs. I've heard groups that only had two speeds—fast and slow. Use a metronome and write down at what tempo each song sounds best. Then get used to varying tempos between songs.
3. Compare what your band is doing musically to what the original band did on the album. Again, don't listen for production quality, but for subtle (or maybe not so subtle) differences between how the song is played. Has your horn player been holding notes long enough? Does the rhythm guitar sound "dirty" like the guitar on the album?

Is Everyone Soloing at Once?

A long time ago, my brother taught me a lesson about being a sensitive musician. He was listening to me drum along with a Beatles record. "What are you doing?" he asked.

"Just a drum roll," I said.

"Why?"

By now I had stopped drumming. "Well, I like that pattern, so I played it."

"Yeah but there's a guitar solo right there. You can't solo while the guitarist is soloing. In order to be comfortable playing, you've got to be comfortable *not* playing."

"Oh."

Many musicians unknowingly overplay their parts. When you have a keyboardist who can't keep his fingers off the ivories, it hurts the band. Popular music relies heavily on the one-solo-at-a-time rule (or "no solos, period"). Busy players, no matter how good they are, can be a real detriment to a band. A tape recorder can solve this problem.

After taping the group, set a time when everyone can meet to review the tape and freely suggest constructive criticism. Have albums or tapes of the originals handy to refer to. Encourage comments on each other's playing and singing, stressing that comments be constructive to the group's sound. Usually, just listening to a recorded rehearsal will embarrass or humble busy players, because it's hard to ignore the fact that you're overplaying when the evidence is rewound and played back again and again.

The purpose of a critical review of yourselves is not to start a heated argument, but to project songs the way they were intended. Musicians who perform together are not called "groups" or "bands" for nothing. The final product is a unified effort. Two or more busy players in the same group can make the music sound like a competition. Any musical "space" is hurriedly filled with leads, crashes, runs, and rolls, creating a musical jungle. While you're all discussing the songs around the tape recorder, bring this up. Solve the problem before it gets out of hand (and you strangle the guitarist). If the guy's egotistical, get right to the point without delay. Confront him with it. Use his ego to the group's advantage by putting him at the front of the stage, where he can be seen, but not necessarily heard. Alternate solos. Egos *can* co-exist in a group, as long as each person is given enough room to feel satisfied.

There's More to This Than Music

If you think making a lot of money as a local live performer hinges on how well your group plays, think again. Here's what leaders of some very successful local acts say:

"Presentation is *the* most important aspect of popular music. The type of material you play and how well you play it is secondary to how well you present it. That includes sound, lighting, and most important, stage presence. It's a theatrical presentation."

"You're entertaining *people*—laymen—*not* musicians. Musicians tend to play more for their own satisfaction rather than the audience's. No more than 10 percent of an audience understand intricate musical movements or appreciate them when they hear them. If you're playing three chords onstage, the average beer drinker thinks you're great because you're up there and he's not."

Most young musicians watch their idols and think, 'Gee, I want to be just like that,' but what they miss is that a star doesn't have to be a superb entertainer. He's got a reputation, so he just goes up and sings. You and me have to work hard on entertainment, 'cause we don't have a reputation. An unknown group has to prove itself every time the curtain goes up."

"The bands that put the emphasis on entertainment are the bands that go furthest and play the classiest rooms. They get more notoriety."

I know from experience that entertainment takes precedence over music. I was in one particularly hot band—every member was a fantastic musician. There were no visible weaknesses until we climbed onstage that first night. In between those beautifully executed songs were giant voids of silence. We thought we sounded so good that the music would *create* excitement. It didn't.

Showmanship and Timing

Since you're a musician, you probably enjoy—maybe even crave—attention. But even if you're shy, you can miraculously turn into a dynamic entertainer. How? By accepting the role of being an actor or actress the moment you set foot upon that stage. You become *two* distinct personalities. One is created, quite unlike your normal self. Whenever you're ready to perform, imagine yourself as someone else—a person who is funny to watch, tells interesting stories, or is sexually alluring. If you have the desire to perform, you'll have the courage to act. The chatter, gestures, and timing can be learned.

Study the actors on television, and count how many different personality types are portrayed. The independent woman who has a searing comeback for every man who tries to pick up on her. The egotistical jock who's too cool for everyone. The dumb, sexy blonde. The "mister know-it-all" bookworm. Almost every television situation-comedy has the same role models; all can be adapted to the stage. Experienced musicians tend to sound like rapid-fire AM disc jockeys, very cool, laid-back FM radio announcers, alluringly sexy nymphs, or brash, indifferent snobs. "It's all practice," said one musician. "Playing a stupid, dorky personality is good for normally shy people."

"Say exactly what you think," another musician says. "Whenever the spotlight hits me after a song and I'm not ready, I screw up my face and try to look as stupid as possible. Then I'll ask loudly, 'Gee, uh, what should I say?' or 'Looks like I'm supposed to talk, huh?' The crowd loves a stupid character."

"I've got a safety valve," one musician told me. "If I'm caught without something to say, I'll blurt out, 'I want to remind you that, uh . . . ' and then just say whatever comes to mind, like 'All drinks are free for the rest of the night,' or 'The nude bathing-suit contest starts in one hour, so stick around.' Lies go over great! The more outrageous, the better."

Experienced musicians usually become incredibly fast with one-liners. Sometimes, however, things become so routine that the same jokes are repeated night after night in identical order. Regular customers get bored with this repetition. "Talk time between songs is the only variation for your following, because they know all your songs," a veteran musician warns.

"I tell my musicians to always be on their toes," says a bandleader. "No smoking or heavy drinking, because their hands and mind need to be ready to react. Drummers in particular should always accent punch lines with cymbal crashes or something, since the audience has no 'applause' sign to read. They need to be told, 'Now is the time to laugh,' or 'Now is the time to participate.' A drummer is the cue card for the audience."

Some bands don't know what to say so they lamely introduce each song by telling which artist recorded it. This is repetitive and boring. The audience doesn't care! Well-prepared groups have written-out set lists and talk about other things. Really clever groups give song cues. Here's how one stage leader works song cues:

"I constantly reassess our situation so there is no predetermined song list. This way I best capture the mood of the crowd, instead of forcing something down their throats. I give my cues through what I say—references to the song. An alert musician will catch my cue."

An advanced form of comedy is a pre-arranged, choreographed skit. This takes rehearsal just like music does. "We do one called, 'Gladys Fright and the Pigs,' where I come out as Gladys Fright," one performer told me. "The two guitarists wear pig masks and do dance steps. A routine like this has to be just right, with an intro, song, and exit all dress-rehearsed." Your band is worth a lot more money when you show a manager this degree of preparation.

Sharp-witted musicians are experts at insulting a crowd to the point of laughter, but just short of animosity. They can use a heckler to their advantage. "A heckler can bring life to a dull crowd," advises an experienced stage performer. "If you work the insults right, the whole crowd will unite with you against the heckler. You've got to turn the tables on him. If you can make the crowd laugh at him, he'll shut up."

Insults can certainly be carried too far. Any ethnic insults must be considered very carefully because they can backfire so easily. I've seen musicians come close to getting into fights by insulting or directing jokes at women they thought were single, until a husband or boyfriend challenged them at stage side.

Comments should always be directed at individuals or groups—not the audience in general. People are more likely to respond when you give them personal attention because it thrusts them into the spotlight.

Watching professional comedians and entertainers is a good way to pick up ideas. Showrooms in New York, Chicago, Seattle, and other large cities regularly feature top entertainers. Be on the lookout for primetime extravaganzas or late night TV comedy shows. Study, for instance, how Don Rickles insults people without alienating his audience. Every time you hear a joke you like, write it down. Then buy a small, open-top flip file and organize jokes according to circumstance, such as "bad crowd," "fat men," "good weather," "Federal government," etc. Keep the file hidden on a monitor or amp, but within fingertip reach onstage.

Some of the best topics to liven up your stage show can be found on TV news programs or in daily newspapers. Political comments evoke loud crowd response. Freak news items, usually buried in the newspaper's national section, are well worth clipping and filing.

When playing out-of-town gigs, find something everyone who lives there would know about, but an outsider wouldn't. A friend of mine makes it a habit to find the worst restaurant in each town. He continually berates it onstage, much to the audience's surprise and delight.

Visual Rehearsing

Now the only question is, are you as funny and entertaining as you think? An excellent way of answering this is to cover one wall in the rehearsal room with full-length mirrors, and set the band up—stage lights and all—so that you perform facing the mirrors. This makes you aware of every motion and expression, and soon good stage presence will be conditioned in you.

Are your expressions obvious? Stage actors are taught the art of exaggerating both mouth movement and facial expression. You want the audience to understand your feelings, so exaggerate your stage motions.

Use the range of your voice to express emotion and emphasize points. The more dramatic your vocal fluctuations, the better. A monotone is boring!

The simplest thing to watch for in the mirror is a smile. A smile says more than anything else about how you feel. Encourage everybody to smile. A stage full of laughing, jiving, and above all, *smiling* musicians is irresistible. That's when an act is really cookin'! Mirrors catch flaws, too. "I never let my musicians wear watches on stage," said one bandleader. "When a performer is constantly glancing at his watch he's telling the audience, 'I'm tired. How long before my break?' "

Rehearsing before a wall of mirrors can improve the band as a whole, not just individuals. Six musicians sending off different, disorganized signals to the audience is less effective than a band sending out one unified, unmistakable message. Everyone should be working together to project one image.

"The only problem we've had is with people who don't understand team effort," a successful bandleader says. "They're more 'self' oriented. I'll take someone like that to watch a big name act. Even though the lead singer might be the focal point, the guitarist and bass player will be on the side doing dance steps together, and always smiling. It's obvious they've worked hard on their portion of the act."

I relate the concept to football. Even though the quarterback gets most of the attention, what good is he without linemen?

Your band should have one or two players for the audience to focus their attention on. Four people fronting the show gets confusing unless you have a dynamite lighting system that will direct audience attention to one person at a time.

When someone is talking, all the other musicians should be looking and listening. Turning toward the speaker shows the audience where to look. By listening attentively, you'll be able to add whatever instant inspiration you get. Timing is the key to effective delivery.

Everyone should be visible to the audience. If the stage is large enough, the drummer should be on a riser, along with the keyboardist if that person plays seated. You can't talk to the audience if you're hidden from their view—"voices from the sky" are confusing.

Mirrors provide a great opportunity to work out synchronized dance steps, or any unison motion. Guitarists standing side by side with guitars swaying up and down to the beat is a classic routine, and it's still effective. Any leads that are doubled or tripled should always be *shown* to the audience, besides being heard, by standing side by side at the front of the stage.

Some bands videotape their acts to evaluate and improve their stage presence. You might want to rent or borrow a videotape camera before your first gig so you can critique your band's visual effectiveness. Then tape yourselves again periodically, say every six months, to stay on top of your show.

Can Your Band Pass This Test?

Here's a list of questions to answer about your group's rehearsal efficiency, and your musical and showmanship abilities. The questions with a "no" response should be jotted down so that you can work to correct these areas.

(circle one)

1. Did all the band members help decide what songs to learn? Yes No
2. Are all of your songs danceable? Yes No
3. Have you found a permanent rehearsal site? Yes No
4. Has everyone agreed to a regular rehearsal schedule? Yes No
5. Is everyone taking rehearsals seriously? Yes No
6. Does everyone come to rehearsal prepared? Yes No
7. Does everyone immediately quit playing and listen when someone is talking? Yes No
8. Does everyone wait until their turn to solo? Yes No
9. Do you still have time for things unrelated to the band? Yes No
10. Will a constructive criticism meeting be comfortable? Yes No
11. Is everyone in agreement that entertainment—not just music—is what the band must present? Yes No
12. Are the band members willing to assume stage personalities? Yes No
13. Do any shy members realize that they, too, must participate in entertaining? Yes No
14. Is anyone in the group particularly good with jokes, puns, and quick comebacks? Yes No
15. Are you starting a joke flip file for the stage? Yes No
16. Can some mirrors be aligned along one wall of the rehearsal room for improving your stage presence? Yes No
17. Do you understand that tonal fluctuations, facial expressions, and body language all must be exaggerated? Yes No
18. Does everyone automatically smile when playing? Yes No
19. Does the band have an agreed-upon, definite focal point? Yes No
20. Will it be feasible to rent or borrow a videotape camera so the band can critique its visual effectiveness? Yes No

• CHAPTER EIGHT •

STACK THE DECK IN YOUR FAVOR!

Even after one or two months of diligent rehearsing, you still have a long list of loose ends to tie together before jumping into the performing arena. The songs are really coming along. Everyone has adjusted to rehearsing two or three times per week. By pooling everyone's microphones and odds and ends, you've got what looks like a P.A. The guitarist has a van and the drummer has a dilapidated—but still running—old truck. The keyboardist's boyfriend is assistant manager for a chain restaurant, and he wants to hear the band. The wheels are turning fast. That's good.

To create the best possible impression on the people you'll deal with, keep one foot on the brakes long enough to take care of these last preliminary details. Then you can concentrate on performing and counting money!

Define Your Image

You know the act has to be distinct. A "band with a purpose," you might say. There will be a semblance in attitude, dress, and music. Before marketing your image—and committing money for its promotion—check out the competition and make sure the market isn't flooded with similar acts. You don't want to stage a show that's conspicuously similar to another group; both bands will hurt each other's job opportunities, since club owners won't notice any difference and will carelessly choose between the two groups. It's your job to make employers want *you*.

Go to establishments featuring live entertainment just to watch and listen. Do you like their clothes? How could they look better? Does the style of dress stand out compared to what people in the audience are

You want to be sure that what you wear on-stage accurately projects your image. This country band wears fringed Western shirts during the week, but switches to tuxes for more formal weekend gigs.

(photo of Cheyenne by Joseph Frenz)

wearing? Is hair short or long, and does it look good? Does their appearance match their music? Which songs does the audience like best? Were they fast, slow, popular, or just danceable? Leave with some ideas about how that act could project a clearer, stronger image. What worked—and what didn't? How will your act be better?

Now go to a record store. With a Top 40 sheet, systematically find each hot artist's new album. How are they dressed? Can you draw parallels between music styles and appearance and see how an "image" is created? Next find albums by artists your group copies and study their appearance. If they're all wearing T-shirts and jeans, maybe that's what you should wear. They have an image their fans associate with, so if you're playing their music, that's the image your audience will relate to. If you're concentrating on current trends, look to brand new releases for signs of coming styles. "When Be Bop Deluxe came out with short hair and formal suits, I thought they looked stupid," a musician told me. "A year later I realized their thinking was a full year ahead of mine, so our band started wearing little ties, baggy pants, and clean-cut hairstyles. Now that's the 'in' look."

After the group decides on appearance, try to imagine if the appearance and music will be complementary. I've seen too many slick, well-dressed groups futilely try to belt out "Sweet Home Alabama" and "Cocaine."

Bizarre appearances sell very well. Devo, Kraftwerk, Bow Wow Wow, Frank Zappa, Alice Cooper, David Bowie, The Tubes . . . the list of successful groups with outrageous personalities and unique costumes goes on and on. If your group is willing to forego all embarrassment and jump headfirst into theatrics, people will return to see you. A daring, off-the-wall show will make you a lot of money because it's a blast to watch.

Appearance Equals $—Look Sharp

A traditional black and white outfit is still the most common dress among the majority of musicians, but thank God for rock 'n' roll! Now virtually anything can be used as a group outfit, from pink satin pants to Keds hightop sneakers. As long as coordinated dress theme is obvious—no matter how bizarre—it'll get your image across (although many employers still have a dress code or "standard" they'll expect you to uphold).

Setting off part of the band in different outfits can catch audience attention. The most common example of dress variation is between male and female outfits, where three or four male back-up players all wear a formal, two-color suit or shirt and pants combination, and the female lead wears whatever showy outfit she wants. If one of the men is a "front person" with the woman, his clothes can color coordinate with her outfit instead of with the other men's clothes. This shows the audience who to watch. The only rule is that the person who is dressed differently should be the focus of attention.

If you perspire heavily, pick material or clothes made out of cotton. A cotton shirt breathes easily, and can dry out between fast songs. Sweating profusely for five hours in a nylon shirt and polyester pants is a terrible feeling.

How many outfits you need depends on how often the band will play and how much you enjoy washing clothes. An act playing five nights a week can manage with two outfits, but three saves detergent and adds visual interest.

Some acts change shirts every set. If you've got enough stage clothes, go ahead. Audiences appreciate variety and love surprises.

Your group image needs to be portrayed in a promotional package that serves as your calling-card for soliciting jobs. Before getting into the nuts and bolts of the package, however, let's look at how an identifiable theme is repeated when writing to and doing business with people, and also reinforced from the stage.

The Logo, Stationery, and Backdrop

Look to the business world to comprehend the incredible importance placed on advertising. Products or services are packaged in distinctive colors and designs in hopes that you'll relate to the product's image, become familiar with it through advertising, and buy whatever they're selling.

With your promo pack, you want to accomplish the same thing. You're selling your services. To influence employers to hire you, it's to your advantage to have specific colors and a distinct design incorporated in a logo, and plaster this logo on stationery, business cards, a stage backdrop, and any other printed materials the group dreams up.

The most attractive logos appear simple and straightforward, even though they may contain intricate detail and have taken a long time to design. They should be easily recognizable. The design should complement and reinforce your appearance and music. In short, the logo should represent your total image.

"Many acts don't need a special logo per se. They can just stylize the way they write their name," said a graphic artist who frequently designs band logos. "Just remember to get the name in the design. You want that visual association. Why make it hard for the audience to recognize your name?"

See pages 116 and 117 for some effective logos.

A commercial artist will charge you plenty to design a logo. The final product might be well worth the money, but before hiring a professional, ask to see a portfolio of previous designs. Are the designs simple and bold enough to be understood from a stage? Do you like the artist's style? Are the designs exciting, modernistic? Do they rely on color extensively?

Frequently, someone in the group knows an artist. If you know what you want and have examples of other logos you admire, an amateur can usually come up with an appropriate design, and this will definitely save you money.

Ask at music stores about artists who specialize in band logos. A logo specialist, priced in between a commercial artist and an amateur, is usually right on top of current musical trends. The biggest printing expense is the addition of multiple colors, so consider this before deciding on a beautiful rainbow-color logo. It'll look great, but the cost of having 1,000 business cards printed could jump from $40 to $200. One, two, or three colors are standard.

After you have an artist draw a preliminary design, ask yourself, "Can this be reduced to fit on a business card without losing effect and clarity?" This is a good test for simplicity. Look for that magic.

Stationery. Matching 8½x11 inch paper and size 10 envelopes, and 9¼x12½ inch manila envelopes should all be printed with logo, address, and phone number. Safe quantities are 250 of each (as long as the address is well-established). White paper is best because of the white ribbons on correcting typewriters. If the cost of printing is prohibitive, have a rubber stamp made from your camera-ready design.

Business cards. Have 1,000 business cards printed with the logo, address, and phone number. The flashier the card you can afford, the better. Many agents keep a bulletin board covered with band business cards, and the brighter, catchier card will get noticed. Have the card printed slightly oversized (larger than the standard 2x3¼ inches), but make sure it can still fit in a wallet. Cards should be included in promo packs and handed out readily at gigs.

Backdrop. A backdrop that coordinates with your apparel does wonders for band identity. All professional musicians have heard, "Hey, you guys sound really good. What's the name of your band?" The audience should know your name by the end of the first song, and the backdrop is the mechanism for telling them. Why make them guess? The expense is worth it.

Backdrop expense, like logo designing, varies widely from amateur to commercial artist. Again, a specialist in band logo designs is probably your best bet. Fabrics used range from rough, matte surfaces to silk.

I've seen some local bands hang large white screens behind the stage and flash multiple images onto them via synchronized slide projectors.

116 Making Money Making Music

The classic top hat and rose reinforce this band's name and stage presence perfectly. (designed by Madeline Green)

Custom artwork combined with the right words will always grab attention. This card effectively conveys the easygoing nature of this group. (designed by Steven Holsapple)

A great name for a circuit band. This logo creates a polished, slick image. (designed by Don Barker)

Although this design is busy and almost confusing to read, it makes it clear what kind of band is for sale: a heavy metal, high-energy act that will blow your socks off. (designed by Don Barker)

This simple design blends the band's name and its namesake into an interesting logo. (designed by Dave Montes)

Here, the way the band name is written, the calm desert night, and the tag, 'fine musical entertainment,' drive home the point that employers can expect a low-key, quality show. (designed by Don Barker)

With bold, modern lettering, this band gets across the message that they provide a fast-moving, high-energy rock show. (courtesy of Jimmy Rehn)

A photo-card enables you to picture the whole band and stands out from the pack with its full color and ability to show detail. (courtesy of Tom M. Dote)

This act had a "cute" image and played new tunes, so they wanted a sexy contemporary design. (designed by Don Barker)

This stylized logo identifies a classy rock act. The card flips open to reveal further booking information.

When timed to the music, it looks great. Buying slide projectors is expensive, but it contributes to a high energy stage production.

Other printed material. A large printed page with the group name, photo, logo, and "Now Performing" printed below with plenty of space to write in details is effective in club marquees and can double as a poster. Bumper stickers printed with the band's name and logo are another good promotion technique. A personal manager of a group I was in had small, bendable table tents printed on heavy paper with band name and booking information. After setting up for a gig, we'd place these stand-up cards on dining tables to let diners know there was entertainment in the bar, and on bar counters and tables in case any members of the audience wanted to hire us.

The Promo Package

"It's just like catching fish," a veteran musician once told me. "To catch the bigger fish you gotta be smart and use the right bait. A promo pack is your bait. If you have a good one, you'll get nibbles from the higher paying jobs. Then you just reel 'em in."

It sounds corny, but it's true. First impressions are a big part of the opinion a potential employer will form of you. I know one good band that repeatedly has trouble booking gigs on the basis of their promo package. They almost have to beg managers to come and see them in person, but when the manager sees their show the group is inevitably offered a job. If their promo pack represented them better, they wouldn't need to hassle with live auditions.

Once established in an area, a group doesn't need to use promo packs because reputation sells the act. But, until your group is known around town, you'll need a promo pack to get the word about yourself out to agents and employers.

A promo pack should be a tightly constructed sales pitch. There should be no ambiguity about what kind of band you are. Image must be crystal clear—it needs to shine through all the separate parts of the package, unifying printed, photographic, and audio materials. Everything about the package must smack of professionalism.

Perhaps more important than knowing *what* to write is knowing what *not* to write. Too many adjectives make you sound like a used-car salesman. Employers know that anything *you* write is self-promotion. As one musician friend said, "Nobody cares if the musicians in your band have a sum total of 270 years experience."

Open with a personally typed cover letter, saying you appreciate their interest in your act. Thank them for any returned phone calls, and express a desire to work with them. That's it. The cover letter should run one-half page *at most*. Besides the cover letter, enclose a single pre-printed page describing the act. Here's your chance to hype the band. Open with a short paragraph describing the style of music you play. Then introduce each member in a short paragraph. Close with a short tag about your potential, how enthusiastic crowds become over you, and mention "This group will be a financial asset to your business."

The most influential thing a promo package can contain is a list of legitimate references and press clippings on your band. If the group is not brand new, contact some former employers who liked the group, and ask them if they mind your listing them as references. Include these names, businesses, and phone numbers on the cover sheet. As for press clippings, the best type are newspaper articles, because most newspapers try to print impartial entertainment reviews. Always call newspapers before playing out of town (entertainment writers consider visiting bands more interesting than local bands). If a reviewer does come out, *make friends*. If you're leaving soon, ask the reviewer to send you a copy of the story. Also save any club or organization promotional prints that have the act's name on it. These are not impartial, but they prove you've worked before. Take all these clippings to a printer, and ask that they be arranged on $8\frac{1}{2}$x11 inch sheets and copied. Staple these behind your promotional page.

Photographs

You shouldn't be stingy when it comes to band photographs, especially the one to be included in your promo pack. Go ahead and pay a *real* photographer the extra money for that crispness, definition, and sparkle so many amateur or semi-professional photographers miss.

The photograph illustrates your group to potential employers. By looking it over they judge your showmanship, personalities, and stage energy. Make sure your photo exudes the positive vibes you want it to.

Wear your stage clothes so the photo projects your image clearly. Before deciding on a setting for the picture, describe to the photographer what image you're trying to project. An experienced photographer is accustomed to viewing life through a viewfinder and can offer suggestions on how to bring out the image you want. The sitting might be in a studio, on a beach, or on a farm—whatever it takes to bring out your image.

Here are some sample promo photographs. Study how each clarifies image. By glancing at your photo, employers should *know* what style of music you play.

Long hair and a sporty "today" look relate a rock style. (copyright Pat Johnson Studios)

This cabaret act uses an alley to underscore a 50s revival image. (photo courtesy of John Jackman)

This hard rock, American new wave band gets across their no-nonsense stage personality. (copyright Pat Johnson Studios)

This photograph shows the good-time, friendly nature of a group that performs upbeat, original music. (copyright Pat Johnson Studios)

A photo of a club circuit Top 40 act in which each musician manages to project the personality he assumes onstage. (copyright Pat Johnson Studios)

This photograph captures a funk band's lively personality. (copyright Pat Johnson Studios)

A stark stairway helps create a modern image. Here composition effectively distinguishes the female lead from the rest of the band. (copyright Pat Johnson Studios)

The photographer has managed to capture this blues guitarist's sensitive stage presence. (copyright Pat Johnson Studios)

This group of hard rockers wanted something to catch your eye. Enter the G-strings. (copyright Pat Johnson Studios)

Cut Tape

After reading your letter, promo sheet, press clippings, and glancing at your photograph, an employer still saves the final evaluation until hearing your cassette tape. For an unestablished band, the tape featuring several "cuts" showcasing the band is the most important part of the promo package. An act with either a good reputation or an assortment of press clippings doesn't need a cut tape—but you do.

The cut tape should exhibit a variety of tempos and styles. Because it will be sent to people hiring live entertainment, the music should sound energetic and "alive"—as close to a live performance as possible, short of taping yourself in a noisy barroom. To accomplish this, use a minimum of studio effects and overdubbings, so the finished tape doesn't sound *too* polished and perfect. You want the music flawless, and the tape merely capturing your sound cleanly, not overly *enhancing* it with compressors, echo chambers, and multiple tracking. Instrumental tracks are typically laid down first—all at once if possible—and vocal tracks are recorded in a second session.

Pick songs which best represent what you play. If you lace your cut tape with unrepresentative style, you'll continually get booked in the wrong places. If you play Top 40 hits, put the most current songs on the tape.

Since you want to show how exciting and versatile the act is in a short length of time, don't bother taping whole songs. One minute of each tune is enough. This allows you to offer a sampling of seven to ten songs rather than two or three.

Pick the one minute out of each selection that contains the strong melody line—the part of the song everyone walked around humming while it was a hit. If you have two lead singers, feature them both; if the sax player is hot, show her off. These "mini songs'" can be arranged two ways: You can either have the engineer fade in the beginning and fade out the end, with a four-second pause between selections, or you can arrange all the one-minute segments into a medley without any pauses. An advantage of medleys is that you play straight through, so less studio time is required. A problem arises if someone has to switch instruments between tunes, since there is no time to do so. Then you'll need to record with pauses between cuts.

Cut tape quality is important, even though tone-deaf bartenders may be listening to it. Buying time in a 24-track studio is a waste of money for a cut tape: a four-, eight-, or sixteen-track studio is adequate and rents recording time for $20-40 per hour, including technician. Master reel-to-reel tape must be bought, and is then duplicated onto blank cassettes. The total cost, depending primarily on your recording time, can range from $100 to $600. Because of this, a Top 40 band which must constantly represent itself with the latest hits is better advised to spend $1,000 on a four-track recorder and tape themselves. (See Chapter 15, "How to Organize a Home Recording Studio")

If you don't own a four-track, flip through the Yellow Pages to "Recording" and shop around for a studio. Talk to the engineer of each studio (who may also be secretary, producer, and owner) and see if you like the person. Ask, "What kind of music do you like? What are some examples of albums you think were recorded very well? What kind of people record in your studio most often?" If the answers are bluegrass and *Flatt & Scruggs' Greatest Hits*, maybe you should take your AC/DC copy band somewhere else. That engineer won't understand how to record "Hell's Bells."

Be sure to ask the engineer about tape duplicating services. Some studios offer a price break on duplication if you record there. If you can't decide, ask for a list of musician references you can call who have recorded there. They'll be able to tell you if the engineer is easy to work with, and how the final product measures up.

Preparing Before the Studio

My first experience in a studio was a sudden one. Some friends decided they wanted drum tracks on their heretofore acoustic album, so they called me. I simultaneously learned the songs and added drums to them in the studio. Since we had unlimited free studio time, money was no problem, but I've regretted my parts on the tape ever since. Any song I've ever played goes through a maturation period while it is learned, torn apart, and added to; it evolves until it peaks out into the best it can be. By learning material in the studio, I short-circuited the entire creative process.

That predicament was made possible by the free studio time, but this isn't the situation in 99 out of 100 cases. Studio time is money, so all learning and rehearsing is done beforehand. When you enter the studio, the material must be performance quality.

The best way to make sure you won't be surprised by what you hear played back through those JBL studio monitors is to tape yourself in rehearsal. A stereo cassette deck works fine. This way any changes can be made before the studio.

After rehearsing to your satisfaction, the key to an efficient and trouble-free session is non-musical preparation. This will suppress anxiety and bolster confidence, letting you concentrate on the music.

Find out what instruments the studio provides for recording. Frequently, they'll have an acoustic piano and a drum set, along wth a lot of percussive paraphernalia. It's wise to use their piano, since moving your own in usually knocks it out of tune, but your drummer will probably want to use a set he's familiar with. As a general rule, drums are heavily padded for recording. Do this beforehand. Tell the engineer over the phone if any of your amplifiers are excessively noisy or "buzz" loudly. If so, he'll probably want to plug you directly into the board instead of miking your amp, so you can leave the amp at home.

Many times it's the minor details that unnerve a musician before recording. Things like arrival time, location, and having new strings, reeds, and heads can make the difference between a $125 and a $300 bill.

Everyone should be aware of how much you're paying for time, and understand the need to move fast. You don't have to sit around and smoke a joint to be comfortable in a studio. By setting up quickly and having confidence in each other's ability, you'll get high when the first take is a keeper.

Videotaped Promotion

Home video machines have created a new way to sell acts to agents and employers: videotaped performances. Videotapes supersede the need for cassette tapes since they record both visual and audio performance.

A videotape can be made either in a studio or at a live show, but since the cartridge really relies more on visual performance, filming a live show is preferred for excitement and crowd enthusiasm. The sound quality won't match what a good studio can produce, so the acts that can benefit most from video taped promotion are those with fantastic visual shows. Cabaret bands, comedy acts, and groups with elaborate lighting can better relate their value through a videotape than through a sound cassette tape. A band suffering from a lack of stage presence should stick with a cassette, lest they draw attention to their weakness.

The biggest drawback to video promotion is the relative scarcity of video machines. If the agent doesn't have a video deck, your tape will be ignored. (As home video decks become more common, this problem will gradually disappear.) Another drawback is price. Video cartridges are expensive to be sending all over the state, and getting people to return them is often a futile effort. But if your stage show is lively and exciting, you should look into video promotion.

Getting the Package Out to Agents and Employers

When you've got a complete promo package and the group knows enough material to play four hours, it's time to send the packages out to agents and employers. You'll want to target the people most likely to be interested, so consult your market research sheets. Pick out all your primary ("A" rated) markets. Which nightclubs and restaurants hire your style of music? Will you appeal to organizations sponsoring large parties or dances? What about agents? Which charge the least percentage and represent places you'd most like to play?

Telephone each primary market and ask the person in charge of entertainment if he'd be interested in reviewing a promo package. Make sure you spell his name right, and use the correct mailing address. Affix a white address label with address typed in on the front of each 9¼x12½ inch manila envelope, and assemble your package like this: In a letter-size file folder, paper-clip together a business card, an individually typed, personally addressed cover letter listing references; the photograph; the promotional page describing the act; and any photocopies of press clippings. The tape should be sent in its plastic box. If you want your videotape or cassette returned, enclose a self-addressed envelope with enough postage on it to cover mailing.

After sending the packages (the more you mail, the better!), wait one week and phone everyone back to see if they're interested. Agents and club managers are notoriously busy, so keep trying to get through on the phone. Then it should only be a matter of signing contracts (Chapter 9).

How to Arrange an Audition—If You Must

Some employers will insist on seeing the act perform (ah ha! The real value of a videotape!). For them, reviewing your promo pack was only a screening process to decide if you're worth their time for a live audition. If the band is already working, there won't be any problem. You'll tell them where the act is playing, and they can come out when they like.

That way, you're not inconvenienced. If the person is from a club or restaurant, it's best to invite him to a place similar to his. The owner of a good-paying dinner house might be scared away if she walks into a rock club right when you're screaming through your heaviest number. It's also a good idea to request they come out on a Friday or Saturday night, since a big crowd will make you look like a popular draw.

If the band isn't working yet, you'll have to go set up specially and play as an audition. Tell her you'll be delighted to as long as the act is paid for a regular night's work. If she balks, suggest the band set up and play for one hour only. Make sure at least your expenses are covered (tell her you have rental fees to pay, whether true or not). If you find yourself bargaining for next to nothing, ask for a commitment pending the outcome of your audition. If she likes you, do you get a three-week run or just consideration for Monday night? What are the stakes? If you can't get payment or commitment, tell her you'll catch her next time.

As a last resort, invite her to an audition at your rehearsal site. The disadvantages of judging an act in the provocative garage atmosphere are plenty; blankets strung up on the walls, the absence of an audience, the bassist's dirty jeans, and the fact that rehearsal rooms aren't organized for listening. If this is the only way, have a dress rehearsal and limit it to four or five songs, played non-stop. Go all out! The excitement you generate at the audition will probably determine if you get the job. Make sure the person is fully aware beforehand that she's going to be listening in a rehearsal room—not a performance setting.

Creating a Dynamic Stage Show

Think back to the best concerts you've attended. What made them great? Was it the energy on stage, the comfortable atmosphere, or the singer's magnetic personality? The whole stage production? The point is, all these things are seen through your eyes. Sight is our dominant sense, so visual experiences are remembered vividly and form a bigger impression than sound, smell, or touch. If your show—the visual experience—is exciting, people will return to see you again and again because you're fun to watch.

Lighting is essential to any stage show. The members of a group invited me to come see their rock club debut. I liked the music, but it was a boring show. Nothing was happening. Two months later the singer asked me to come out again. I was blown away! My eyes were riveted to the stage, led from performer to performer. The evening passed before I knew it. How were they transformed from boring to captivating without changing any songs? They bought a $4,000 light set-up, and hired a lighting technician (they still mixed sound themselves from the stage). The technician knew all the songs, had strobes synchronized to the beat and illuminated the featured musicians with dazzling white spotlights. Everyone was visible at the right time, and their backdrop sparkled brightly from behind. Expensive, yes, but crowds loved it. The band was now in heavy demand.

Audiences are spellbound by the lighting shows illuminating Yes, the Who, the Rolling Stones, and Styx. Good lighting doesn't allow audience attention to wander. It acts as a cue card, showing everyone where to look. It also eliminates "cross talk" or "double talk" by two or more musicians at the same time. When the tight circle of light illuminates you, it's your turn to talk, and no one else's.

The light fixtures usually owned by touring bands and lighting companies are parabolic aluminized reflector (PAR type) lamps. Intensity ranges from 150 to 1,000 watts. A PAR-64 1,000 watt fixture is the professional standard. PAR lamps are not good at focusing or narrowing light direction, so their primary use is "color washing" the stage in reds, greens, and blues, and creating general moods. More elaborate fixtures are used as "specials" (spotlights). One of the more effective globes for creating a special is the 28 volt aircraft landing light, used on 747 airliners. As you can imagine, they create a very compact, *bright* light (this is the *real* reason punk rockers wear sunglasses onstage!).

The number of lights needed varies from stage to stage, and group to group. For nightclubs, a 24-light system will provide very good illumination and variety of color and effect. Some stage fronts can be covered with four to six lights, but then support musicians and any background will be lost from sight.

The light globes and fixtures are not the expensive components of a lighting system. The expense is in the switching and control box. Simple foot switches can be bought for $50, but with dimming capabilities, power distribution, and low voltage control, cost of a new commercial control box can soar to $800 to $2,000. To see what's available, call theatrical supply companies, or ask for lighting catalogs at local music stores. Some boxes are built especially for musicians, such as the six-channel Rocktronics model. Its controls, including momentary contact switches, individual on-off channel switches, and a foot-activated dimmer, are positioned for convenient foot operation. Other popular brands are Electrosonic, Pulsar, and Zero 88. Make sure the fixtures you buy are built for touring and heavy use.

Since it takes a lot of time to arrange new lighting positions according to where you're playing, you should have modular, telescopic tripod stands to mount fixtures on. These allow for quick assembly and easy height adjustments.

Possibly the best effect to come out in a long time is the wireless audio system. At last a guitarist or lead singer can roam offstage into the audience, free from tangling cords. Crowd reaction is fantastic! And just as important, the technology previously available only in $1,000 units can now be purchased for under $500.

Smoke machines are rock band favorites and can be bought or rented through theatrical supply companies. There are two types: oil-burning and dry-ice units. Vapors created from the oil machines can leave a sticky residue on equipment, so dry ice machines are preferred. Besides price, a major drawback of smoke machines is that they require a lengthy set-up and warm-up period (about an hour) before becoming operative.

Some acts rely on fireworks to thrill audiences, and there's no doubt brilliant flashes, flames, and explosions are exciting. Musicians who understand basic electricity and pyrotechnics (or licensed pyrotechnicians as required by some areas) can set off blinding flash pots, shoot flames 30 feet in the air with lycopodium torches run off acetylene oxygen tanks, and appear to breathe fire (remember Kiss's pyrotechnical wizardry?). Playing with fire around unstable chemicals is dangerous, however, so extreme caution must be observed. To find this kind of equipment, call a professional pyrotechnician or theatrical supply company.

Theatrical companies will also rent or sell costumes, curtains, and stage props. Many will custom design backdrops and cloth grills for P.A. mains. Small props, masks, and gimmickry can be mail-ordered.

Most visual effects can be home-built, saving hundreds of dollars. For someone electrically inclined, light switching boxes are easy to make. Smoke machines are easy, too. Here's how one keyboardist built his:

"My partner and I patterned it after a commercial machine, but ours heated quicker, took more dry ice, and produced more smoke. We found a 55-gallon drum with a removable lid and clamping ring. We rust-proofed the inside, and then had two pieces of threaded pipe welded onto the drum, and connected two 30-amp heating elements on each side. These were wired to a junction box with eight 20-amp circuits, which made it safe to plug the unit into any 220-power outlet. The drum would be half filled with water, and the heating elements would heat the water. Dry ice would then be placed in the drum over the hot water and *slowly* lowered down, producing 'smoke,' which was channeled out the two pipes through big flexible plastic tubes lying on the stage. The whole thing cost $60 to build."

Where allowed, flash pots can be made for under $5, and a flame thrower for $120 (price depends on the tank deposit).

Visual effects are in part limited only by your imagination. "I've got an idea I want to try," says one musician. "I'm going to use hydraulic lifts to raise my organ off the stage, so it'll look like it's floating. That'll be a great trick!"

As you acquire a more elaborate stage show, you'll be under greater pressure to operate everything from the stage. All the effects mentioned here can be controlled from the stage, but eventually a lighting technician, pyrotechnician, or effects coordinator will be needed. That's one more mouth to feed.

The Band Needs Ears

Perception from the stage of what the audience is hearing should never be considered accurate. "I've found that when we're too loud onstage, the volume is low out in the room, and when we're nice and soft onstage, it's too loud for the audience," says an experienced performer.

We're all picky about how we sound. It's maddening to whip off a hot solo, only to be told that no one in the audience could hear it because the drummer was too loud. Even with only two performers, levels can get out of balance. The rhythm guitarist can obliterate whatever lead the soloist is playing. And the bigger the group, the harder it is to achieve a balanced "mix."

How much help are friends? Not much, unless they happen to be musicians whose judgments you respect. When your best friend has downed three pitchers of beer and keeps telling you to turn it up, you have to take his perception into consideration. Loved ones are even worse judges of musical balance, since they come to hear you, and fail to consider the rest of the group's sound fairly. When I spot a musician in the audience, I invariably ask how we sound. Is the volume too high? Can the lyrics be understood? Are the leads distinguishable? When I get to talk to a drummer, I'm even more specific, asking about things only another drummer would listen for.

With experience, sound balance can be controlled from the stage. Sound checks, conducted hours (or minutes) before performance time, are your primary source of information on volume levels and equalization. Of course, it's easier if you don't have to worry about the sound. It's simply a matter of economics. A sound technician is one more person to pay. Still, local bands are willing to sacrifice the extra money for a technician because it's the best way to be sure the audience hears what you want them to hear. While playing in groups without a sound technician, I worry about my overall volume and tone. I know the audience hears something different from what I hear, but is it good? Does my bass drum have enough presence? Does the snare snap crisply? With a technician watching and listening, I don't worry. Those worries become *his* worries, not mine.

There are four considerations about any prospective technician:

1. Does the person have equipment, or will everything used in the P.A. be the group's? Musicians have to supply their own equipment, and technicians should be no exception. They don't have to supply *all* the P.A. components, but a mixer and equalizer would help out.

2. What experience with electronics have they had? The problems that crop up with a P.A. far outnumber the problems of all the instruments combined because there are so many things to go wrong. You need someone who can think clearly, make an educated guess at where the trouble lies, then systematically trace down the problem and fix it. Knowledge of electronics theory and hands-on experience running P.A.'s both help.

3. Does the person have a good musical ear? This is a prerequisite for any sound technician. Without someone who hears balances well and can distinguish instrumentation and harmonies, the purpose of hiring a technician is defeated. This is why so many technicians are former or aspiring musicians.

4. Is the person likable? This is just like adding another musician—someone else to cope with. Try all sound technicians out on the Musician Personality Test in Chapter 5.

Affording a technician is the major problem. Some bands only hire technicans for the first night of an extended-run gig. You can also hire a technician to come to the group's sound check before the performance and set levels. The problem with hiring a technician part-time is that sound levels change with the number of people in a room. Feedback and individual volumes also fluctuate. Full-time technicians can be paid an equal cut of what each musician earns or a flat weekly salary. Payment varies widely according to what jobs you include with position. Does it involve mixing, setting up equipment, driving an equipment truck, or fixing broken equipment? Duties and salary should be clearly agreed upon before hiring.

Answer "Yes" to These Questions and You're Ready to Fly

1. Have you gone to see other groups in your area and think your image and format will be unique?
2. Does your image match those of the artists you're copying?
3. Do you have any bizarre costumes or gimmicks to present to audiences?
4. Does the group have at least one set of matching outfits?
5. Has stationery been printed and photographs taken?
6. Have you completed a cut tape?
7. Have you phoned your primary markets and asked the appropriate people if they'd be interested in a promo package?
8. Have promo packs been followed up with phone calls asking about job openings?
9. Have you agreed to and signed any contracts for shows?
10. Are you experienced at running a P.A. from the stage, or has a reliable sound technician been hired?

For Further Information . . .

To spruce up your stage show, check out *Designing with Light*, by Michael Gilette, Mayfield Publishing Co., 285 Hamilton Ave., Palo Alto CA 94301. Although geared for the theater, its practical advice is applicable to music productions. *Designing and Painting for the Theatre*, by Lynn Pecktal, Holt, Rinehart & Winston, 521 Fifth Ave., New York NY 10017, provides excellent advice on drawing, painting, and building stage props and scenery. *Handbook of Stage Lighting Graphics*, by William B. Warfel, Drama Book Specialists, 150 W. 52nd St., New York NY 10019, shows how light position and selection of colors can create special moods. For practical advice and to keep abreast of lighting trends, *Lighting Dimensions Magazine*, 31706 S. Coast Hwy., Suite 302, South Laguna CA 92677, offers comments from well-known lighting designers.

If you'd like to learn more about staging a truly spectacular show, read *Fireworks Principles & Practice* by Ronald Lancaster, and *Handbook of*

Pyrotechnics, by Karl O. Brauer. Both books are available from Chemical Publishing Co., 155 W. 19th St., New York NY 10011. Be sure to phone your local fire department to find out about any restrictions on the use of pyrotechnics.

• CHAPTER NINE •
BUSINESS LEADERSHIP

You can be dynamite onstage and do nothing but lose money if your offstage act—the business side of a band—is inept. Not incidentally, business leadership also determines which bands stick together—and which don't.

If you don't understand how a business operates, learn! There are plenty of resources available. Colleges offer classes in small business administration, accounting, management, negotiation, and secretarial skills—all of these apply to the successful operation of a performing act.

The Unseen Offstage Duties

People know musicians rehearse for performances, but that's about as far as popular perception of our profession goes. What else could it take to play in a band? Don't successful musicians just lie around smoking joints and drinking Budweiser all day long? Such a carefree life we lead!

Well, not quite. We're viewed this way because the public only sees us during the fun part of our job. They never see the business side of entertainment.

Organization, books, accounting, and taxes are all integral parts of a band. All require attention. To neglect any one area is to jeopardize the group's integrity. All of these areas are interrelated, so communication between each is important. The musicians handling these tasks must tell each other what's going on at a bi-weekly business meeting (explained at the end of this chapter).

What shocks (or discourages) most musicians is the amount of time and energy these tasks require. Your stage hours won't equal the time devoted to business-related matters. But business doesn't have to be a drag—some musicians actually enjoy the hustling and paperwork. I do.

By being involved with the inner workings of the group, you're more aware of where you really stand, where the group is headed, and how to advance faster. Thus you'll "control your own destiny."

A fundamental requirement of anyone involved with the act's organization, bookings, accounting, and financing is honesty, and always having the good of the band in mind. The group's well-being is the main concern. If a member is too self-centered, or has questionable ethics, that person shouldn't be trusted with responsibility in any of these areas.

Dividing Business Leadership

One person can't—and shouldn't—do it all. It's possible until the act grows from part-time to full-time employment; after that, it's just too much work. Why kill yourself? You could be earning money at another musical job! Besides the value of your time, here are some more reasons to divide business leadership:

1. More involvement leads to more interest.

If you give members reasons for staying in the group other than just performing, their commitment to the group will be greater. Their interest will be higher if they've invested time to make the enterprise successful. If the drummer isn't involved, his concern for the group's fortunes is minimal.

2. More involvement leads to more trust.

Authority is *always* suspect to some degree. Musicians become critical of their bandleader if he writes the checks, books the gigs, makes the decisions, etc. The way to create trust is to make the critical musicians leaders. Give them some authority, some decision-making power—make everyone a manager. Obviously, "Financial Manager" and "Guitar Pick Manager" are not of equal importance, but self-esteem can flourish even in menial jobs. Even a little managerial authority makes people feel important.

3. Business outweighs music, so business must be divided up.

In Chapter 5, I said, "The band as a unit must be stronger than any one member." Any musician who has worked with (or "for") a strong personal manager soon realized music is secondary to business. If the act doesn't book gigs, all the hot chops in the world won't do you any good. Money is generated—and profit preserved—by good business sense. Business dictates; don't allow one person to have all that responsibility.

4. The most successful business people don't try to do it all.

Would you rather do acceptable work on three projects or outstanding work on one? People often spread themselves too thin, and it shows in mistakes, oversights, and incompleteness. Learning to delegate authority is a key to advancement in business.

5. Someone might be better qualified than you.

If you've got a singer who works part-time as a secretary, why not use his skills? If the trumpet player manages a fast-food joint, why try to manage the group yourself? Realize your own limitations. Each musician should be asked what he likes best and does well in order to make maximum use of resources. I once played with a woman who worked part time as a tax consultant. And *I* did the band's taxes! How stupid!

Some musicians are no good at business in any way, shape, or form. They add 2 + 2 and get 5. They call an employer and get into an argument. Leave business klutzes to musical responsibilities *only*. I've found they're unusually good at musical decisions, like song selection, picking apart harmonies, and arranging set lists.

Should You Be Paid for Your Time?

I'd like to shout, "Yes!" but it's not that easy. If band duties are divided up, then time and effort are also divided up between members. You can't justify giving yourself a 5 percent cut if two or three others are putting in just as much work. If everyone contributes equally to offstage duties, then no one should receive an additional cut.

After you figure out everyone's abilities and interests in non-musical duties, draw up a chart of what each person is responsible for and how many hours a week the task requires. If possible, rearrange duties without sacrificing efficiency in order to even out each person's time investment. If a balance between hours spent on the band can be arrived at, you'll have it made and everyone will be happy. If, on the other hand, you and the conga player are the only ones resourceful enough to handle business matters, you two should be reimbursed for your time. You can be paid a straight percentage or an hourly wage. For example, if you're booking all the gigs and keeping the ledger and checking account up to date, you could ask the band to pay you 5 percent of all the gigs you line up, or $5 an hour. If you're booking long-running engagements (i.e., a month at each restaurant) it would be to your advantage to be paid the percentage, since you might only need five hours to book a $6,000 job. If you're booking one-night stands, an hourly wage works out better, since a lot more time would be spent phoning, organizing, and negotiating contracts. But the percentage arrangement involves less paperwork and avoids any questions from other members about the accuracy of your hourly wage computations.

A Representative Must Be a Natural Salesperson

You know that despicable persistence of door-to-door salespeople? After wedging their foot in the door, they talk 90 miles an hour nonstop while pushing candy, utensils, vacuum cleaners, and other incredible bargains in your face. That's the attitude and energy needed to represent your band. You'll have to use those same tactics (unless you can persuade the local Avon representative to drop perfume in favor of selling your act).

You'll need to be well-dressed and act businesslike. Promptness and preparedness can make or break a contract negotiation. Employers pride themselves on being businesspeople, and if you give the impression that you're one of them, that's half the ball game.

You must be able to lie. I was going to say "hype," but it comes down to effectively lying about the act. Your job is to sell the group, and all salespeople stretch the truth about their product. That's part of selling. Of course, if you promise an eight-piece brass section, you'll have to deliver, but if you call your act "the hottest country-swing band in northern Ohio," who's going to doubt you? That's just your opinion.

In order to lie and sound convincing, you must believe what you're saying. I've never been good at pushing a group I personally didn't like. I'd rather tell the truth about a crummy band, because then my reputation won't be tarnished. However, if I really think a band sounds great, I'll describe it with all kinds of superlatives. In describing the song list, I'll say, "It's a mixture of new and older hits" instead of saying, "It's a little outdated." About the musicians I'd say, "They're all young and really hot" instead of "They're inexperienced." Is this lying? Yes, I think so. It's also what promotion is all about.

Agents do everything I'm describing. They make phone calls and schedule business lunches with employers. If you and/or another band member can learn these salesmanship skills, you can represent the act and pocket the 15 percent agent cut. I know plenty of groups that refuse to work through agents, instead opting to divide representation among themselves by geographic area. This can be a major savings.

If you're handling negotiations with clubs 1, 2, 3, and 4, David is handling 5, 6, and 7, and Debbie is handling 8, 9, and 10, take care to keep these segregated so two of you don't book the same club. Too often if more than one representative is talking to the same employer, band strategies and communication become jumbled. You might offer the act for $300 a night and one hour later Debbie quotes the going rate at $260. The employer is either going to take Debbie's offer or hold out for $225.

Never tell an employer you are the pianist for the group. Employers regard musicians as poor businesspeople, so don't allow them to get this impression. State clearly that you are the agent. That's all. It's none of their business that you just happen to tickle the ivories. The amount of money an employer will offer an agent as opposed to a musician is astounding. One band in my area was topping out at $1,000 a week until they hired a representative. Their average weekly salary jumped to $1,500 in one week, from the same employers. Project a confident, no-nonsense personality to employers and never, never let them know you're in the band; by the time they see you onstage the negotiations will be over. One guitarist-band representative I know is purposely omitted from all promotional pictures so customers won't know he's in the band. The group has business cards printed that read, "Alex Johnson, Agent" and a phone number. The phone number is the guitarist's house, but "Alex Johnson" is an imaginary person. When someone calls for Alex, they're under the impression they're talking with an agent, so they accept the fact they'll have to pay big bucks. The funny thing is, it works!

It's reasonable to assume a representative should have experience in selling, but musicians with experience as buyers shouldn't be dismissed. Whereas they might lack the persistence and effective "sales pitch" of a salesperson, someone who's been involved in hiring musical entertainment knows what concert promoters, planning committees, and nightclub owners can really afford. They know what a bar can gross on a good night, and can use this information during negotiations.

The only exception is in large cities, where you'll probably need a bona fide agent to get steady gigs in high-paying clubs. Competition is so intense in big cities that clubs get away with abusing bands—they "audition" them for one night and pay them peanuts. A good, reputable agent will save you a lot of hassles.

Booking the Act Can Be a Full-Time Job

An agent's work is never done. There's the organization who wrote a bad check; the chain nightclub that always strings out payment till month's end; the benefit concert promoters who want the band but can't afford expenses; countless employers to convince; and the cliff-hangers, nail-biters, and lost deals you still hope to pull off. It's terribly time consuming.

Representatives must enjoy talking with people. If you don't relate well to strangers, you'll have trouble selling yourself. Pick out something unique about each person you deal with and write it down. When you talk with them again, you'll have a personalized lead for the conversation, and the other person will reason that, "Hey, this guy remembers me. I like him." Getting to know and then developing friendships with employers assures you of work.

If your group isn't filled with musicians anxious to book gigs, an incentive plan might work. At a band meeting, suggest that anyone who successfully books a gig receives a 5 or 10 percent commission, on top of their regular cut. Soon you'll have several eager representatives. But before the inexperienced 15-year-old organist begins ambitiously contacting employers, have him read Chapters 4, 9, and 10.

Never Talk Money on First Acquaintance

Since you might talk with a few employers before reading Chapter 10, this is an important principle to mention now. There are three reasons for not blurting out your price:

1. It can turn an employer off.

I was once trying to sign a deal for our group to perform in an exclusive San Francisco club. "Playing in this big club will really pay well," I thought. They could certainly afford to pay us a lot! With this in mind, one of the first things I asked their agent was, "How much do you pay?" I got the cold shoulder from then on. He wouldn't return my calls. The problem was I had insulted him. He knew any unknown band professional enough to play his club did it for the exposure and publicity, not just the money, which was also good. If you ask about money right away, you're effectively saying, "We're desperate and we need a job." Employers don't want desperate bands; they want bands in demand.

2. It can ruin a harmonious business friendship.

Making contacts, meeting people, and nurturing friendships are an immense help to a new business. Struggling bands have been saved by the resourcefulness of a business-related friend. One of the unwritten rules governing good business relations says that prices be fair, understood, and *not* the only reason for doing business together. Friendships and fringe benefits can supersede money, so when you only ask about price and don't attempt to socialize and create a friendship, many people will back off. They might know a group of musicians who will play for the same money *and* are really nice people.

3. You might undercut yourself!

Musicians cut their own throats every day. I've done it, too. I met with a woman two years ago who wanted to hire my band for a wedding. "Great," I thought. "Weddings are easy money." Soon after introductions and sitting down for lunch, she said, "Oh! I'm supposed to find out how much you charge for weddings."

"Well," I said, "As a policy, we charge $125 an hour for wedding receptions." Boy, that sounded sweet!

"Oh, that's fine!" she exclaimed, obviously delighted with herself.

"We didn't want to exceed our $1,500 budget."

I sat dumbfounded. I could only mutter "Oh," under my breath. I had just committed us to play four hours for $500, when it was obvious she was prepared to offer $1,500.

Always let the employer quote a price first. Then you can act shocked, embarrassed, and insulted at what might be a very fair offer. After an employer says, "We pay $950 a week," you then have a point from which to go up. Until you get their opening offer, avoid quoting prices.

Sometimes all the high-powered hype in the world won't help you. A smart employer will act very uninterested, and you'll find yourself comin down, down, down in price. With this kind of employer, make your proposal—very low key—and let him do *all* the talking. Just sit back and wait. The balance of power will shift to you as the employer digs into a deeper and deeper hole trying to explain things to you. Patience is the secret with this kind of employer.

Cover These Points in a Contract

When an employer pulls out a contract and says, "Sign here," you must know what should—and shouldn't—be included in that agreement. If you are a member of the American Federation of Musicians (AFM), your local will supply you with a union contract. If you're not in the union, you should type your own contract to present to employers or send along with promo packages. (See sample agreement on page 142.)

The decibel-volume clause is important to many dinner houses, because blaring rock bands may give diners indigestion. Likewise, the liability section is important to musicians because drunken dancers have been known to fall into P.A. mains.

It's okay to sign an employer's contract as long as it contains these specifics, and you've read it carefully for any hidden clauses.

Always take an original and a photocopy to be signed, and give the employer the copy. If working through the mail, sign both papers, and send them with a self-addressed, stamped envelope so the employer will promptly return the original to you.

The only payment term that's really taboo is a personal check, since it might bounce or be hard to cash. Large hotels that allow you to cash their personal checks at the bar are an exception to this rule.

Written agreements are certainly preferable to a handshake, but a verbal agreement *is* binding by law. One act I was with was cancelled the night before the gig. We had no contract, only telephone conversations with the employer. Even so, we were awarded full payment ($450) in California Small Claims Court with no trouble at all!

PERFORMANCE AGREEMENT

Terms CHAKRA heretofore agrees to perform to the fullest of their professional abilities on the date(s) _____ from _____. The business/organization/person, _____ (the employer) will pay CHAKRA _____ in exchange for this (these) performance(s), in the form of _____. Payment is due _____.

Rights CHAKRA retains all rights concerning the material which they perform. CHAKRA also reserves the right to break for 15 minutes of every 60 minutes or an equivalent thereof. The employer, _____, shall have the final say concerning music decibel level.

Liability The employer, _____, is liable for any damage to CHAKRA's stage equipment resulting from a patron-incurred infraction only during the hours specified in paragraph one of this page.

Please return the original of this performance agreement as soon as possible; the copy is for your file. The employer's signature above the word "employer" will constitute this as our agreement.

X _____ X _____
EMPLOYER   CHAKRA REPRESENTATIVE

_____
ADDRESS

_____
CITY, STATE, ZIP

_____
TELEPHONE

_____
DATE SIGNED

You Don't Need a Business Manager (Yet)

Have you dreamed of turning over all those bothersome details to a manager? You can certainly do it, but it'll cost you 10 percent (rarely), 15 percent (likely), or 20 percent (increasingly!). A manager who is sincerely concerned about the group's welfare can do a world of good by professionally representing you to clients, and negotiating smartly to keep you on an escalating income. Managers handle books, make sure there's a stage, give the band directions, and are responsible for any employee-employer conflicts. A good one will be able to increase your net income immediately. Judge them by sales ability (ask for client references), sincerity, promptness, and how much you like them. Experience can mean a lot, but I know beginning managers who were instantly successful with bookings.

Where do you locate a "competent" manager? Most managers are in some way friends of the group's. Maybe it's your wife, boyfriend, college professor, or someone who's been to see the band at every bar for the last year. Though they may lack education in business, finance, and management, they do possess the most important criterion for your manager: *They care about you.* This will assure you of their honesty and good intentions. When a musician doubts his manager's financial integrity, the working relationship is doomed. Find someone you can trust.

A business manager will usually circumvent agents—that's part of his job. A business manager is not a personal manager who babysits the band. These are two different jobs. Of course, one person can do both jobs, but this increases their importance, power, and usually their percentage. Keep control of your destiny.

If business duties are divided among band members, you shouldn't feel pressured into hiring a business manager until things really become hectic, or you feel the act has peaked under its own leadership and you *need* a manager to expand financially. In the meantime, always remember the things the extra cut is paying for. That'll bring you back to your senses!

Becoming a Band Accountant

Accounting. The word alone sends a shiver of fear through many musicians and inspires visions of torturous hours spent bending over columns of numbers. Is accounting really that hard? Let me put it this way: You can learn band accounting in less than one hour. After that, it'll be a breeze to keep your records up to date.

"I went to a CPA and had her set up our books initially," says one guitarist who keeps his group's books. That's fine if you have the money; otherwise, you can set up your own books. Here's what you'll need:

1. A band checking account and/or band credit card
2. A two-column entry ledger (analysis pad)
3. A month-by-month cash disbursements chart
4. A stack of file folders for expense and income receipts
5. An inexpensive pocket calculator

If you have a personal checking account, you're already familiar with how records are kept. The principle is the same; band records are just a bit more detailed.

Since you are a self-employed musician, many expenses can—and should—be written off against your taxes. To make deductions acceptable to the Internal Revenue Service, accurate records must be kept. That's the law. Receipts legitimize the records.

If your band is a partnership, expendable items (strings and sticks) and large group purchases (P.A. equipment) are considered band expenses and kept track of in the band ledger. Instrument purchases should be deducted as personal expenses, and shown on your private ledger.

Here's how it can work: When you and the drummer buy strings and sticks, make sure you get a receipt. If you paid cash or wrote a check, get the register tape or handwritten receipt. If you paid with a credit card (I'll go into the benefits of each type of payment later), the receipt will be sent to you in the mail by the credit company. In any case, the money is drawn from the group's expense account. Now, back to our hypothesis: After leaving the music store $26.35 poorer, did you go anywhere else? Lunch with an employer maybe, or to the gasoline station? If so, get receipts!

When you return home, pull out your receipts and enter them in the band ledger, with the $26.35 and whatever else under "expenses." When you get paid, enter the amount under "income" in the ledger. Expense receipts and income check stubs should be filed in order of date received in your monthly file folder. At the end of each month, go down the description column in the ledger and figure out how much money was spent for each category by filling in your "cash disbursements" sheets. This allows you to look back and calculate where the bulk of the money was spent and figure how to effectively cut costs.

Most musicians pay for expenses with a wad of green bills (when they're lucky). This is fine as long as you keep receipts, but writing checks is safer, since every purchase can be proven to other musicians by the cancelled checks. "Everything is paid by check," one musician told me. "Every deposit is authorized. I hand out income statements and balance sheets so they know assets, liabilities, gross income, expenses, and profit, as well as what share profit they and everyone else drew. Then no one suspects any wrongdoing." Checks also provide you with a register of expenses to refer to. Paying with credit is the easiest, since all you need to do is make a notation of what you bought, and the receipts are mailed to you. Credit, however, is hard for a beginning group to receive.

A good way to handle band expenses is to skim 10 or 15 percent off the top of each gig and deposit it in the band's account. This pays transportation, booking, and expenses related to music or performance. If an expense account isn't opened, you'll spend half your time collecting money *back* from everyone when the group needs hotel rooms, gas money, or equipment repairs.

Following are a sample ledger page and cash disbursements calendar:

SAMPLE LEDGER PAGE

Date	Description	Expenses	Income
April			
14	drumsticks & guitar strings	26.35	
	business lunch w/ Dan Jacobs, owner	17.-	
	gasoline	15.-	
15	check from Red Baron		1000.-
19	cords for monitors	45.30	
22	check from Sutter Creek Showcase		1200.-
23	Benefit for CSUS recycling center		100.-
24	gasoline, van	18.-	
25	post office	2.22	
27	gasoline	14.50	
28	stationary	47.02	
	post office (stamps, package)	9.66	
29	Baron check		1000.-
	gasoline, van	20.-	
	rehearsal room rent	180.-	
30	telephone bill	67.13	
	April totals	462.18	3300.-
	April net profit		2837.82
May			

CASH DISBURSEMENTS CALENDAR

Expenses	Jan.	Feb.	Mar.	Apr.	May	June	July	Aug.	Sep.	Oct.	Nov.	Dec.
Gasoline												
Auto repairs												
Auto payments												
Telephone												
Postage												
Office supplies												
Printing												
Tapes, albums, singles												
Entertaining employers												
Educational activities												
Publicity												
Insurance												
Food												
Hotels, motels												
Medical												
Clothing												
Cosmetics												
Staging equipment												
Lighting												
P.A. equipment												
Manager												
Roadies												
CPA												
Other musicians												
Studio												
Rehearsal room rent												
Equipment rental												
Equipment purchase												
Miscellaneous												

Income-Tax Time

April 15 is the ultimate reason records and receipts are kept. Filing shouldn't involve much work if the records are legible and each month's expenses and income have been tallied in the ledger.

Both federal and state tax agencies tend to watch musicians closely, since the opportunities for not reporting income are numerous. To be safe, always write down income. Although many part-time bands don't declare income tax, if you keep expense receipts, you probably will have enough write-offs to counter taxes owed, and you won't be breaking the law. The best way to set up the group for taxation is to form a partnership. This limits the tax responsibility of any member to only himself, and makes keeping accurate records easier than if everyone keeps his own. Partnerships report either a profit or a loss and then divide responsibility equally among band members, who file individual returns.

When a band is organized with a designated bandleader and he is paying the musicians, problems can arise. "I hire musicians as independent contractors, but the IRS doesn't see it that way," says one disgruntled bandleader. "They try to make me responsible for every one of my musician's taxes."

If you have questions concerning how to organize your band for tax purposes, have a CPA go over it with you. In some areas, songwriter services are available for legal questions.

Have a Bi-weekly Business Meeting

Several bands I knew broke up due to suspicion and doubt. Two of the groups even had very good interpersonal relations, but the failure—or, more precisely, oversight—of the members in charge of business and finances to provide updates and open accounting systems fostered mistrust in the other members. Everyone should know where the group stands. If these two groups had scheduled regular business meetings detailing policies and actions, chances are they would still be together.

While business and accounting updates are crucial to your act's integrity, other areas can also be discussed at meetings. Long-term goal direction should be re-evaluated periodically to make sure everyone still wants to pursue the same direction and understands how the group is trying to attain goals. Short-term goal accomplishments should be reviewed so everyone can sense progress. Upcoming goals should be planned and tasks delegated. All booking possibilities should be explained, with their respective advantages and disadvantages. Personal problems between members should be tactfully solved. Rules governing performance behavior can be debated. All except musical matters (rehearsal) can fit on an agenda for discussion at business meetings.

At your first business meeting, the group should decide who will play the role of group leader. The responsibilities of the designated leader are to keep the meeting progressing on an agenda, encourage diffident members to talk while quieting overly talkative members, control conflicts between members, and keep a record of what the group has done, what's in process, and what the group plans to do.

How these duties are carried out by the discussion leader determines the effectiveness of the meeting. Do all the members understand now? Are the singers friends again? Did everything that was supposed to be discussed get discussed? It's the leader's style that most influences group interaction. Here are four styles of leaders:

The democratic leader. This style of leadership is ideal for a band. This leader does not make decisions for the group. He acts as a *guide* rather than a director. He summarizes or offers opinions in a neutral voice, thus indicating his openness to other suggestions. He walks the delicate line between heavy-handedness and absence of control. The pressure he exerts on the group is just enough to get things done, but in the process he allows the group time to explore alternatives. This is why a democratic style is so desirable: It compromises and tries to achieve both efficiency and creativity.

The authoritarian leader. This person makes all the decisions for you, often without consulting you. Things get done very fast, but the choices, solutions and policies might not be the best ultimate answers. Creativity—the input of the rest of the band—is ignored for the sake of efficiency. Many groups are ruled by authoritarian bandleaders who assume this power because they started the group, own the equipment, and book the gigs. The ever-present problem, besides forsaking better answers for quicker answers, is keeping everyone happy. Most musicians don't like being oppressed and will eventually rebel against the leader.

The permissive leader. This person takes the opposite approach of the authoritarian leader. She may keep notes of what has been discussed, but she doesn't attempt to influence, direct, or even guide the meeting. This style of leadership encourages creativity, but sacrifices efficiency. Decisions and goals may be delayed. About as aggressive as the permissive leader gets is to steer discussion back to the meeting's agenda. Members need to be capable of subtly leading themselves for this style to work.

The absent leader. Some acts sort of "fall" together, with no one clearly in charge. In a leaderless group, natural leaders usually emerge and assume initiative. If they are not the most able, it will quickly become apparent. This trial and error style of leadership takes time, but weeds out ineffective leaders.

As long as everyone is aware of these varying leadership styles, the group can elect to adopt a cyclical style; in other words, for maximum efficiency, a forming band might follow the authoritarian style of one member until the group is solidly booked, at which point it has been agreed that the authoritarian leader will step down, and a democratic style will be substituted to assure each member equal input and the group maximum creative problem-solving ability.

No matter what style of leadership the group initiates, the other members need to behave in certain ways to expect comfortable interrelations and long-term goal realization. Here are personality traits that will keep communication honest, open, and non-aggressive:

Willingness. Be willing to say what you think. The trick is that you must share your views and participate in discussion *without* advocating your own idea. It's not easy. You have to offer your idea as a suggestion, and let the others decide its value; you don't try to persuade them.

Aptitude. Permissive or democratic atmospheres are best for intelligent members, since creativity is encouraged. Discussion can be made more intelligent by asking everyone to prepare ideas in advance on paper and discouraging talkative members. Quantity of verbal output is usually not commensurate with quality of suggestions. If the bassist and guitarist are constantly talking back and forth in circles, the singer—who has the ability to solve the problem—might remain silent out of frustration.

Cooperation. Certainly members should be able to cooperate with each other. This is especially important for group meetings since once something is decided, the goodwill of other members is imperative if the decision is to be carried out.

Insight. Members should be able to see suggestions through the eyes of others. Ask yourself questions such as, "How will Bill respond to this?" and, "Does this put Carol in a sticky predicament?" before verbalizing the suggestion.

Patience. You might think you could have solved the problem better yourself, in one-tenth of the time, but by running it through the group process, ideas get examined, questioned, added to, twisted around, and resubmitted—usually in a much stronger, mutually pleasing form.

Objectivity. Members should critically question and openly compliment ideas whenever appropriate—which is more often than not. When you challenge suggestions, offer a specific change or a new idea so your critical remark isn't interpreted as a slight to the original contributor.

Comment on the proposal's consequences, not the proposal itself, or worse yet, the person who proposed it. Be careful to include as much positive feedback to members as negative feedback. If a person's suggestions are continually dismissed, he'll eventually quit contributing.

The meetings should be scheduled every two weeks for a full-time act, and last one or two hours. The atmosphere should be a neutral, comfortable setting—behavioral studies conclude that ugly rooms produce fatigue, irritability, and hostility, whereas beautiful rooms produce pleasure, energy, and a desire to continue the activity.

The agenda created by the leader can vary widely in degree or specificity. You might just scribble out a few key words to remind yourself of the topics, or you might type up a detailed agenda of discussion and hand a copy to each member. Before starting each meeting, just as with rehearsals, allow 10 minutes at the beginning for gossiping and telling jokes. This assures the meeting will follow the agenda with little deviation.

Interpersonal Skills

Decision-making and problem-solving are two very different procedures. "Decision making refers to *choosing* among two or more possible alternatives," says John K. Brilhart, in *Effective Group Discussion*. To contrast, says Brilhart, "In the process of problem-solving many decisions must be made, such as what factual data to accept as true, which is the most probable precipitating cause of an unsatisfactory situation, the order in which to arrange several criteria, when and where to hold a discussion of the problem, and even when to take up a specific issue." Before you can solve problems to the group's full advantage, however, you must understand the less complex guidelines of decision making. Following are five suggestions from *Psychology Today*, in an article by Jay Hall:

1. Don't argue stubbornly for your own position. Present your position as clearly and logically as possible, being sure you listen to all reactions and consider them carefully.

2. When a stalemate seems to have occurred, avoid looking at it as a situation in which someone must win and someone else lose. Rather, see if you can find a next best alternative that is acceptable to everyone.

3. When an agreement is reached too easily and quickly, be on guard. Don't change your position simply to avoid conflict and reach agreement quickly. Through discussion, be certain that everyone accepts the solution for similar or complementary reasons.

4. Don't use such techniques as majority vote, averaging, coin tossing, or swapping off.

5. Seek out differences of opinion; they are to be expected and can be most helpful in testing ideas. Get every member involved in the decision-making process. If you have a wide range of information and ideas, the group has a better chance of finding a truly excellent solution.

These guidelines work well in democratic-style leadership. What Hall proposes are the same tactics I'll discuss in the next chapter for integrative bargaining. If you apply integrative principles to band interrelations as well as the customers you deal with, the whole business will work in harmony.

• CHAPTER TEN •

How to MAXIMIZE PERFORMANCE EARNINGS

> Musical skills alone can get you a job, because at an audition they aren't looking at your books. From then on, however, you've got to be a skillful negotiator.
>
> —Rick Van Horn, columnist,
> Modern Drummer magazine

After leaping into the marketplace and landing on both feet, you want to be off and running as quickly as possible. To keep from tripping up, everyone has to be happy. How do you keep everyone happy? It's easy. Start out making better than average money, and keep your salaries on the rise. Sure, other things contribute to happiness, but in the beginning, nothing can make a bigger difference between a psychologically healthy or sick band than money.

This chapter shows you how to get more money—or its equivalent—out of employers, while cocking a watchful eye on burgeoning expenses.

Figuring Your Bottom Pay Scale

What sounds like good payment to me may sound lousy to you. Because of differences in talent, experience, reputation, organization, and business skills, musicians have varying pay scales they will accept. How much more money will you play for? What's fair, and what's unreasonable?

Just to check whether your expectations are in the ball park, ask some working musicians how much they're getting paid. Their answers will either excite you, reassure you, or shock you, depending on how much you value your time.

The first step toward setting your bottom pay scale for the act is deciding how much money you yourself will play for. Lump sum figures can sound very enticing until broken down and handed to you. I remember jobs I agreed to enthusiastically—until I realized how much time they entailed in traveling. Decide what you will accept in terms of an hourly wage. Is $5 an hour beneath you, or does it take $10 an hour to make you feel satisfied? For casuals, is your minimum $20, or is $30 an hour the

School dances, weddings, and Christmas parties can do wonders for your hourly wage. Some bands specialize in casuals because they can earn close to a week's salary in just one night.

(photo of Sweet Onion by Mark Kenworthy)

least you'll accept? Come up with a figure that's comfortable, reasonable, and slightly daring. After checking other musicians' rates, you'll know at what point you're pricing yourself out of the market. For now, figure the minimum you'd play for. Let's say you decide on $10.50 an hour as the minimum you'll accept because your last job paid $10, and you want a raise.

The next step is to talk this over with the entire group. What's the least amount each person will accept? Well, damn it, the bassist thinks at $10.50 you'll have to pass up a lot of offers, so you come to a consensus figure of $9 an hour. The saxophonist mentions that an hourly figure should include travel time. "Oh, yeah," you sigh. Finally, everyone agrees on $8 an hour per musician as the bare minimum.

While you've got everyone together, set financial goals for a year-long period. How soon can you expect to nudge your wages back to $10.50 an hour? That depends on how often the act performs, and how smartly you deal. Let's say you expect to make $1.50 more apiece per hour every three months. That means in 12 months you'll be pulling in $14 an hour from band income. I think that's a modest escalation, and one you should be able to attain.

Of course, some gigs will pay you $25 or $50 an hour, but the minimum you'll accept for now is $8 an hour, take it or leave it. You may compromise and accept a job figuring out to only $6 an hour, because you need the money, but this isn't the gig that'll help you increase your income. Keep tight reins on your time, or you'll get stuck on the same merry-go-round that so many musicians do. They play year after year after year, but never increase their income because they're accepting all jobs, regardless of hourly wage. Now let's budget your jobs, and rate them according to how well they really pay.

Rating Jobs

There's a lot more to a professional performance than just standing up and singing. Is an offer worth your time? Before answering, you have to figure how much time the total job will consume. Dividing $350 by performance hours alone doesn't tell the whole story. If you pick each job apart, piece by piece, you'll be surprised which ones *really* pay the best hourly wage, and which ones are *not* helping the act achieve its long-range financial goals.

Here are typical tasks required for an average booking, assuming you don't use an agent:
1. Market research
2. Telephoning
3. Mailing promo package
4. Organizing and agreeing to the deal

5. Travel
6. Set-up and tear-down
7. Performance
8. Administrative and bookkeeping

If you do all of the pre-performance and post-performance duties yourself, you'll have to be paid more than other band members to uphold your $8 an hour wage. If these tasks are divided up evenly, however, no one would draw an extra salary and everyone's time investment would be minimal.

Now, let's see how these tasks work out in an actual gig. Let's say I want to book my band into a restaurant in Auburn, California. After checking my market research sheet, I would phone the manager and tell her I have an act that would fit beautifully in her restaurant. She expresses an interest, so I mail her a promo package, and a week later she calls me and we agree on a three-night, $225 a night deal. Our three-piece group plays and then Ralph, the bassist, cashes the check. We have a policy of paying whoever arranges the booking 10 percent (better our pockets than an agent's!), so I have an extra share coming. Ralph gets 2½ percent of each gig for handling administrative and bookkeeping duties. This is how I figured my hourly wage for three nights.

Market research	15 minutes
Telephoning	15 minutes
Mailing promo pack	30 minutes
Travel time (three times, up and back)	3 hours
Set-up and tear-down	2 hours
Warming-up period	1 hour
Performance	12 hours
Total time investment	19 hours

After subtracting my 10 percent "agent" cut, Ralph's 2½ percent, and dividing by three, I earn $265 for the three nights. My hourly wage is $13.95 an hour, while Ralph, who put in 30 minutes of administrative work, gets $11.49 an hour. John, the guitarist, doesn't do anything but travel, set-up and tear-down, warm-up, and perform, yet he still earns $10.97 an hour.

Always assign everything you do a time amount, so an hourly wage can be figured. A group at that Auburn gig who only counted performance hours would think they were making $18.75 an hour! To compare job offers accurately for the best hourly wages, all your business-related time must be accounted for.

Often the gig that pays less actually yields a higher hourly wage. This is vividly illustrated by the following comparison.

I had two one-week offers from agents for my four-piece group. One local rock club was offering $1,200 for four nights. The other offer was from a restaurant in Berkeley, California, which is about 90 miles from where I live in Sacramento. This one was a $1,600 offer. I didn't have any initial time invested in either of these due to the agents. This is the chart I scribbled out to decide which offer to accept:

Local Rock Club ($1,200)
1. Travel time — 1¼ hours
2. Set-up and tear-down — 2 hours
3. Warming-up period — 1 hour
4. Performance (4-hour nights) — 16 hours

Total time — 20¼ hours
Per hour wage — $13.33

Berkeley Restaurant ($1,600)
1. Travel time — 12 hours
2. Set-up and tear-down — 2 hours
3. Warming-up period — 1 hour
4. Performance (5-hour nights) — 20 hours

Total time — 35 hours
Per hour wage — $10.29

Even though the Berkeley job paid $400 more, it yielded $3 *less per hour* than the in-town gig. To build my hourly wage—the *real* indicator of advancement—I took the local job. The time saved was easily used for other money-making projects. Time is your measure of a job's value.

Obviously, expenses change with jobs, too. After transportation money is scraped off the top of the Berkeley gig, hourly wage plunges downward even further. Always compute expenses after figuring your total time investment, or an offer's real value won't be known until after you've already played.

No Fee Is Final

Ask and ye shall receive. I've proven this over and over again to my own astonishment. There's so much money available it's incredible. Many musicians are underpaid simply because they lack the confidence to tell people what they're worth. They don't get it because they don't ask for it!

We have an unusual buyer-seller relationship in North America. The seller scribbles a price on a tag, and the buyer pays that amount. Most countries in the world operate on a bargaining system. The seller sets a price, the buyer offers half that much, and the two either compromise or don't make the transaction.

As a musician, you're the seller. The problem is that we traditionally allow buyers—the employers—to set prices. Why do we do that? Because we've been raised in this non-bargaining culture.

This means you have to begin standing up for your own worth and questioning job offers. It means breaking a deeply ingrained bad habit. Do you think you'll feel uncomfortable asking for more money? It might be uncomfortable the first few times you gather enough courage to ask, but as soon as you see how successful it is, you'll become a confident—maybe even aggressive—bargainer.

Any price you're quoted is the *least* that person or organization can afford. Here's what one nightclub owner told me: "My auditor keeps me posted on how I'm doing, and how much I can afford. If she tells me I can afford $6,000 a month for entertainment, I'll only budget about $4,500, and plow the other $1,500 back into the business." If your band is making $1,200 a week, chances are good that your employer can pay you $1,400-$1,600 without needing to draw more customers. That's the amount he budgeted for you, but you didn't negotiate for it! You accepted his first offer, the $1,200.

Always regard a quoted price as a place to *start* bargaining. An offer is an offer, not a finalized, official figure. What authority does a quote price carry? Is it a divine, magical figure of some unearthly creation? NO. It was arrived at by an auditor and an owner. It represents what they think they can hire any unsuspecting band for. It carries no "official" status. You assume that they offer that much money to you for a good reason, but many times there isn't any reason at all. They just pick a figure out of the air and recite it to you in a very serious, confidential voice. They quote a low price in case you've got enough guts to hold out for more.

One effective trick some agents and employers try to pull is showing you the figure on paper. "Oh, my gosh," you say, "it's already typed into the contract!" Don't let it faze you. Tell them the contract is unacceptable, and they must draw up a new one. Better yet, produce your own, pre-typed contract (with a high amount written in), and bring a sheet justifying the exorbitant fee, listing hourly wage, expenses, and rental costs. Who cares if you don't really have any rental costs? Just as the employer tells you he can only afford $1,200 when he really can afford $1,600, you can tell him you need $1,600 to make your hourly wage, when you might need only $1,300.

Welcome to the world of business!

Wheeling and Dealing with Customers for Cash

It's hard to discover creative solutions when working with a fixed, defined resource, such as money. An amount of money is being negotiated, and the only question is how each negotiating party will fare. Will you get the money you want, will the employer get the best of you, or will you evenly compromise? In the next section, I'll discuss how to enlarge your share of the take by concentrating on variables *other* than cash. This is cooperative bargaining (integrative), and the ramifications of cooperation—building lasting relationships—are more beneficial than strict competitive bargaining. Still, competition is sometimes the only means available. Distributive bargaining is the practice of getting as much money as possible from a negotiation—at the employer's expense.

Distributive bargaining promotes a subtle—or at times obvious—adversary relationship. You're in competition with the employer. If you are offered $300 and you accept right away, you've lost the competition. Occasionally, of course, you won't be competing, or at least it won't seem like it. The gig might be for a friend's wedding, or you might regard the offer as very generous. In such cases you wouldn't bargain, you'd gladly accept. But these same emotions and logic—doing a friend a "favor," and judging an offer "more than fair"—can be used against you by a skilled bargainer without you knowing what hit you. Only after the gig (if even then) will you realize you've been taken for a ride. It pays to understand competitive bargaining, how to use it, and how to defend against it.

Every negotiation has an inherent conflict. At the base of the conflict are two parties (in the case of a musician-employer negotiation), a proposal by one of the parties, and the consequences of that proposal for each party. The proposing party will reap positive consequences from the proposal, and the other party will be affected negatively. Thus distributive bargaining produces "win/lose" consequences.

To illustrate this relationship, let's say you approach an Elks Club about performing at their Fourth of July celebration. Here's how it could be diagrammed:

Parties	Proposal	Consequences
Your act	We play at dance for $800	We get paid $800 (+)
Elks Club		We spend $800 (-)

As you can see, the $800 expenditure by the Elks is viewed as a negative consequence by them. They'd rather pay $500 (then they could afford a Thanksgiving party, too). But you want $800. The band is great, you've got some monitors to pay off, and besides, you're worth every penny of it. Obviously, we've got a conflict here! A compromise at $650 might appear logical, but that won't pay the monitor bill, will it? No. You need $800. How do you make sure you get the $800, and don't settle for $500? You make the representative lower his aspirations. This is the goal of distributive bargaining. Your job is to make him feel lucky to get you for $800.

The relationship is best illustrated by the following Aspiration Level Theory chart:

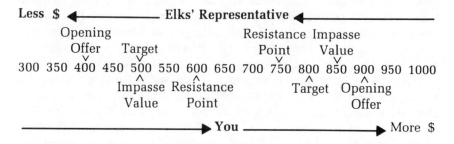

As you can see, your goals directly oppose the Elks' representative goals. Your strategy is outlined underneath the money figures; his is outlined above.

Your *opening offer*, $900, is the only amount you quote to the representative. Even though you don't expect to get this much, that's what you say you want. An opening offer should be only slightly unrealistic.

Your *target*, $800, is how much you want to get. You expect to come down from your opening offer, but only to your target.

Your *resistance point*, $600, is the least amount of money you'll accept for the gig. You hope you won't be pushed all the way to this point.

Your *impasse value*, $500, is the insultingly low level at which you will abandon any ideas of agreement. You would rather take the day off and go fishing—or try for another gig—if this is all the representative finally offers.

In a typical negotiation, all you'll know about what an employer will pay is from the opening offer. You won't know their target, resistance point, or impasse value.

Theoretically, if you can find out an employer's resistance point, you can push him all the way to it. This makes any information you can gather about your "opponent" vitally important. Call musicians who have worked for him previously and ask what they got. Salaries paid to different bands vary widely. If you can start by accurately reciting how much money the Elks Club paid to various groups last year, a pale look of defeat will mask over the representative's face. Chances are, you'll then get whatever you ask for.

Without indicting information—and even with it—you need to act in certain ways and appeal to certain emotions in order to come out ahead. You want that Elks' rep to give more and bigger concessions than you do. Here are some concession behaviors guaranteed to help you win the distributive negotiating game:

1. *Before going in, limit your own power.* You know how frustrating it is to try and get something from someone who lacks the authority to give

it to you? Say you're trying to return a pair of shoes. Every time you arrive, ready to present your case and argue if necessary, a dumb sales clerk stares blankly at you and repeats, "I'm sorry, but you'll have to talk to the owner." Problem is, every time you come in the store the owner always seems to be out on his yacht.

In that negotiation, the sales clerk won. That's because she purposely claimed limited authority. She knows that after a few more futile attempts at cornering the owner, you'll give in and keep the damn shoes. It's the same with a band employer. If you receive an offer that's less than you desire, say, "Oh. Well, I'll have to talk that over with the act." After taking time out of a busy schedule to negotiate with you, the employer may give in to time pressures, and say, "All right. Let's get this thing over with. How much *can* you accept?"

2. *Make it clear there's competition for your act.* I don't care if no one else but your neighbors have heard of the group! *Generate* competitive interest in yourself before going into a negotiation. Say you're weighing several possibilities. Employers must feel they are competitively vying for your act. Otherwise, they'll offer you whatever they feel like offering. Make 'em think there are ten others anxiously waiting in line.

3. *Act very patient while negotiating.* If you rush into a luncheon appointment with an employer, your nonverbal message is, "Let's get this over with, I'm willing to compromise." This is a huge concession: The employer knows that all he has to do is take his time, remain uncommitted, and watch you drop your asking price by hundreds of dollars.

4. *Talk a lot.* Usually in distributive bargaining, the more aggressive of the two parties comes out ahead. If you talk the most and control the mood—a strong "take charge" attitude—the other party will be swayed by your arguments and agree with some of your fast-talk reasoning— even if he doesn't understand what you said.

5. *Flinch at every offer.* If you want $2,000 a week, but she only offers $1,500, show your dissatisfaction. Look as pained and uncomfortable as possible. The idea is to make her feel guilty for suggesting such a paltry sum. *Embarrass* her! If you have too much pride to admit that $1,500 is ridiculously low (even if it isn't), you won't get what you want. *Haggle.*

6. *Be slow to counter-offer.* When the club owner says, "Okay. I'll pay you $1,250 instead of $1,200," should you immediately lower your demand from $1,400 to $1,350? No. Leave your offer where it is. Reiterate why you're worth at least $1,400. If you can stall long enough, the owner might forget he made the last concession and raise to $1,275 or $1,300. What does this mean? He's bidding against himself! Be slow to agree with an offer. Whenever you're ready to say yes, say no a few more times.

7. *Be stingy with concessions.* When you do make a concession by dropping your asking price, make a smaller concession than the employer made. If she came up $50, make your next concession $30.

The increments of concessions reveal how much money each side needs or can afford. If you drop from $2,000 to $1,750 to $1,500, I'd think you're only expecting to get $1,000 or $1,250. On the other hand, if you drop from $2,000 to $1,800, to $1,750, to $1,725, I'd believe my offer would have to be $1,600 or $1,700 to hire you. It's the same with the employers. Pay attention to their consecutive increments. If I go from $1,000 to $1,300, to $1,600, what impression do you get? That I've got a lot more money than I'm offering.

One good tactic is the "Fake Final Offer." To be effective, you must show considerable pain in dropping your price this far. "Gee, I'm sorry, but $1,725 is my final offer," can work if you look and sound sincere. It shouldn't be the first concession you make, but it needn't be the last! To retain your credibility after your "final offer" is ignored, take up a good deal of time, reiterate your needs and give your "absolute, rock bottom, last offer." Make it obvious that you're doing him a favor and will be performing virtually for free.

8. *Always ask for compensation.* Every time you come down in price, ask for something in return. I've dealt with employers who will grant me a small concession—something other than money—every time I come down in price, because I ask for it. Say things like, "Well, if I reduce my price to $1,700, will you double the band's bar tab from $25 to $50?" Then after you've got a few of these small concessions, offer to trade them back for additional money.

9. *Have ready reasons for the money you want.* Always come completely prepared with cost breakdown sheets and an hourly wage list. Justify your demands. Don't act frivolous. If you can show a breakdown for the price you're requesting—listing all expenses—an employer will realize you've got bills to pay and take you seriously.

10. *Try to find out their deadlines.* An employer—just like you— delegates a certain amount of time to negotiate contracts. He wants to be finished by that time in order to take care of other matters. When you greet an employer before negotiating, ask how much time he has for the meeting. If he asks you, say you've got plenty of time. You might really have to be out of there in 15 minutes, but by not revealing your deadline, you don't commit yourself to reaching agreement. Since you know his deadline, however, you can refrain from offering any real concessions until just a few minutes before he has to leave. The majority of concessions are saved for the very end of a negotiation, so if you can hold out until then, you'll have room left to bargain. The employer will be under a time pressure to reach agreement, and will give proportionately more than you. Just sit back and relax!

If the person you're dealing with is especially hardnosed and unwilling to bargain, these five social norms might soften him up:

Equality. Emphasize the fact you're not getting a fair deal. Make the person feel unjust and dictatorial.

Equity. Show how much time and effort you've put into preparation with the group, and stress how hard you work on stage. You *deserve* better!

Social Responsibility. Appear in desperate need of all the money you want. Tell them the band's financial problems. Make it into a soap opera!

Reciprocity. Emphasize the point he owes it to you to pay the higher price. Have you worked for him before? Make it clear you did him a big favor the first time—at great financial hardship to yourself.

Precedent. Have you played for this amount before? Is this really a reduction in wages due to inflation and extra expenses? Show that you deserve more money because you've earned this much before.

Here's an example of how I once used these tactics for my maximum gain:

Bruce Young, representing an organization that we had previously played for, the Dirt Diggers Club, called me about another job. Was our band available to play September 25? I hesitated, trying to seem busy, but then I told Young that yes, we were still available for that evening. We arranged to meet Friday the 23rd to sign a contract.

I drew up a chart detailing my bargaining strategy. Since we were paid $750 by them before, I figured this would be his opening offer. I set my opening offer at $1,000. My target was designated as $850, and my resistance point at $500. This was a four-hour job, and our usual rate was $125 per hour, so I only *needed* $500 to satisfy myself. Anything above was icing on the cake. I planned to use the norm of precedent if he tried to go less than $750, since we were paid that sum before. That same day, I sent Young a letter to thank him for the call, remind him of the meeting, and *increase his commitment.* The more time he spends thinking about me, the greater his commitment will be to culminate a deal.

When I walked inside A&B Cycle Shop and asked for Bruce Young, I was told that he had just left. "Bruce told me that you were coming," said Dick Gavin, "so he left the contract with me."

Gavin handed me the contract. It was all filled out except for my signature (power of legitimacy). When I saw the terms, I balked—$650 (opening offer).

"Everything is fine, except for the price," I sputtered. "The price is wrong?" asked Gavin incredulously.

"Yes," I answered, regaining some composure. "It's below our normal rate for casual engagements."

"That's too bad," responded Gavin, sympathizing with me, "but I can't change it." Limited authority! I couldn't believe it. He was using all of my tricks.

"When will Bruce be back?" I asked, fearing that he was off to the Bahamas for a couple of months.

"In about 10 minutes," said Gavin.

"Fine," I replied. "I've got *plenty* of time."

When Young returned, I explained to him that we usually got $1,000 for casual jobs, since it breaks up a weekend run at a club, and could actually cost us money (competition). Young responded that he understood (sympathy), but the Dirt Diggers had gone over their heads the last time paying us $750. They could only afford $650 this time. Besides, he added, the last time they expected a bigger crowd.

"Gee, Bruce, I'm sorry, but we have *never* played for one price, and then come back and renegotiated *down*" (precedent). "I thought that we were doing you a favor last time playing for $750," I added (reciprocity).

"Well, I guess I could pay you guys $700, but I can't go any higher" (final offer).

Then I started talking a lot, telling him about the expensive stage monitors we had just bought, and explaining that we could make more money playing a Friday and Saturday that weekend in a club (competition). I added that $900 was a break-even point for us (false information, but still a large concession). I looked at the clock and noticed it was 4:50 p.m. I wondered if Bruce usually went home at 5:00 (deadline information).

"I'd love to work this out today, Bruce, but I can come back tomorrow. I have *plenty* of time." I didn't think he'd want to come back on Saturday.

"Okay, Jim. "I'll pay you guys $750" (final final offer).

"That was six months ago when you hired us," I replied, trying my best to flinch. "With inflation, expenses, agent, manager" (neither of which we had), "and equipment rentals, I need more money. $850 is as low as I can go" (final offer).

"Well . . . you can't go any lower, huh?" he asked.

"That's about it," I said. "Maybe . . . well, $825" (final final offer). Concessions were getting frequent now.

"I can go to $800," he offered quickly.

"All right," I said. "$800 is fine."

It was 5:00.

Money Isn't Everything in Negotiation

It's very important that you're on friendly terms with several primary, secondary, and tertiary employers. You'll need the goodwill of these business contacts to increase your income. They can't be used and discarded—cordial relations are vital. You save time and money by negotiating with previous employers because they don't require any sales pitch or promo package.

Sticking to a policy of straight distributive bargaining is not in your best interest because competitiveness doesn't win long-term friends. Some large chain operations, due to time limits and ease of negotiation, prohibit anything but distributive bargaining, but most employers are receptive to bargaining with integrative goals in mind. Integrative bargaining eliminates competition between participants, as both you and the employer work to satisfy each other completely. Instead of a winner and loser, the result is two winners!

To successfully find integrative solutions to a negotiation, more than money is discussed. Transportation, hours, lodging, food, and drinks are considered. Advertising is thrown into the hat. Additions or limitations of the stage show, such as leaving behind an electric piano, the lighting system, and the lighting technician, are possible. The key is to come up with a package deal containing maximum benefits for the act *and* the employer.

The tactics you use for integrative bargaining differ markedly from those used in distributive bargaining. Listening is more important than fast talking. You never embarrass the other party by dismissing their offers. Aggressiveness is replaced by passivity. No secrets are kept regarding your expenses or needs. It's truly an atmosphere of cooperation.

Here are seven rules for successful integration with employers:

1. *Integration requires flexible resources.* Both you and the employer must realize that many resources substitute for money, such as radio advertising, hotel rooms, meals, and laundry services.

2. *Competition is not part of the negotiation process.* The goal is no longer defeating each other, but defeating the problem. Ask the employer, "How can we both get what we want?"

3. *Avoid commitment to the proposal.* Don't worry about pride or making sure you get what you set out to get. The emphasis is removed from your proposal ("We want $1,500 a week") to the consequences ("How can I get what I want?"). You may still get the $1,500, but it might not be in the form you proposed.

4. *What satisfies you may not satisfy me.* Everyone has different needs. Though money is your overriding need, a manager may need a crowded bar room because the owner will be in Friday night, or he may need an out-of-town band for publicity reasons. See his needs through *his* eyes.

Maybe the boss has dealt with several successive acts who didn't know what W-2 forms were, or who got soused on stage. Cater to these special interpersonal needs, and employers will gladly pay you for relieving their headaches. Talk to them and listen for clues to hidden needs.

5. *Approach negotiations optimistically.* A "let's solve this" attitude is infectious. Employers, once they realize you're concerned about their needs, too, will quickly adopt a positive attitude toward finding a mutually satisfying solution. Enthusiastically ask for their help!

6. *Share important information.* Be open and frank with employers. Tell them what's most important to you, and ask them for a similar list. Bare your soul: Once employers realize you're telling the truth and being sincere, they'll confide in you, helping to speed the negotiation along.

7. *Sit down together and brainstorm ideas.* It's vitally important to think of as many solutions as possible. This insures total, mutual satisfaction with the final solution. When brainstorming, write down every suggestion, regardless of how bizarre it sounds. Save any evaluations for later. When you hear something intriguing, modify and build upon it until it sounds feasible.

What you're really doing is expanding the mutual resources. Instead of cutting the pie in half (compromise), you're looking for ways to *each* get a whole pie. This requires expanding the resources, or pie. I've found that needs of live music employers and those of musicians vary a tremendous amount, so expanding the resource is easy, as long as you try.

Here's an example of an integrative negotiation I was involved in. Compare it with the distributive example for effectiveness.

On November 24, I received a message from Chuck Speddan, owner of a nightclub in Longbarn, California. He needed a band.

My four-piece act will usually play for $225 per night, but we prefer a minimum of $250. Longbarn is a long drive from Sacramento, so gasoline for two vehicles—approximately $50—was a big factor. We'd need to rent a couple of rooms ($25 each) and buy food to prepare or eat ($50 per day). This estimate of what we needed, just to earn our standard wage, came to $375-$400 per night. Could he afford $400 per night? I hoped we could cut some corners short of sleeping in tents at a 6,000-foot elevation in December!

I phoned Speddan to hear his proposal, and search for a mutually satisfying solution.

"Jim," he asked, "are you available on December 17, 18, and 19?"

"Sure, Chuck, we'd love to get up in the mountains for a few days." This admission that he was offering something attractive to me would have been forbidden in distributive bargaining, but in integrative bargaining, information is freely exchanged.

"I just got back up here myself," he said. "I tried to call you when I was in Sacramento picking up produce."

"Yeah, I'm not home too much. Chuck, I've got a list here of what

I'd need in order to come out all right."

"Okay. My only problem is that bar traffic has been light, but this new snow should bring more skiers. Right now all I can offer you is $200 a night with room proposal."

With a minimum need of $225, plus $150 in expenses, how would we settle? Quickly I subtracted $50 from my nightly target of $400 since he could provide rooms. After a pause, Chuck added, "I've been short on cash because of the slow bar." I struggled to remain uncommitted as I searched for a way to transport and feed the band.

"I understand your problem (legitimizing his position). We sometimes play for $225 in town, Chuck, but I'm afraid gas would take a big chunk—we have to take up two vehicles" (information).

"Yeah, I know," he responded. "My van really ate it up coming from there this week."

The word "van" triggered a brainstorm. "Chuck, when's the next time you come down here?"

"The middle of next month," he answered.

"Would you have room for some P.A. equipment and cases?"

"I've usually got room," he said. "Would that save you guys from having to take two cars?"

"I think so," I replied, deducting $25 from my shrinking nightly sum. "But with food for four of us, I still need $325 a night. Could you serve us any meals?"

"Sure!" said Chuck, brightening at the thought of not having to expend more cash. "Breakfast and dinner, plus a day's free ski rental!"

Finally we were both brainstorming ideas to accomplish our mutual goals: Speddan needed a good, out-of-town band, but he would only have enough money from his meager bar tabs to pay the band $200 per night. I still needed $225 to pay four musicians, but most of the food, two rooms, and half of the travel expenses were taken care of. And we were going to go skiing! Would the band sacrifice a little money to ski for a day? I wasn't sure. Then I got an idea.

"Chuck, could we charge a $1 cover at the door?" (expanding the resource).

"We've never done that." He hesitated. "But if we split the door 50/50, I'll try it."

Only 50 customers a night would guarantee us our $225. It had worked! Speddan was going to get a band for $175 (with his one-half share of the door money) and we were going to make $225 plus room, food, half of our travel expenses, and entertainment. This positive negotiation has rewarded us again and again with a long-term business relationship.

Clubs That Pay, Clubs That Promote

"We're not getting paid much here," Nicki said, "but the place is always packed, so it doesn't really matter."

She didn't mean the shoulder-to-shoulder crowds were more fun to perform for, although that's also true. Nicki meant the minimal wages were compensated for by the exposure the act was receiving. This was the most popular club in town, because management allotted a tremendous amount of money for radio advertisements. Though this didn't leave much money for the band, it gave groups the chance to win over a following. And a successful band can name its own price all over town.

So not only is there a difference in the amount clubs pay, but there is also a difference in the form of "payment." A club that advertises vigorously can be worth more than a club paying twice as much cash.

Large chain hotels and restaurants generally offer the most money to musicians. These organizations are large enough to afford an extra $100 or $200 per night in order to please guests by hiring seasoned, entertainment-oriented acts. Small chain restaurants and privately owned dinner houses sometimes rival what larger operations pay, and are generally more receptive to booking local groups. Bars and small- to medium-sized nightclubs offer less.

If you have built up a large local following, nightclubs will offer money well above what even large hotels pay. If they want you, $3,000-$4,000 for a three to four night run is not uncommon. Before you can touch this kind of money, however, you need a loyal following to pack the bar and pay the bills. To build a following, you must play at clubs that advertise.

Every area has clubs that consider themselves rivals. Rock clubs battle rock clubs, country music clubs fight for the same audience, and jazz clubs mix it up, too. In my area, the rock clubs dominate. Their battles take to the airwaves, where partiers are encouraged to patronize their favorite spot. The incentives mentioned on radio are endless, but usually the band is the main attraction. Occasionally, wet T-shirt or best-dressed-dog contests are the focus of the ads, but inevitably it's the musicians who benefit by playing before 400 people instead of 40.

This makes advertising very desirable for bands. Even though you don't make your $8 an hour this month, next month you may double it! If you can win the fancy of those big crowds, you'll have the trump card for the next negotiation.

Playing for the Door

Before agreeing to perform in exchange for a cover charge, check a few things out. Playing for the door can be lucrative, as long as you're confident of the band's drawing power and trust your employer.

One problem is a guest list. If you let all your friends in free, their money will go to the bar (the owner's pocket), rather than the door (your pocket). Negotiate for a guest list only if the owner is taking the cover charge.

Before agreeing to the deal, ask employees how busy the bar was last week. If the waitress says, "Oh, it was *dead*. I only made $15 in tips," you have ample reason to believe it'll be dead again (and the *band* will split $15).

Make sure this is a club that advertises. Have you heard their ads before? Will they run a special on mixed drinks the night you play, and publicize it? Since the employer doesn't feel confident enough to guarantee you a minimum salary (or does he?), ask for guarantees of advertising, and *get it written in the contract!* How many 30-second spots will he buy? How many times will the group's name be mentioned? Nail down these specifics. If money isn't the deciding factor for the group, buy advertising yourself! Radio spots can be surprisingly inexpensive. By spending $90 on radio spots (and making the commercial yourself), you might pull an additional 100 people in at $2 a head.

A good strategy is to ask for 100 percent of the door until a certain number of people have come in (enough to pay your hourly wage). Anything over that, split 50/50 with the owner. This gives him incentive to advertise. Also, I would recommend knowing and trusting the employer before allowing him to supply someone to collect the money. Offer one of your friends free beer to stay at the entrance and collect money. If you're taking a chance on playing for the door, it's *your right* to handle the money and pay the employer any percentage agreed upon.

When to Play for Free (or Next to Nothing)

Some situations warrant accepting less than your hourly wage. If you've performed around at all, you've swallowed your pride more than once and played for free. First of all, you'll have to decide what the gig is worth to the act. If it's a charity dance or benefit concert, you may believe in the cause sufficiently to leave empty-handed, or figure the free publicity might make it worthwhile. Still, you should receive expense money. If you're a union member, you'll have to inform your local of the event, and fill out a form in order to be reimbursed by the AFM for your performance donation.

Is it really an audition? This is an infamous employer excuse for getting good entertainment cheap. Exhaust all options before agreeing to a free audition: Has she heard the tape? Can she come out to see the act perform somewhere else? Go ahead and pay their expense money to come see you perform at a job. This is cheaper than the whole group driving, setting up, playing, tearing down, and not getting paid.

If, in the end, it comes down to a special live audition, exercise some distributive negotiating principles. Instead of playing the whole night for $50, offer one hour free! When the hour is up, the employer must decide immediately whether she likes you, in which case you perform the remainder of the night for a full-scale price (negotiated beforehand), or doesn't like you, in which case you tear down and go home. If there's one thing employers hate, it's musicians disturbing customers by carrying and loading equipment during business hours. When they're confronted with that scenario, you'll usually get paid, *in full*.

How to Court a Following

I'll never forget that song. Once every night my group would play a comical original number, "The Worm." During each chorus of "The Worm" everyone dancing would fall on the floor and wiggle their feet in the air. We got more requests for that song than any other, much to our displeasure (we were serious musicians, you see). But "The Worm" did more for our band than anything else, because audiences *loved* it! Everyone who "did the worm" got a worm diploma, and many wormers came back again and again. (One woman told me she was wallpapering her bedroom with diplomas.)

Interaction like this with your audiences will build a steady, loyal following. Alternate jokes, keep up on the news, and concentrate on spontaneity in delivery. Remember that talk time between songs is the only diversion for your fans, since they've heard your songs plenty. They're listening in hope of hearing something new, something exciting and revealing about the band. Give it to them!

On breaks between sets, mingle with the audience. Get to know individuals. Share information about yourself—the more personal, the better. Always keep in mind you're selling something: yourself.

Even though it's expensive, gathering names and addresses for a band mailing-list is the single best assurance of creating a following and keeping them notified of where you're playing. Mail postcards printed with next month's schedule, and list a P.O. box where they can write the group.

Giving away prizes from the stage is another crowd pleaser. "Every time I sign a contract," a pianist says, "I ask for a four drink-per-set bar tab. Then instead of drinking ourselves, we hand out pairs of drink tickets each set to the best dancers." This not only endears you to the audience (especially the best dancers), it also creates a flurry of activity on the dance floor, which employers love.

Getting into the Act

A limited amount of freelance work is available in small theaters and comedy playhouses. Your duties vary widely, from just playing a chart to writing, scoring, hiring musicians, directing, and performing. The pay is equal to or slightly better than standard nightclub money. The major difference—which extroverted musicians despise and introverted musicians enjoy—is that you play second fiddle to the visual theater, and are usually hidden from the audience.

The playhouses I'm familiar with will frequently call the musician's union when they need an instrumentalist, unlike most clubs; hence, small unions have a little more control over theaters than they do over the club scene. It may be difficult to break in unless you are a union member, although if you can write and score well, playhouse producers won't care if you're union or not.

If you're the music director for a play, expect a small musical budget. The emphasis (and the money) is on the visual production: actors, scenery, writers.

Performing music written for a play is very different from usual types of live musical performances. Songs are fast, short, and require a wider dynamic range than those played in nightclubs. The sounds you'll be asked to make won't be in your normal bag of licks. "I feel much more like an effects person who just happens to play piano," laughed a keyboardist.

Wedding Bells Are Music to Your Ears

It's time to review your market research sheets and pull out those high-paying organizations, associations, and businesses that hire acts for special occasions. If you can get your foot in the door with a few of these employers, the potential for garnering future high-paying jobs is astounding! Rates *at least* double compared to steady gigs, though if $300 is your normal night, $1,000 or $1,500 is certainly common. The work involved is minimal. Just cooperate with them!

The way big casuals influence your hourly wage is sheer magic. The $15 an hour you made last week jumps to $30, $60, or $90 an hour this week. Despite this fact, many musicians don't aggressively pursue these gigs because, "We have to pass up a four-night run in order to play that casual." My answer to that is, "So what?" If you can earn a week's salary—or close to it—in one four-hour show, why not do it? The time saved can be spent in rehearsals, recording, teaching, or any number of musical ventures. It can also be used to vacation!

The people who hire entertainment for big school dances, weddings, or company Christmas parties are not professionals. They might have volunteered to pick the band, or just been given the bothersome job by the boss. They're planning a big party, so they have a lot of chores and responsibilities. Graciously offer your assistance and ask if there's anything you can do to help. If you make hiring your band easy for them, and guarantee a successful show, you can name your own price. Relieve them of their worries.

Include any special expenses in your asking price. Tuxedos, elaborate lighting systems, smoke machines, and extra P.A. equipment are all common rentals for big bashes, and the rental fees can be exorbitant.

Holiday Rates

New Year's Eve has traditionally been the best-paying night of the year for musicians. Employers seem to be uncharacteristically generous that night, as if trying to make amends for screwing you all year. Now if we can only get them to feel the same way about Ground Hog Day, Cinco de Mayo, and Grandparents Day. . . .

You should hesitate to book holiday weekends too early. Big parties are usually planned for these nights. It always hurts to get a one-night, $1,500 offer *after* signing to play a four-night run for $1,200.

Often nightclubs and restaurants throw their own holiday celebrations. Costume parties, with tickets presold, are common. Anytime a club goes to extraordinary lengths to promote a special party, you should charge casual rates. After all, the bar revenue will double or triple, so why shouldn't yours? You can still agree to $300 for the other nights, but the party night should pay big bucks. Query employers on what they've got planned so they don't take advantage of you. They will if they can. An employer's idea of "just a regular night" can turn out to be the party of the century.

Cutting Corners Is the Name of the Game

Any successful business is constantly looking for ways to reduce expenses while continuing to grow. A group of musicians should be no different. How can the group trim the fat and pocket the extra dollars?

The area that consumes the largest share of expenses while wasting the most money is transportation. It's easy to fall into the habit of driving separately to gigs. With soaring gasoline costs, your profits are poured right into the tank.

Always keep an eye on the number of people the group is employing. State-of-the-art electronics make it sensible to consider replacing expendable musicians with tape recorders, rhythm boxes, delays, and computers.

How much are you depending on agents? That 10 or 15 percent can pay for a lot of things. Are you letting an accountant organize tax returns? If so, you might want to reconsider and pocket the fee.

Many bands also become accustomed to renting staging or P.A. equipment. Maybe you should buy the stuff. Check around at music stores and theatrical companies for any "rent to own" policies. Also, look for bargains in used equipment.

Integrative bargaining can save more money in the long run compared to distributive bargaining since you become good friends with employers. They'll be more likely to treat you better and help all they can in saving you money. Friendship will prove your biggest asset.

For Further Information . . .

If you're interested in learning more about bargaining, *The Social Psychology of Bargaining and Negotiation*, by Jeffrey Z. Rubin and Bert R. Brown, Academic Press, 111 Fifth Ave., New York NY 10003, explains techniques and principles in understandable language. *Negotiations, Social-Psychological Perspectives*, by Daniel Druckman, Sage Publications, 275 South Beverly Drive, Beverly Hills, CA 90212, contains chapters by experts in the field of negotiations, and covers buyer-seller relationships, decision-making, and the effects of behavior on negotiations. The easiest to read—and most humorous—guide to everyday bargaining is *You Can Negotiate Anything*, by Herb Cohen, Lyle Stuart Inc., 120 Enterprise Ave., Secaucus NJ 07094.

• CHAPTER ELEVEN •

YOU'RE A PROFESSIONAL, SO ACT THE ROLE

When you sign a contract to perform, you're indicating that the act is fully capable of delivering a quality show. The employer's idea of what he's buying may differ slightly from your idea, so it's important to make everything as clear as possible before signing. Inevitably, some things will still be overlooked or misunderstood. Since you're the one being paid, it's your responsibility to provide the service and behavior expected of you, within reason (you don't have to empty the trash or mop the floor).

Another touchy area is musician-audience interaction when this interacting involves more than just performing and clapping. Female performers especially need to know how to control a predominantly male audience.

What Employers Want—and Get—from Professional Musicians

You're a professional musician. If not, you soon will be. A professional is *anyone* who has received payment for performing, even if it was only $60 split six ways. The title "Professional Musician" applies to you and Doc Severinson both, so employers expect certain qualities from you, regardless of the modesty of your musical experience.

Employers expect you to be better musically than their cousin who strums guitar at family picnics. After all, why are you being paid, and not their cousin? You're expected to have practiced repeatedly and learned your parts, and it's assumed you're talented enough to perform the music well. The act is billed as professional, not amateur.

Employers expect a total effort. They hire under the assumption you'll try hard to do well. Even if a mediocre effort for you is a colossal achievement for anyone else, employers still feel they deserve your best effort. Besides, you'll feel better if you know you've done your best.

They'll also assume you're not a group of deadbeats who slouch around onstage. Again, it all comes back to entertainment value. They want to see you enjoying yourselves, besides just trying hard and sounding good. Boredom can pass through music without being heard, but it can't escape unseen in your actions onstage. A stony, straight expression is a dead giveaway that you'd rather be somewhere else.

Employers expect acts to have enough confidence in themselves to pull it all off. Amateurs are allowed to act shy, embarrassed, and a little shaky when convinced to perform, but you're expected to show initiative by aggressively walking up and playing. No hesitation. They assume you're confident of your abilities.

Of course, many acts don't deliver what employers expect at all. I've seen musicians run around like chickens with their heads cut off, worried and upset. Some don't mind performing without knowing the material, and these are often the same performers who only give a 60-percent effort. It shows. Some look like they're reading in the library, so solemn is their demeanor. And a few players and singers are so obviously shaken by being on a stage that the word "amateur" instantly pops to mind. Audiences will feel cheated.

These are exceptions to the rule. Most musicians practice long hours and try damn hard to put on a good show. This is what employers want from professional musicians—that desire to give it all you've got, even if you are a little raw. Just as long as you're sincere, it's okay. If the act's hot, that's another thing (and you'll be hired back!).

There are several responsibilities you owe the employer before arriving for a gig. Assuming you've negotiated a price and received signed contracts (prior responsibilities), you now need to arrange your arrival time, notify the employer of any equipment you need, and find out who will be in charge when the band is playing. Your arrival time must jive with a good time for the business. You don't want to lug equipment past tables of people trying to enjoy dinner. The boss will kill you! If there's no way a sound check is going to fit into the day, don't complain about it. You'll just have to do without.

Getting into an argument with the employer or some of the employees is completely unprofessional, and therefore unacceptable. No situation warrants a temper tantrum by the lead singer. "Scenes" like these can permanently damage your reputation. If word gets around to other clubs, you may have trouble booking gigs.

Working Musicians Are Time-Accountable

"Punctuality with musicians is pretty sad," bemoans one guitarist, "and when they do arrive, they're not ready to play."

"I fired the last group playing here," a manager told me, "because of the lead singer. She was getting here 15 to 20 minutes late every night, so I had a talk with her. The next night she was an hour late! There's no way I can overlook that."

If any one trait is most important to an employer, it's arriving on time for work. Yet, promptness is not a habit with many musicians, because they frequently haven't had to work steady 9-to-5 jobs, or regular hours of any kind. We move around a lot! Our employers, on the other hand, keep regular hours and expect their employees to follow time schedules. They don't appreciate tardiness, and often won't tolerate it, either. Being late to a job, or arriving at show time but then tuning up for 10 minutes, earns you instant disrespect from exactly the people you want to impress. Punctuality is a firmly cemented rule of the business community, so to be accepted you must learn to be on time.

Acts that show respect for established business ethics relate an eager willingness to work *with* employers, not against them. One group I was in a while back didn't have the greatest equipment or stage show (we were really green) but the owner of one club loved us because we were always on time. He interpreted our promptness to mean we cared about our job. Eventually, he bent over backwards to help us with our band.

Many bars set their clocks ahead about 15 minutes so that they can get patrons out the door at the end of the night, and still close on time. Always ask an employer if he's running on "bar time," because if he is, you'll need to be ready to start 15 minutes earlier than the posted starting time.

Writing down phone calls, appointments, and work hours helps in developing punctuality. By seeing the times on paper, you'll become conscious of their existence. It serves as a constant reminder of where you have to be, by when. Count the minutes it takes you to get ready for work, and then clock how long it takes to get there. Allow a slight buffer time—five or ten minutes—just in case traffic is heavy or something unexpected happens. My mother always set her clock ahead 15 minutes to get out the door on time, and that worked for her. Do whatever it takes for you to arrive on time.

How to Handle Management Disputes

You're in a different position than waitresses, assistant managers, or managers when dealing with the boss. Entertainers are almost exclusively hired as independent contractors—not employees—so employers are not required to give you the benefits employees receive, but neither are you restricted by rules regulating employees. This means that when there's a problem to be solved, you shouldn't necessarily act as a subordinate, like an employee would. Rather, you can work on an equal basis with the employer. He is not your "boss."

All this may change for union musicians. The AFM has been lobbying Congress to change the status of musicians from independent contractors to employees for some time. This is long overdue, since employers don't make contributions for your FICA taxes, unemployment, or Workmen's Compensation, yet they exercise the rights of employers by establishing work hours, days off, discipline, and working conditions. Until that time, however, union musicians will remain independent contractors. Don't let an employer push you around like an employee.

If you have a business manager or personal manager, any disputes or issues with an employer should be immediately referred to that person. If your manager can't be reached, one band member should confer with the employer—not all six of you.

If you don't have a manager, one person should be designated "group representative" for all gigs. That means if the keyboardist is the band rep, the drummer has no business proposing suggestions to the employer. The drummer should go to the keyboardist with ideas. This presents a clear consensus of group leadership to the employer, and minimizes distraction. It's confusing when five people are talking at once!

Any talks with employers should be done offstage, preferably behind closed doors. Getting into an argument onstage with the boss or any employee is inexcusable. I've seen it happen more than once, and besides putting the band in a bad mood and alienating the management, it really turns off an audience.

Your representative at live shows must be someone who can sympathize with employers, but also make the band's position clear. The overriding concern should be to solve the conflict to mutual satisfaction by using the integrative techniques described in Chapter 10. Instead of saying, "We want to do this," say, "This is *why* we want to do this."

It's best if all problems can be cleared up before getting onstage. However, if time runs out, finding a solution has to be put off. This is acceptable for all disputes but one: payment. The amount, form of payment, and when you get paid must all be agreed upon before starting; otherwise, you might end up playing for free. What bargaining leverage do you have if the show's already over? None! Negotiating after a show guarantees you won't get what you want. If the issue of payment is unresolved at showtime, corner the person in charge and *resolve* it. In this position, the pressure is on the employer, not you.

"May I See Your I.D.?"

I started performing before I was old enough to drink (21 in California), and I am probably the rule rather than the exception. I know musicians who started playing clubs at age 12. I've found that both alcohol restrictions and child labor laws can be bypassed as long as you are honest and up-front about minors in the band.

Alcohol is the biggest obstacle. Most employers, when informed the lead guitarist is only 16, turn white in the face and defiantly announce the kid can't have any beer. That's easy to deal with. Some employers will ban the minor from the bar area on breaks, or limit the minor to the stage area. That's fine, too. Occasionally, an employer will tell you that hiring a minor is illegal, but this is misinformation on his part. Call your local police or sheriff's station and ask if a minor can perform where alcoholic beverages are served. The answer is inevitably yes, with some restrictions.

With a minor in the band, honesty is the best policy. Even if the 16-year-old guitarist looks 26, notify your employer of the situation. The substantial fines (and possible liquor-license suspension) slapped on businesses for serving minors are feared by employers, and a band with an underage guzzler can quickly earn a bad reputation and be out of work.

When the Song Ends, So Does the Noise

If the audience notices a guitarist tuning or doing something other than listening to you, they won't listen to you, either. Why should they? Your own group isn't listening. The band must give whoever is talking their undivided attention. That means no twanging guitars, piano chords, or kicks on the bass drum. If the instruments are used to emphasize something the speaker said, that's great, but any other instrument noise detracts from the speaker.

In fact, tuning or otherwise making noise can attract more attention than the speaker. Notice how everyone stops talking and stares while someone tunes up? The audience thinks a song is starting, so they look to see who's making the sound. The other musicians look on with consternation, trying to hurry things along.

Tuning is not aesthetically pleasing to hear. The incoherence of sound is annoying, and if two or three musicians are all trying to tune in between songs, the effect is like listening to "The Twilight Zone" played backwards.

Electronic tuners are the best thing to happen to guitarists in years. For $70 you can buy a tuner that allows you to tune silently. Strobe tuners are more precise and faster. Tuning out loud should be completely prohibited.

One musician I know runs through the first two or three chords of the next song just before starting. This isn't necessary! It's a bad habit. You should know your starting position for each song without reviewing onstage. Think it out mentally if you have to, but don't clue the audience in before each song.

If your drummer persists in snapping the snare a few times between every song, ask him to stop. Drums cut through and confuse the audience as to what's being said. Everyone needs to be quiet and pay attention to the speaker.

Get everyone to practice keeping quiet from the end of one song to the beginning of the next at rehearsal. By not making any instrument sound between songs, you can appreciate something else: silence! It's very impressive when a group stops together, is silent, and then starts together. Silence is refreshing and professional too.

Conflicts with the Audience

Hecklers and agitators sound like nuisances, but more often than not they benefit an act by stirring up excitement. The conflicts with audiences that pose problems are much more serious. Jimmy Buffet called them "sharks that can swim on the land," and the Little River Band labeled them "nightowls," but everyone knew they were talking about smooth-talking singles who go out "picking up" on men and, especially, women.

From the stage you can watch all the slick operators at work, smiling, talking, and buying drinks. It can be fun unless you're not into playing the game or have attracted someone who's overly persistent in wanting to jump in bed with you. For musicians—gorgeously illuminated in spotlights—the problem dramatically increases. For female musicians in particular, a room full of drunken men can pose quite a predicament.

"You can try to make it funny without getting serious, 'cause it *can* get serious," says Barbara, a lead singer. "I'll say, 'Hey, I thought I told you to wait in the truck.' If the band and audience all laugh along with you, most guys will get embarrassed and shut up. If he's really smashed, though, one joke won't faze him."

Many women performers rely on sex appeal as part of their stage personality, and this, of course, invites trouble. "The main thing is to never let down your guard," Jenni says. "Once you show that you're permissive, you'll have continual trouble with men. If you dance with one, you've got to dance with them all because they won't let up until you do."

A convenient escape is to attach yourself to one of the band members, whether he's really a boyfriend or not. Then most advancing men will politely back off.

"Whatever you do," says a female guitarist, "don't string the guy along. It'll just delay a confrontation. Guys will either get pissed off at you or wait around till the show's over, expecting something."

Always Make Friends

You're going to need all the contacts you can make. The person you dismiss as "a real jerk," or "unimportant to my musical advancement," will probably be in a position to make a pivotal decision about your career later on. If you've gotten along well, there won't be any problem, but if he likewise thinks you're a real jerk, you'll get it in the end. You need friends to get ahead.

Your personal feelings can be kept separate from your business relations. That's professionalism. Divest yourself of personal feelings. If you develop a friendship with employers, that's great: There's no better position. In business relations, though, intimate relations are not necessary. A polished business facade swiftly gets things done. You can fume about it later over a martini, but not in front of an employer. If you absolutely cannot stand dealing with someone, stay away from him. Meet only when necessary.

Always remember you're representing more than just yourself. There's a band out there depending on you. Learn to swallow your pride for the sake of the group. If you come back from a meeting saying, "I sure got the best of her! But, uh, we did lose the deal," you'll feel victorious, but you've really lost. You missed the goal, which was to make the deal, not compete verbally with the employer.

At least be on speaking terms with the people you deal with. If I staunchly refuse to deal with one employer, that's one less job opportunity for the group. Partings should be cordial—with smiles and compliments—so that you'll feel friendly toward each other next time. Then you'll be projecting a highly professional personality.

• CHAPTER TWELVE •

STAYIN' ALIVE

The public in general considers musicians a slightly bizarre breed. You know the stereotype: eccentric, erratic souls involved in counter cultures and drugs. Beatniks. The rough lifestyle of the road. Though people are fascinated by musicians, they don't envy us our nomadic existence. "Musicians age fast," they say. Stars like Jimi Hendrix, Janis Joplin, Jim Morrison, Keith Moon, John Bonham, Bon Scott, and Lowell George serve as ready examples of musical tragedies.

Although we cannot be lumped together as beatniks any more, alcohol, drugs, and occupational health hazards are still very real problems. Yes, there are greater dangers to musicians than Pac-Man or Space Invaders.

Since we aren't "employees," but are instead "independent contractors," employers are not required to protect our health and well-being. As for the drugs, they're readily available if you want them. Following is an explanation of the pitfalls of performing, and how to avoid them.

The Secret Damage to Your Ears

There's no doubt about it. Because musical equipment continues to be made more and more powerful, the time has come to examine the consequences of performance on our ears. At what volume does noise injure the ears? How can you judge the effect music is having on your hearing? Most important, how can you stop the damage without stopping the music?

Currently, more than 16 million Americans suffer from noise-induced hearing loss; another half million are completely deaf from noise exposure. Clearly, this is not a problem unique to musicians, but as a group we probably get more than our fair share of loud noise. Hearing loss is our most common health hazard.

The ear is divided into three sections: the outer, middle, and inner ear. After sound "waves" enter the outer ear and are transmitted through the middle ear, the waves pulsate a fluid called endolymph inside the cochlea (inner ear), where the nerve cells are located. These cells lie on the basilar membrane that runs the length of the spirals in the shell-shaped cochlea. Complications occur when sound waves are too great, causing violent undulations which throttle the basilar membrane. Unfortunately, the ear has no warning device to tell us when sound waves are too powerful. Hearing loss won't be noticed for many years—when it's too late.

Most of us hear sounds between 40 and 15,500 Hertz (our talking range is between 500 and 3,000 HZ), and within this range the ear is especially sensitive to certain frequency bands. To accurately measure sound, we must use a specially weighted scale that corresponds to our ear's sensitivity: the decibel scale for "natural" sound (A-weighted) that ranges from 0 to 140 dBa.

Frequency intensity can imperceptibly but greatly increase while on stage. A dBa jump from 110 to 116 will not sound appreciably louder, but the actual energy which your ears are subjected to will have *doubled*. Also, as you go higher on the decibel scale, the magnitude of energy increases substantially, so that the difference between 110 and 116 is much greater than the difference between 40 and 46.

The Occupational Safety and Health Administration (OSHA) requires that workers be exposed no longer than eight hours at 90 decibels, and for every five dBa increase exposure time must be cut in half. Environmental Protection Agency (EPA) Standards are even more stringent.

OSHA Permissible Exposure

Duration per day (hours)	Sound level dBa
8	90
6	92
4	95
3	97
2	100
1 1/2	102
1	105
1/2	110
1/4 or less	115

What risks are we running as musicians?

A 100-watt Marshall amplifier pushes out 115 dBa to your ears as you stand six feet in front of the amp, facing to the side. A full set of drums kicks out 112 dBa at the drummer's ear; the level is 108 dBa fifteen feet out in front of the set. Now add the bass, rhythm guitar, keyboards, horns, monitors . . . What an audible arsenal attacking our ears! We are handily exceeding OSHA guidelines. As a matter of fact, OSHA warns that at levels of 115 dBa, people should only be exposed for fifteen minutes *per day*!

Listening and interpreting is your livelihood. How can you save your ears? The first course of action is to have both ears monitored. Request an audiogram test, which shows on a graph which frequencies, if any, you're losing. Pay particular attention to a noticeable dip occurring in the 4,000-6,000 Hz range. If you show a loss in this area, ear protection should be worn while you play. Audiograms are inexpensive, and are usually offered by community service centers; colleges; ear, nose, and throat doctors; or any large health care clinic.

The safety devices useful to musicians and sound technicians are numerous. Stock ear plugs are inexpensive and available virtually anywhere sold as swimming plugs. They don't discriminate between which sounds they block out. To my knowledge, Sonic II Sound Filters are the only ear protection device sold nationally in music stores. While wearing Sonics, you can hear conversation because the device's tiny diaphragm is wide open, but when the intensity raises, the diaphragm closes to shield your ears from loud noise.

Other alternatives include wax-impregnated cotton, ear muffs, sponge ear inserts, and custom-fitted ear molds (available only from specialty laboratories). You could also inquire at sporting stores for ear protection devices. If one type blocks out the bell of your ride cymbal, or too much high-end from your amp, try another.

In rehearsal, practice hearing conservation by wearing protection at all times. If you sing and need to hear better than protection allows, save vocal practice until after instrumental practice, when the P.A. and amps are turned off. A very practical band purchase is a decibel meter (A-weighted scale). Give it to the sound man and vote him veto power over the group's onstage volume.

Our auditory system is versatile, but it was not designed with powerful instruments and amplifiers in mind. Your ears are your bread and butter—take care of them!

Clearing the Air

The smoke-filled air musicians breathe regularly while working has been proven harmful to your health—even if you personally don't smoke. If you value good health, you should collaborate with your employers to improve working conditions.

In nightclubs, ambient smoke is derived from two sources: sidestream smoke, which enters the air directly from the burning end of the cigarette; and mainstream smoke, which is exhaled by the smoker. Of the two, sidestream smoke is the more dangerous.

A cigarette smoker inhales—and exhales—mainstream smoke eight or nine times with each cigarette for a total of about 24 seconds. But the cigarette freely burns for 12 minutes and pollutes the bar room continuously with sidestream smoke.

Besides contributing more smoke to the room than mainstream exhaling, sidestream smoke also contains *higher* concentrations of noxious compounds than mainstream smoke. Over two thousand gases, liquids, and particles have been identified. The deadly results of these chemicals—lung cancer and heart disease—have been well documented.

Carbon monoxide is of particular concern. If the bar you're performing in combines a low ceiling with poor ventilation, CO levels can jump sufficiently to induce acute CO poisoning. The signs and symptoms are easily recognized: headache, nausea, vomiting, dizziness, drowsiness, and collapse.

"It's disgusting," says a director of public education for the American Cancer Society. "So many facts relate secondhand smoke to cancer, but we're still stuck breathing it. Musicians are in a very precarious position because of the working environment—what worse place is there for cigarette smoke than a nightclub?"

Ambient smoke has posed a problem for the Occupational Safety and Health Administration (OSHA) because they haven't been able to classify it as "leading to injury or illness." This may be changing. According to a 14-year study by Dr. Takeshi Hirayama, published in a 1981 issue of the *British Medical Journal*, secondhand smoke has now been directly linked to lung cancer. A 1980 study reported in the *New England Journal of Medicine* found that nonsmokers exposed to tobacco smoke in the work place suffer lung damage equivalent to that of persons who smoke from one to ten cigarettes a day. Conclusive evidence like this will eventually strengthen OSHA worker standards.

Following are some important standards presented in OSHA's pamphlet, "A Worker's Guide," that musicians should be aware exist:

> Every employer is required by law to provide a safe and healthful work place and work conditions for employees by identifying possible job hazards and correcting them before they lead to worker injury or illness.
>
> Employers must allow workers to watch monitoring or measuring of worker exposure to hazards or substances regulated by OSHA standards.
>
> Employers must allow workers or their representatives to see accurate records of worker exposure to potentially toxic materials or harmful physical agents and medical records.
>
> Employers must tell any worker who has been, or is being, exposed to toxic materials or harmful physical agents in concentrations or at levels which are higher than the limits for exposure set by occupational safety or health standards; and tell this worker what is being done to eliminate harmful exposure.

But are you covered by these standards? Only if you are an actual employee, not just an independent contractor. This distinction, however, is often unclear.

"It depends on the contract and its wording," says an OSHA field consultant. "Most contracts are an agreement. Are you under direct control of the owner? Is he truly a superior to you, as in a normal hiring situation? If you answer 'yes' to these questions, maybe you're actually an employee—not just a contractor. There is one way that even the contractor is protected by us. If you call your local OSHA office with a complaint against a bar, we'll come out free of charge to investigate. Your name is kept confidential so that your job will not be endangered. We will inspect a premises for an independent contractor, like a band, as long as we can justify that *other* employees—waitresses, cooks, bartenders—are also being exposed. If the owner is the only worker besides a contracted band, then we really can't do anything."

Smoky barrooms are usually caused by poor ventilation. The trend in club design is toward installing electro-static precipitators—air filtering systems that suck up dusty air, filter it, and send the same air back into the room. Filters trap dust particles, but gases (CO) go right through the filter to recirculate in the room. A better type of ventilation system pulls fresh air into the club while sending the polluted indoor air out. Unfortunately, these systems are comparatively expensive to operate since the fresh air usually must be cooled or heated.

Often just telling an employer of your concern will solve the problem. By going into a discussion with a no-compromise, defiant attitude you'll surely alienate him. Try to satisfy both him *and* yourself fully. Practice the integrative skills you learned in Chapter 10. Can a back door be left open? Maybe you can get a friend to watch the door to make sure no one uses it. Can the ventilation system be turned up so that it will work faster? Maybe the band can pay the owner five dollars a night to cover extra energy costs. Can you set up a fan in front of a window? Search for creative solutions. If you feel comfortable doing so, talk to the owner about having OSHA come out to monitor smoke levels. Many times they can suggest simple ways to alleviate the smoke. If OSHA isn't available, try your local Environmental Health Agency, the owner's insurance company, or the American Society of Heating, Refrigeration and Air Conditioning Engineers (ASHRAE). The variety of advice and helpful suggestions you'll turn up will be refreshing. Maybe then we won't all need to become "gas mask musicians!"

Physical Conditioning

I've always likened what we do to what an athlete does. It's a performance. Standing up four hours per night with a guitar is fatiguing. It's even more tiring to drum, or dance all night as a lead singer. To avoid tight and sore muscles, strains and tendonitis, a regular physical fitness program is almost essential.

Routines can be broken down into three groups: stretching, cardiovascular, and muscle-building exercises. For the working musician, stretching and cardiovascular are the most urgent. To insure good flexibility, practice static stretches (slow, constantly applied pressure) rather than ballistic stretches (quick, bouncing motions). Stretch prior to cardiovascular and muscle-building exercises, and immediately prior to and after performance. Cardiovascular exercises, like jogging, brisk walking, bicycling, swimming, and racquetball, develop endurance and strengthen the heart. This is *vital* for playing in clubs, bars, and restaurants. It's murder to play that last set at 1:30 in the morning! Muscle-building exercises can contribute to your comfort onstage and when traveling. The many variations of weight lifting develop your muscles to easily support your body. Being well-conditioned also enables you to put on a lively show (how do you think leaping David Lee Roth broke his foot?). An ideal workout schedule could read like this: lift weights Monday, Wednesday, Friday; jog or swim Tuesday, Thursday, Saturday; stretch all six days prior to exercising, and prior to and after any performance.

How Does Alcohol Affect Your Music?

I've felt the effects of alcohol on my playing. You probably know the feeling—a slight numbness, relaxation, and carelessness that sets in. Having a drink before playing or during the show can free the mind of worries, allowing you to immerse yourself in creativity. But is this really creativity, or something else? Is your ability enhanced or inhibited by drinking?

The answer varies from person to person, depending on *why* you're drinking. Sometimes having a drink will calm nerves or ease depression. Better ways than alcohol of getting ready for the show are discussed in the section "Getting High Without Drugs," but in the meantime, let's look at the physical and mental effects of this most common drug, alcohol.

In small amounts alcohol slows reflexes. Discriminate control, dependent on nerve-muscle interaction, is quickly lost. If you're anything like me, you don't like to give up your musical control voluntarily! Right down to your fingertips, telltale signs of alcohol consumption can be felt because of neuromuscular inhibition. You just won't react as quickly.

Alcohol, like other general anesthetics, depresses those parts of the brain involved with the most highly advanced integrated functions. First affected are those mental processes that depend upon training and previous experience. Rehearsed patterns, key changes, dynamics, and cues all suffer. Memory, concentration, and insight, all vital to a musician, are dulled and then lost. Obviously, your musical execution while drinking is severely hampered.

Several musicians I know, explaining how alcohol affects their playing, revealed that they felt alcohol, even when consumed at rates faster than their livers could possibly process, improved their musical abilities. This is a fallacy and clearly demonstrates alcohol's powerful influence on individual perception.

Perception is not necessarily the same as reality. You can feel as if you are really performing well, but since your perception is altered, you can actually be performing sloppily without realizing it. If more than moderate amounts of alcohol are consumed over a short period of time, performance will definitely decline.

But how much is too much?

In moderate amounts it is very difficult to measure alcohol in the bloodstream. The body contains approximately five liters of blood; therefore, 5 percent of a 12-ounce beer is not very substantial. This quantity would most likely still enable you to perform without dramatically altering perception or neuro-response. One drink per hour (one a set) has little effect on blood alcohol level.

A very real factor, however, is how you feel about your abilities after consuming alcohol. If you have a drink, believing that the consequent feeling will subtract from your effectiveness, chances are it will. Performance is so sensitive that one drink *can* inhibit thoughts and reflexes.

Much has been made of the fact there there is no remedy to revive a person from a drunken stupor. Time and rest is the only proven method, since it allows the liver to process the excess of alcohol. Temporary escape from the effect of moderate drinking is possible, however.

The caffeine in coffee will counter the depressant effects of alcohol quite well. If you come to work after downing a few drinks, have a cup of coffee between each set. The stimulation from the coffee, however, creates a complication: Since you are arriving at an awakened state artificially, your body will need to recover from the "high" as well as the alcohol-influenced "low" which the caffeine is obscuring. Expect to be tired the morning after.

Doobies Should Be Listened To, Not Smoked

It took a long time to get any conclusive data on the effects of marijuana, but the results are not surprising. According to a 1982 report issued by the Institute of Medicine of the National Academy of Sciences, marijuana has the same effect as tobacco on the respiratory tract and lungs. A performer needs good physical endurance and strong breathing, so stay away from pot before or during performance. As with tobacco, total abstention is the best policy.

In some ways, marijuana is more like alcohol than tobacco (that's why everyone smokes it!). The principal active chemical in pot, delta-9-tetrahydro-cannabinol (THC), impairs coordination. THC also inhibits short-term memory, slows learning, and distorts perception. Not good. Even worse, whereas a drink is metabolized quickly in about an hour, the effects of THC may linger four to eight hours!

At least avoid smoking marijuana on performance days. The effects just last too long. As for the smoke inhalation and lung cancer, you'll breathe plenty of tobacco smoke in the club. Why compound the problem?

Of Musicians and Amphetamines

If you perform till 2:00 a.m., have to commute 80 miles to your home, and are expected to work at 9:00 a.m.—for two weeks straight—you're going to be a walking zombie. If the bassist offers you a pill to help you stay awake, you'll seriously consider popping it. The physical and mental effects of an amphetamine, however, whether the bassist calls it a black beauty, Christmas tree, bean, pink heart, upper, crank, or just speed, can be very unreliable unless you know from experience what effect it'll produce. Some people develop a sense of increased energy and self-confidence, faster decision-making ability, and feel euphoric. Others, with the same dosage, exhibit toxic psychosis that closely resembles paranoid schizophrenia. And either person may become dependent on the drug, using increasingly larger dosages to get the desired effect.

Entertainers who need a "lift" before performance turn to amphetamines for stimulation. Even though you may derive confidence and energy from the drug—and both are elements of good stage presence—these "heights" come at the expense of your body. Amphetamines increase blood pressure and shift the body into "overdrive," a condition where you go, go, go because your mind ignores the body's signals that you need rest and food; thus you feel a need for neither. The result is weight loss and a terrific need for sleep.

I know musicians who use amphetamines only in what they feel to be extreme cases, like the example first mentioned in this section. As long as the dosage is very small, I can sympathize with them, though I rely on coffee for my boost.

If you consider using stimulants like these, allow yourself some recovery time. Most important, only take amphetamines on an occasional basis. Don't allow it to become a regular habit.

Getting High Without Drugs

Though people may still link drug indulgence and musicians together, many popular musicians have begun a new age of anti-drug crusading.

"No-no-no-no! I hate drugs. The hell with drugs!" says Paul T. Riddle of The Marshall Tucker Band. "I would rather be dependent on myself and my music, not on something so artificial as drugs. I may have two or three little bitty light beers, but only *after* the show."

Derek Pellicci of the Little River Band agrees. "Drugs and booze get a large zero in my whole way of life. If I can't do it naturally, I wasn't meant to do it at all."

"I don't need that kind of getting up," says Molly Hatchett's Bruce Crump. "Personally, I see drugs as a hindrance to performance. Relaxing after the show is easy because I get so worked up *naturally* before a show that I sleep like a baby!"

"Take care *not* to depend on drugs," Jeff Myer of the Jesse Colin Young Band says. "Once you start, you need them to keep going."

To freely avoid drugs you need another way of getting high. The answer is proper mental preparation! Be secure and confident of your ability and approach each show with a positive attitude.

Not being ready to perform can result in a formidable foe: stage fright! Stage fright is perfectly normal. Even established pros feel some nervousness. When you step onstage, you're welcoming critical review. The audience expects something exceptional. How are you more skilled than they? Can you play a part or create a feeling they can't? For confidence to replace nervousness, your practicing should include more difficult passages than the performance will entail. "Remember that each performance is unique," says guitarist Michael Lorimer. "The reason to practice and carefully prepare is not to determine what will happen, but to be ready for it." Experiment at home. Go wild! This will make the performance seem easy in comparison.

The best preparation involves more than just rehearsing day and night, because the elements and emotions confronting you in a live performance differ greatly from the comparatively simple pressures of rehearsal. Violinist Kato Havas writes in *Stage Fright, Its Causes and Cures* (Bosworth & Company) that emphasis is wrongly put upon physical practicing. The differences between physical and psychological conditions are enough to create stage fright and breakdowns. Havas adds that it is no wonder some instrumentalists appear to hide behind their instruments:

> This reliance on repetitive, muscular training can become such a burden that one tends to forget what a wonderful gift it is to be born a musician; that in fact the task lies not in the hours of practice but in learning how to appreciate this gift entrusted to us *which entails learning to love ourselves.* And how can one do this through finger exercises and through constant self-doubt? Especially when a certain amount of self-depreciation is actually encouraged because it is considered modesty . . . In fact, when dealing with stage fright, the first thing one must set out to eliminate is the reason for self-depreciation and self-doubt. For how can a musician com-

municate the meaning of music unless he knows what love is all about? How can he "give" unless he is free to love himself, his fellow beings and, most of all, his audience?

Here are 10 simple rules you can practice to ease stage fright:
1. Like yourself.
2. Understand your instrument.
3. Arrive prepared.
4. Be comfortable in your surroundings.
5. Review the show before starting.
6. Acknowledge your nervousness.
7. Release your tension physically.
8. Be innovative and imaginative.
9. Anticipate mistakes.
10. Don't dwell on mistakes.

To complete your preparation, work on adopting an optimistic, positive attitude toward people and surroundings.

The value of positive thinking cannot be overemphasized. This is especially true for a performer, since you must not only *think* positive, but also *appear* positive. You must entertain the audience—in many cases they've paid money to see you.

A good first step toward refining positive attitude and appearance is to gauge how important music is to you. The more devoted you are to music, the more enthusiastic your performance will be. You can't take more energy out of the music than you put in. "When the entire concentration of all your force—physical, emotional, and spiritual—is brought to bear, the consolidation of these powers properly employed is quite irresistible," says Norman Vincent Peale in his bestseller *The Power Of Positive Thinking* (Fawcett Crest Books). "Results do not yield themselves to the person who refuses to give himself to the desired results. . . . In other words, whatever you are doing, give it all you've got. Give every bit of yourself. Hold nothing back."

Before you'll realize it, positive thinking will lead to thinking positive. What was once an effort to uphold now stands by itself. Your personality will have changed. Another delightful aspect of positive, optimisitc thinking is that it is contagious. The rest of the band will appreciate your attitude, and subconsciously imitate your positive behavior. This band "face lift" will be easily apparent to the audience—they'll be floored by this inspiring, vivacious group of musicians. Result: Return customers for the bar, and more bargaining leverage for you!

Is Touring Right for You?

Touring used to be standard procedure for all musicians. It was a way of expanding income. But is touring the answer for your band?

"An agent contacted us about touring Canada and Alaska in the spring," Steve told me. "She offered more money than a fall tour because the weather is worse then. That was fine, but we didn't take into consideration the inflation up there. We could't save any money."

Sheila's group was able to save money, but the time out on the road hurt their in-town reputation. "We expected to make better money when we got back because we'd toured, but no one seemed to notice that we'd been gone."

Anyone who's toured in some capacity, whether a single week of one-night stands or a year-round itinerary, knows the life to be something less than wine and roses *all* the time. Unless you're putting out albums, you should be choosy about touring. Weigh it against the jobs you have now. A local band needs a damn good reason to tour. If you're not careful, touring will cost you a lot of money simply because you won't be home to pick up opportunities. This is the biggest disadvantage of touring. You can't teach students or rent equipment out if you're on the road. You can still write lyrics, but the bulk of your non-performing income is cut off. Touring isn't economically attractive unless these auxiliary markets are extremely limited in your home town, or you've got an album to promote.

Touring enables you to meet new people, but it also separates you from long established acquaintances. Friends and lovers tend to drift away. Couples try to stick together when thousands of miles apart, but it's tough. Nightly telephone calls just don't make it. For some musicians, the answer is to take the spouse or lover along. When this nonmusician has band-related duties, such as manager, travel director, or sound technician, the chances of things working out improve. Since they're not performing, they need to be busy with either their own work or band work. Ideally, both partners of a couple are musicians. This solves most relational problems associated with traveling.

But what are the reasons a local group should tour? Here are five:

1. *It can be considered paid vacation.* "This was our second USO tour, and it won't be our last!" said Bonnie. "The money is great. It's tax free. And the shows are so easy! Their roadies set up all our equipment, we'll run a quick sound check, and then play for an hour. Then they fly us to the next base. It's hectic, but it's a great way to see Europe."

"We make better money than this in Atlanta," said Duane, whose Miami trio gigs on several Caribbean cruise ships, "but who cares? We see the Bahamas, Virgin Islands, Barbados, Trinidad—I've always felt we're just getting paid to vacation."

If you want to travel, there are few better ways. There are usually no more than six performances a week, so you can go on an overnight trip. Daytime hours are usually open to do as you please. Offers abound for groups willing to tour in North America, and foreign tours are available through the right channels. It pays better than enlisting for two years in the military to see the sights!

2. *Tours can pay well.* Certainly there are instances when agents offer tours paying better than what you can earn from local band employers. This can be particularly true if the group is specializing in a style of music that isn't cutting it in the local night spots. A good agent can match your style into receptive places and make a tour out of it.

3. *It can end the monotony.* Maybe you need a change of pace. Hitting the road will certainly turn things upside down for awhile. Playing in the same clubs night after night can become monotonous (although touring for too long can become boring, too).

4. *It's a guarantee of steady work.* At least it's as close as musicians usually come to a guarantee. Not knowing where—or even if—the act is playing in two weeks is a harrowing experience, one that happens plenty with local bands. A tour enables you to accurately project income and pay the bills on time.

5. *It might be a necessity.* Is your area an exceptionally difficult place to find work in? Are musical jobs scarce? If so, touring may be your only route to full-time live music employment. In this case, you'd have to weigh what you'll make from touring against earnings from the auxiliary musical jobs coming up in Part Three.

Planning a good time to tour is vital to your negotiating success upon your return. There's simply a right time and a wrong time to leave. If you pull the band together, learn the songs, and immediately solicit offers from agencies for tours, when you return you'll have to start from scratch. No one will have heard of you! It's preferable to firmly establish the act first in your own locality, then when you return from touring you'll be greeted with open arms. Clubs work up considerable publicity when a group is "leaving tomorrow for Europe," or "playing their first engagement since returning home from an East Coast tour."

Finding a Reliable Agency

For extended touring either with chain companies in North America or in countries outside the United States, it might be stipulated that you belong to a performer's union. More and more large operations, however, are refusing to sign union contracts. The problem is not money. Employers are objecting to having disputes arbitrated by the musician's union rather than an impartial mediator. I don't blame them. The booking agents I talked with said this problem is decreasing since the majority of groups they book on tours are nonunion anyway. This is a a loss of protection, but still the agents are answerable to performer's unions, since agents are most commonly licensed by the AFM and the American Guild of Variety Artists (AGVA). The licenses regulate agent commission, how and when you're paid, and arrangements particular to traveling.

By the time you're ready to consider touring, you will have made many friends in other groups. Ask their opinion of various agents. Working experience with an agency is more valuable than any other advice or union protection.

If you can't locate a safe agency by word of mouth, you'll have to seek out interested agents by phone or mail. Start by looking in the *Billboard International Talent Directory* or the *Songwriter's Market*, both annual publications. Each lists agencies throughout the country, but the *Songwriter's Market* includes information on what type of acts each agency books and where they place them. An agency booking 30-100 acts might provide easier access into choice tours, but a smaller agency counters this with more personalized, careful attention to your needs. Look for aggressive, smaller agencies.

Whether you telephone potential agencies or write letters, you'll need to ask where they book tours and what type of acts they represent. If they interest you, ask if they'd like to see a complete promo package including cut tape (or videotape if possible), photos, bio sheet, list of references, or an upcoming performance schedule. Booking agents' commissions are currently running 10-20 percent. When you find an agent you like and are offered a tour, ask specific questions about the places you'll be playing. What style of music do these rooms want? What has worked in the past? What's the age group of the clientele? Are there any peculiarities about the employers you should know? An agent who has booked these rooms before will have these answers.

A common musician complaint is that agents frequently don't allot enough travel time on tours to get from gig to gig. If you're finishing the night in Bismarck, North Dakota, and you're due to play 459 miles away in Duluth, Minnesota, the next night, you won't have time to eat between the tearing down, driving, and setting up. Ask prospective agents how far they'll ask you to travel between gigs.

Whether you're touring Ramada Inns or Japan, the first thing a tour agent looks for is entertainment. Can you thoroughly please a crowd? Is the routine classy and polished? The clothes have to look formal yet sharp and the attitude should be bubbly, unless your image is distinctly different—like a blues act. The overall musical sound has to be tight, but the proper appearance and stage show are just as important.

The next question in the agent's mind is your credibility. How dependable is the act? Can you be trusted to make it to the next gig? Is everyone sober on the job? Even if you don't have a reputation for reliability, you can project it by good business etiquette. Return phone calls, write thank you letters, and show an interest in the business side of the tour.

Always negotiate. When an agent tells you he's got an opening paying $2,000 a week, that's his opening offer. Give him itemized reasons why you need $2,500!

Timing is sometimes a problem with agents. When an agent gets a call from a cruise ship entertainment director for an additional band, the pressure's on that agent to deliver in a hurry. Otherwise, the entertainment director won't call him next time. When the agent calls you, then, he might want you in two weeks for a two-week cruise. Has the pressure shifted to you? Not yet. You can bet that agent penciled himself a healthy percentage, so bargain for a better offer if you're going to assume his time deadline. An agent always wants to settle contracts quickly to move on to other deals and keep his hourly wage high. If you offer to agree immediately—for a chunk of his percentage—he'll often go along with the deal because you save him time. Of course, this means the band must be willing and able to leave on short notice.

Touring can be the most educational and fun experience you've ever had. "There's something about having dinner at a gourmet restaurant and then being happy to follow that with a snack cake and soft drink at an all-night filling station for your next meal, that gives you a certain perspective on the variations of life in this modern world," writes Gary Burton in *A Musician's Guide to The Road*. The special moments are counterweighted with hairy ones, however, so you should deliberate carefully before signing up.

For Further Information

To do your best in performance, psyche yourself up with any one of a handful of inspirational paperbacks by Norman Vincent Peale, such as *The Power of Positive Thinking* or *You Can If You Think You Can*, both available from Columbia Book Service, CBS Publications, 32275 Mally Road, P.O. Box FB, Madison Heights MI 48071. Whether you are religious or not, the common-sense measures advocated can help with many preparation problems associated with performance.

There are plenty of books written on small group communication. Two of the better books are *Decision Making in Small Groups: The Search for Alternatives*, by Albert C. Kowitz and Thomas J. Knutson, Allyn and Bacon, Inc., 470 Atlantic Ave., Boston, MA 02210, and *Small Group Decision Making: Communication and the Group Process*, by B. Aubrey Fisher, McGraw-Hill Book Co., 1221 Avenue of the Americas, New York NY 10020.

Gary Burton has packed a lot of good advice into his book *A Musician's Guide to the Road*, Billboard Books, available from Watson-Guptill Publications, 1515 Broadway, New York NY 10036. Burton covers everything from alarm clocks to Hertz credit cards.

To assist in finding an agency that's right for you, the annual *Songwriter's Market*, edited by Barbara Norton Kuroff, Writer's Digest Books, 9933 Alliance Rd., Cincinnati, OH 45242, lists over 40 pages of booking agents, including quotes from each agency on where they book and the types of acts they want.

The most comprehensive listing of booking agencies, personal managers, festivals, concert promoters, charter services, rental services (of musical instruments, stages, sound and lighting equipment), unions, and rehearsal studios is the *Billboard Talent Directory*, 9107 Wilshire Blvd., Suite 700, Beverly Hills CA 90210.

• PART THREE •

THE HIDDEN
(And Richly Worth Investigating)
MARKETS

• CHAPTER THIRTEEN •

GUESS WHAT— YOU'RE A MUSIC TEACHER!

"I never considered teaching," said William. "I don't know why. It just never seemed like something I could do." That was before William met Dave, a keyboardist who taught guitar as well as piano.

"Technically, I'm a better guitarist than Dave. If he could teach, why couldn't I?" Now William teaches in the daytime—averaging $310 weekly—to boost his music income far beyond what nighttime performing alone brings in. Many proficient musicians, like William, dismiss teaching as a profession beyond their means, yet some could undoubtedly become successful teachers.

The teaching field is diverse. There are so many instruments and so many styles that finding your own teaching niche is not difficult in most communities. It's best if you teach in an area with active elementary school, high school, and college band programs since this insures a constant source of students. Public classes don't cater to individuals, so private teachers are kept busy by students who, for various reasons, want personalized instruction.

Unlike studio work, acting as a choir director, or running a home studio, which are part-time jobs, private or public teaching can provide a full-time income. There's a lot of money to be made teaching!

A Good Teacher Needs Only Two Qualifications

What do you need to be a good music teacher? To teach at the elementary, high school, or college level, you obviously need a degree. To teach privately, however, you don't need that piece of paper. All the music education you can absorb helps, but a fancy Ph.D. isn't necessary. Some public instructors even find it uncomfortable to offer private lessons. "It seems awkward to me," confided a high school band director. "I feel it's

202 Making Money Making Music

The best music lessons are more than just reading exercises. Exercises in finger dexterity, discussions of music theory, and lessons in construction and acoustics all mean better informed, more proficient students—and more of them!

(photograph by Ellen Forsyth)

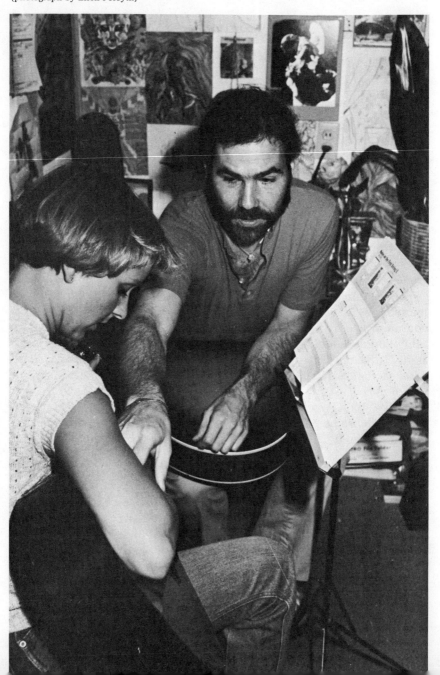

a conflict of interest to be helping kids at school, and then turn around and charge them at night."

To teach in the private sector, you need musical talent and teaching ability. Often musicians possess one of these in ample amount but come up short in the other.

Many fine musicians relate perfectly through music, but poorly through the spoken word. They can be confident, aggressive performers, but withdraw meekly in a one-on-one situation.

Most colleges and universities offer classes in music instruction and communication for musicians who need help explaining how they do what they do. Taking classes like these provides short-term benefits for private teaching and the long-term option of earning a credential.

Besides possessing communicative skills, you've got to be able to play well enough to interest students in the first place. A beginner doesn't want to put her trust (and money) in the hands of another beginner. She wants a pro!

If you're unsure whether your talent authorizes you to teach others, remember you don't have to be expert in all aspects of your instrument, or be fluent in all musical styles. Private instructors teach jazz guitar, modern vibraphone technique, timpani, and rock vocal lessons. The vocalist, for instance, may not feel comfortable teaching classical style because of limited experience in that field, but he may be a great rock and roll singer and know a lot about that technique, so he's qualified to teach rock vocals.

If you do have a diverse basic grounding, but lack full expertise in any one field, cater to beginners rather than accepting all comers. Plenty of teaching supplements and lesson guides are available for the "beginning student" teacher.

A teacher is never just a teacher. Even good teachers are forever pupils, learning both from student interaction and other teachers. The best teachers can answer any student questions, from instrument construction to intellectual theory discussion, and are versatile, active performers as well.

But why wait to become great to start teaching? Being "good" is enough. As long as you don't misrepresent your knowledge or talents, people will sign up to learn from you.

You Can Teach at Home or at a Music Store

You already know this, right? What you might not know are the circumstances that determine which choice is best for you. If you are not a well-known in-town performer, working out of a music store is to your advantage since music students will come to the store asking about lessons. Then the salesperson simply recommends you; you won't have to advertise. On the other hand, if you've played around town frequently and a number of people know who you are, your home will make a better studio. Listeners will approach you on breaks and compliment your ability. If you mention that you give lessons, you'll recruit students without even trying.

If a store is the logical place to teach, check out several before agreeing to a deal. Store owners are anxious to grab up teachers they think will build a large clientele, since your presence brings foot traffic into the store. Also, the more popular the store, the better!

Next, consider what kind of musician patronizes each store. Some cater to middle-aged, upper-income customers, whose taste may be considerably different from that of "Rock City's" clientele on the other side of town. If you're teaching rhythm and blues, find a store that draws R&B musicians. Will you cater to younger students? If so, find out which stores supply orchestra and marching instruments for the local high schools. Then school band directors will send business your way.

Stores handle finances differently. Some require students to pay the cashier; then, based on how many hours you've accrued at month's end, the owner will write you a check. Other stores will ask you to collect the money, log your hours, and pay the store a rental fee for your studio space (usually a cubbyhole near the washroom). A few owners will expect you to wisk the student out onto the showroom floor if they express an interest in buying something. If you're supposed to act like a salesperson, find out if you'll receive a commission on sales.

Working out of your home or rented studio allows more flexibility than a store, since teaching times won't be dictated by store hours or limited studio space. If you teach in your home, you increase your income by avoiding rent and transportation costs. The room you use to teach in is also tax deductible as a business studio.

But personal distractions can be a problem at a home studio. Young children must be watched and ringing phones answered. Students feel cheated if much time is spent on personal matters.

If you're going to teach at home, you'll need instruments, a record player or tape deck, music stands, chairs, and maybe a couch. A friend of mine teaches organ and piano, but since he only has a piano at home, he travels to each aspiring organist's home and teaches on their organ. If you live alone, have the phone nearby to answer calls. Soundproofing materials, discussed in Chapter 7, should be applied to the walls. I visited one apartment studio that was insulated so thoroughly that none of the neighbors knew they were living next to an electric guitar teacher.

The Initial Meeting

The first time you talk over the phone or in person with an interested student is a crucial moment for you and the student. You should find out as much as possible about the student's interests and abilities. Then you can assess where he stands in his musical development and explain where you're going to take him using what teaching methods.

Freely explain the limitations—if any—of your musical and teaching abilities. Will you only teach six-string bass? Make sure students know what they're getting into. Remember that you must only teach your strengths, and the things you'll enjoy teaching. If you cater to a student's whims, both you *and* the student may lose out.

"I don't let a student dictate to me," said a guitar instructor. "I'll get specific with a few, like if a girl comes in and says, 'I don't want to read notes,' there's no ways she's going to, but if a rocker comes and says, 'All I want to learn are licks,' I won't teach him. I can see a student's weaknesses better than he can."

For students who want something other than what you teach, or students who are too advanced for you, be ready with a list of other teachers to refer them to. This helps the student find what he's looking for, and it also means the other instructors will send students your way.

Even if you need the money, always be honest and refuse a student who isn't right for you. Your reputation builds up your clientele, and it can knock it down even faster. Once the word gets around that you waste their time and their money, you'll quickly experience the "death of a teacher."

Lesson Plans

How should you plan your lessons? First, become very proficient at what you will teach, by working through as many lessons yourself as possible. The array of lesson "methods" to choose from is bewildering in a well-stocked sheet music store. Study a variety of guides so that you can either assign lessons directly from a book or write out lessons yourself, incorporating what you consider the most helpful sections from several books.

A broad-based, diverse learning plan is generally recommended. It should involve more than just chart reading. Study of available chart books, along with lessons emphasizing syncopation, skill studies, broken-chord studies, learning via recordings, music theory, and instrument mechanics and construction add up to a "total musical awareness" for the student.

Some teachers don't use sight-reading in their lessons at all. Although reading is an excellent shortcut for learning parts, a great many notation-illiterate musicians don't care to read, so there is plenty of demand for teachers who offer unconventional lessons, including memorizing parts by tape. I once organized a "rhythm section lesson" with a bassist which used no written music. We concentrated on teaching improvisation, syncopating parts, and nonverbal onstage communication.

You'll have to develop a system—or adopt someone else's—for assigning homework. Teachers usually wrestle with how much or how little homework is right for each student until they know the student well enough to measure personal achievement. Still, it can be difficult. Some super-motivated students learn slowly, while other lethargic musicians might learn effortlessly. Due to differences in learning desire and rapidity, a private teacher is best off matching each student to a personalized homework plan.

"I'm a different teacher with each student," said a voice instructor. "In order to teach someone, you have to know how he thinks. Everyone thinks differently."

"With some, it's more of an intellectual approach," said Stu, a guitar teacher. "They want to know why this chord goes here, or why this is called what it is. Other students have a more emotional approach. They listen to what comes out and enjoy the feeling of the music."

"I don't teach one basic lesson," said another teacher. "After I can see where they're at, I teach whatever I think they need."

When Do You Drop That Kid?

Once you begin assigning homework, you'll run into the same question posed to all teachers: How do I draw the line between helping a student along and carrying him? It's not easily discernible. How much discipline or persuasion should you use? A wise rule of thumb is to continue to encourage the student, as long as he is trying to learn. You're under pressure to teach well, since the kid's parents are picking up the tab.

"I don't care if they always pay on time. I don't enjoy accepting their money if they haven't learned. I'll drop them," said a teacher.

Use your intuitive sense to help you decide if a student has practiced. Five minutes after a student walks in, I know whether he's prepared. You can feel it. Working one-on-one, you learn what they're capable of, even on a bad day. "If the kid is working at it, and I know he is, I'll help him over a hurdle by going deeper into the lesson," said a trumpet teacher.

Your approach and discipline must change according to what age group you teach, because each advances differently.

"With a beginner, you see steady, upward progress," said a teacher with 35 years experience in public and private music instruction. "Advanced students hit plateaus more often. This means you have to work them over these roadblocks. They get discouraged easier than kids. You have to psychologically stimulate them. That's why teaching advanced students is harder, takes more energy, and can be more satisfying. Then when they get to the improvisational stage, it's all kinds of fun."

"Adults have a lot more 'whys'," said another teacher. "They doubt a lot more. A kid just assimilates it. An adult has to be spoon-fed.

"Kids are used to doing things they don't necessarily like to do because they're sitting in school half the time. With adults it depends more on mood and inspiration. Their personal life can interfere easier. If they break up with someone, they'll start writing a lot of songs, though they may miss class too."

Several teachers expressed their concern about dropping non-productive students, reasoning that students often feel embarrassed and insecure after being rejected. One way to handle it is saying the equivalent of, "I'm going to let you have a month off to get caught up with your lessons. You give me a call." They usually won't. While this doesn't solve *their* problem, it'll solve yours, and perhaps not scare them away from trying music again sometime.

How Money-Making Teachers Do It

"I had 30 students, but I wasn't making any money," remembered a sax/flute teacher. "Most of the time they'd call 15 minutes before the lesson: 'Oh, I can't make it today,' or 'Can I switch my time?' I'll bet I only averaged $75 a week."

How to handle cancellations has always been the biggest question facing private teachers. A last minute schedule change completely ruins your hourly wage. What kind of a make-up policy will protect you from getting burned? The "no make-up policy." Does that sound coldhearted? Just change your perspective! Instead of selling your services, which can be cancelled, sell your *time*, which cannot be regained. By requiring monthly prepayment, this system works. Listen to Stan, a percussionist, explain it:

"I charge by the month instead of the week, the concept being they've got me reserved once a week for a half hour, and if they don't choose to come, that's fine, but I was here, and they paid me for it. Business-wise it works out great. Everybody shows up. I don't have to hassle with makeups. It was driving me crazy before!"

Make sure your students understand this concept and agree to it before the first lesson. Work with the student to find a weekly time that is best for him, since he must pay for the lesson even if he can't make it. You should consider being less particular in your scheduling, for the student's benefit.

Half-hour lessons are more popular than hour lessons because teachers can make more money this way. Most teaching depends on the student's practicing during the week, and lessons function as a quick review and a time for a new assignment; thus a lengthy time together isn't necessary. For in-depth practicing with advanced students or theory discussion, an hour is better.

Regardless of lesson length, sessions frequently run over the allotted time period. Although this can be exasperating for the teacher (and the kid in the waiting room), most instructors eventually modify their schedule to allow periodic breaks, sometimes as often as after each lesson. The breaks can also help the teacher. "I found that three students in a row was all I could legitimately do without getting burnt out," says a keyboardist.

A violin teacher I know thought up a novel way of providing an intermittent break without sacrificing hourly wage. "I was charging $15 per half hour. Now it's $25 for 45 minutes, which leaves 15 minutes at the end of each lesson to talk with the student or get a cup of coffee."

If you're talented and have plenty of potential students in your area, the only factor deciding how many students to teach will be how much time you can or will want to spend teaching. Plenty of teachers carry a roster of 25 to 45 students, working days only. I met one guy who taught 70 students weekly! If you're going to school or performing nightly, you might top out at 12 to 18. Start out gradually until you can estimate how much time the preparation and lessons will consume; then when you reach your limit, start a waiting list.

How much will you charge per half hour? An accomplished classical or symphonic player can often name her own price. If you've got a degree in music, you're worth more. If you're a popular local performer—regardless of style—you can probably get double or triple what other, lesser-known teachers are asking. Actual half-hour rates range from $5 to $25.

An unknown local organist thought up a clever way to buy an organ, quickly amass a clientele, and teach out of her house: She taught in-store, compiling a list of 24 dependable students, until she could afford a new keyboard. Then she quit the store, pocketed the 20-percent rental fee, set up the organ, and began teaching her students in her family room! Always look for ways to cut your overhead while maintaining clientele.

Group Teaching

In recent years, an increasing number of private music teachers have been replacing individual instruction with group instruction. The reason? Efficiency and money. Instead of 20 half-hour lessons per week, the instructor can teach 2 one-hour lessons. The students, instead of paying $10 per half hour, now pay $5 per hour lesson, so they win. The instructor wins, too, collecting $10 per week from each pupil, or $100 per hour.

Despite those incentives, some teachers dislike the group method. The main objections are: (1) The group teaching style is impersonal and competes with public school courses, so it defeats the purpose of individualized instruction, and (2) Group formats penalize fast learning students because they usually proceed at the rate of the slowest student.

Group teaching presents other obstacles, too. Most private teachers don't have access to a facility that can hold 20 to 40 students. And where do you get 30 electric pianos with head sets? Luckily, some colleges will rent classrooms to nighttime private instructors through adult education classes. Park and recreation districts also sponsor adult ed courses consisting of private instructors teaching in group formats. Instructors are paid a flat hourly wage, or they receive about 50 percent of each student's enrollment fee.

The problems of penalizing fast or advanced students and not providing personalized attention are partially solved by making the advanced students "teacher assistants" to help you in the classroom. This provides personalized attention to slower students while advanced students learn from a different perspective—that of the music teacher. This is one of the greatest benefits of group teaching—it prepares the assistants to become teachers. It also makes you a better teacher, since a group of students requires more time spent in lesson preparation. This makes the group-teaching experience more valuable for serious teachers, says Guy Duckworth, Professor of Music at the University of Colorado. "Group lessons can develop communication skills and pedagogical principles essential to teacher effectiveness that private lessons seldom, if ever, deal with." If you plan to earn a music degree and work in pubic schools, teaching private group lessons will prepare you for the classroom.

Create Student Interest Through Community Involvement

One of the best ways of stimulating student interest in your teaching program and building your clientele rapidly is to host regular student recitals. "Student showcases" enable your students to meet one another and provide a way for less experienced musicians to perform, thus building confidence. They're also a lot of fun. "Just playing and studying privately is great, but students need an outlet to perform, whether solo or with an ensemble. For them, the recitals make going to the lessons worthwhile," said a brass instructor.

City and county officials are usually happy to donate a public park, amphitheater, or small performance hall for the recitals, as long as the shows are free and open to the general public. Learning workshops like this are always encouraged as a public service to the community. Approach nursing homes or senior citizen centers about providing a series of free recitals. Or you might know a private club owner who would be willing to host the recitals on a regular basis. This works out well because a stage and chairs are already set up. But no matter if you look to the public or private sector for a recital spot, it'll definitely be better than cramming 75 students, parents, and relatives into your living room.

Recitals help strengthen parent commitment to providing music lessons for their child. Says a percussion teacher who hosts regular recitals: "The parents love it! They share in the kid's progress and can hear, month by month, what their money has bought. It makes the families closer too. Instead of saying, 'Oh, my wacky kid is driving me nuts banging on those damn drums,' they say, 'Boy, I was so proud of my kid! He played side by side with six other drummers and didn't make one mistake!' That's the kind of parental attitude that pays the bills."

I know one tacher who has a fantastic method for his student recitals. For three weeks, each student works on a piece until it is performance quality. Advanced students go through several lessons, picking the one they enjoy most. The last week of each month, every weekday student shows up on Sunday for a two-hour recital lesson at an outdoor amphitheater. The students benefit from particpating in the show, and the teacher comes out a winner, too, by having a whole week off each month!

Freelancing to Schools

"This is how I get most of my students," a trumpet player said as he wrote out parts for the high school marching band. "I help the band out organizing their parts, and every season about five or ten ask if I'd teach them private lessons."

With tax revenue drastically cut, schools can't hire additional instructors, so they are requiring more work out of their present teachers. While this "hiring freeze" hurts the chances of full-time music teachers looking for work, it is creating many short-term jobs for freelancing musicians who'll help a band director with a work overload.

Most of the work is available through high schools and colleges with active music programs or large marching bands. For the fall season, instructors are expected to write the show and music, rehearse both, handle an expanded drum line, write their solos, train color guard on both flag and rifle, and arrange theatrical settings. See why they're relieved to put you on the department payroll?

The jobs are usually that of a teacher assistant. If you're a sax player, you'll be helping the reed section with their parts by leading them through rehearsal. The instructor may ask you to write out solos for the reed group if the song calls for it. In any case, you'll have to be a quick reader and very good musician, with enough imagination to arrange parts and write solos.

Since the sectional jobs involve working with students, you'll need motivational and communication skills, along with a feel for when your section is on the verge of strangling you if you keep them five minutes late *again*.

Public teachers who need help will either phone a private teacher they're familiar with (often a former student) or request a sectional teacher at the music store they buy charts and instruments from.

If school teachers don't know you and you are not working in a store, you'll have to take the initiative. Prior to marching season, you should visit your local schools and talk to the music directors about possible sectional work. Bring a resume and be prepared to demonstrate your musical ability on the spot. Most payment agreements will be for a specific number of sessions, and a flat rate per session you teach. Thus if you agree to lead a sectional twice a week for five weeks at $25 per session, you'll be paid $250.

Some instructors expect teacher assistants to work for free. Even though the experience of directing a group of students is valuable if you intend to pursue a teaching career, you should be compensated for your time. Here's one possible solution: Agree to teach for free, on the condition that the teacher will refer any students looking for private lessons to you. This way, the fund-strapped school doesn't have to come up with any money, but you still get paid (although payment, if any, will be delayed). If the students like you and respect your musical ability, they'll want to take lessons from you.

Public Teaching

A college degree in music is a proven way to land good paying musical jobs. Nursery schools, kindergartens, elementary schools, middle, junior high, and high schools, or colleges and universities function as great "career bases" for music teachers. Once established as a teacher in a public or private school, it is much easier to land jobs conducting church choirs, community music organizations, or recreational programs.

I know university teachers who use their education to land a variety of jobs. One teacher annually arranges music for the California State Fair, while another conducts a local symphony. A third sings professionally, another is a symphony player, and a fifth conducts a church choir. All give private lessons besides teaching at the university, and all pursue other freelance opportunities as well.

"The credentials certainly help in getting jobs," said one teacher. "You have a much better chance for survival—getting a job and keeping it—if you can do a variety of things, and when you go through a program like ours, you learn a variety of skills. The most important factor in landing a performing job is still that you can perform well, but a degree in music can really help."

One field that pays well and allows you to practice is music therapy. People with emotional and/or physical disabilities are helped by the use of music in psychiatric centers, hospitals, health clinics, day-care centers, and nursing homes. The National Association for Music Therapy,

Inc., says opportunities are presently available for qualified therapists, and the field will continue to grow. Besides payment, rewards include the satisfaction of helping and healing patients. Therapists must enjoy working with handicapped people, and have a great deal of patience and perseverance.

Here is a list of jobs requiring a degree, published in 1979 by the Music Educators National Conference, the Music Teachers National Association, Inc., and the National Association of Schools of Music, in the brochure "Careers in Music." Note that salaries are quoted in 1979 dollars:

	Opportunity for Employment	Approximate Earnings	Personal Qualifications	Minimum College Training Required
Teacher/ Supervisor	1. Public school. 2. Parochial school. 3. College, University, Conservatory. 4. Administrator, University.	1. $7,500-$20,000 2. $7,500-$17,000 3. $9,000-$30,000 4. $18,000-$40,000	Musical talent. Ability to work with people. Ambition to continually study and improve. Be inspiring, convincing, patient. Enjoy people and desire to help them learn.	Public school: teaching certificate, bachelor's degree. College, university: doctoral degree or equivalent training.
Music Therapist	1. Hospitals: civilian, veteran. 2. Clinics for handicapped children. 3. Corrective institutions. 4. Special education facilities.	$8,200-$25,000	Musical talent and skill. Ability to work with handicapped people. Human understanding. Enjoy people and desire to help them attain physical and mental health.	Bachelor's degree in music therapy.
Music Librarian	1. College, university, conservatory. 2. Public library. 3. Orchestra, band, chorus (very limited). 4. Radio, TV station music coordinator.	1. $9,000-$16,500 (may be augmented by teaching) 2. $8,000-$16,500 3. up to $12,000 4. $8,500-$14,000	Ability to work with people. Interest in music, books, recordings, professional problems, and research.	Bachelor's degree with major in music history or theory (preferably plus at least one year graduate study in musicology). Graduate library degree.

You should pursue your music education while actively performing, teaching private lessons, or otherwise working with music. Rushing through a four-year music program and then expecting to begin your career will set you at a distinct disadvantage, since you won't have practical experience or contacts within the employment world. "In the music field," says David Baskerville, author of the *Music Business Handbook and Career Guide*, "the shift from schooling to employment is rarely sudden. Unlike such professions as law, engineering and medicine, people heading for careers in the music business break in gradually, land part-time jobs or become involved in various projects while still in school. As a matter of fact, it has been my observation that the student who waits until he has "completed" his education to get going professionally probably won't make it anyway. A person becomes a pro in the music business gradually, as a rule. As he acquires skills and know-how, he starts out part-time, perhaps semiprofessionally, then moves on to full-time work."

A music degree is a versatile tool which will open new doors for you. Classes are typically offered both at day and night, allowing you to plan classes around most any musical job. If your schedule becomes unbearably crowded with a band, studio work, and private teaching, remember: One of the greatest advantages of education is that it's always available! Carry a light load of one, two, or three classes if necessary.

The Joy of Teaching

Every teacher feels satisfied when a student masters a part. Sometimes it'll take a student three weeks of agony to play a chart fluently, but in the end, it sounds good. (Is it Miller time yet?) The joy of teaching is that when he finally clears that hurdle, you do, too. This instructor sums up the feeling:

"That's where I get off on it, when I can see and hear progress. A lot of musicians come in after fiddling around with the instrument for years, totally sick of playing the same thing, and in a month or two I can completely turn around their concept of music, and improve their whole self-image. They might say, 'Oh, I could never play a lead,' and then suddenly they realize they can. If you can give them the confidence to get out and perform in public, you've changed their life."

For Further Information

If you're a hot player, but need to brush up on your academic understanding of music before you'll feel comfortable teaching, read *Instruction of Music Theory*, by Allen Winold and John Rehm, Prentice-Hall, Inc., General Publishing Division, Englewood Cliffs NJ 07632. The book concentrates on notation, music reading, and ear training.

To move on to a more advanced text on theory, incorporating musical space, language, time, and color, check out *Sonic Design: The Nature of*

Sound and Music, by Robert Cogan and Pozzi Escot, also available from Prentice-Hall, Inc.

Over 35 colleges nationwide offer four-year degrees to become certified as a music therapist. For information on these, write the National Association for Music Therapy, Inc., P.O. Box 610, Lawrence KS 66044, or the American Association for Music Therapy, Education Building, Room 777, 35 W. Fourth St., New York NY 10003.

• CHAPTER FOURTEEN •

LAYIN' DOWN TRACKS

Since there aren't even 15 successful studio guitarists in New York, one of the largest recording centers in the country, this [pursuing large studio gigging] isn't worth considering.
—Bruce Bergman, How to Make Money Playing Rock Guitar

The majority of printed material about studio operations and opportunities only applies to the big studios in the recording centers. The smaller studios, from converted garage four-tracks to the "just short of industry quality" 24-track operations, are ignored. For musicians, this is a gross oversight, since smaller studios provide most of the available session work in the country. This chapter explains smaller studios, takes a look at their clients, and shows you how to cash in on all that reel-to-reel taping going on.

Studio Life—Facts and Fiction

Studio recording is a vague fantasy to most local musicians. You read interviews with the Brecker Brothers or Jeff Porcaro and try to figure out how you can get involved. Unfortunately, the big-time studio scene is reserved for an elite few, and competition is fierce even among these musicians. Important information, like how to get your foot in the door, isn't common knowledge. Luckily, this doesn't matter a whole lot to you, since big studios and small studios operate differently. But it does create a lot of confusion for musicians. Following are the most common questions I hear, and the answers that apply to session players in smaller studios:

"What if I can't sight read at the speed of sound?"

It doesn't matter, especially for the instruments laid down on basic tracks, such as piano, guitar, bass, and drums. You *should* be a very proficient reader, but studio producers rate reading ability a middle to low priority when hiring.

"Don't studios employ their own musicians?"

You don't need to travel to New York, Los Angeles, or Nashville anymore to find a quality recording studio. And since demo business has fallen off, you can book time in a 24-track studio such as this one (Heavenly Recording Studios, Sacramento, California) for under $50 per hour.

As a rule, no. They might have some favorites they'll call first, but no 9-to-5 salaried workers.

"Am I good enough to play sessions?"

Talent is very important in studio gigs, but other variables, such as your personality, are even more important.

"Don't small studios pay small wages?"

Not necessarily. A better price indicator than studio size is a list of clients. The money spent locally on radio advertising, for instance, will shock you.

"Isn't all the pressure scary?"

Sure, if you let it get to you. But remember, you're not in New York City taping $1,000 sessions for Coca-Cola. Your clients are local car dealers, restaurants, and city council election committees. Not as much money is at stake for local clients, and studio time isn't in such great demand.

"Can I send a promo tape as an audition?"

No. Letters of interest are no good either. The qualities that make up a good studio musician can't all be heard on tape or read on paper. A producer needs to hear you, meet you, and work with you before calling you a "regular."

"Do I have to join the musicians' or singers' union?"

Not unless you try to crack the big studios in New York City, Los Angeles, Nashville, or large jingle studios in other big cities. The large studios in these recording centers are held in a tight grip by local unions.

"Doesn't the union closely regulate the studios?"

Except for the large recording centers, absolutely not. In other areas, union studio policies are routinely ignored by everyone concerned—the unions included.

Independent Recording Studios

Independent studios come in all shapes and sizes, from soundproofed one-car garages to state-of-the-art 24-track mix-mastering operations. In between these extremes are four-track and eight-track demo studios, and 16 and 24-track hometown studios. Lately, 24-track mix-mastering facilities have sprung up outside of the industry recording centers (there's even one in Sacramento!). Studios of all sizes provide good opportunities for you.

Studios operate round the clock, but certain hours are more popular than others. The most common recording times are between noon and 6:00 p.m., which fits in nicely with a band schedule.

Average wages for musicians are difficult to calculate. Payment varies between studios, clients, and the musicians hired. AFM scale starts at $158.57 per three hours, but union influence is terribly weak. Still, the money is good. "It's $75 to $100 for two hours per musician," said the producer of a 24-track studio. "Arrangers and writers get anywhere from $100 to $150. Head string player will get $150, string players $100 per session."

Unlike the major recording centers, where a Tom Scott or a Linda Ronstadt can command more than union scale, variance in pay for well-known local singers or musicians is minimal. This is mostly due to limited budgets. A musician cutting his own album might consider paying you more, but an ad agency or car salesman will tell you to take a hike.

Studio Organization

Size and activity determine the number of people a studio employs. Figure 14.1 shows how clients and musicians interact with studio personnel. A busy, but not quite state-of-the-art, 16 or 24-track studio might employ more people than this, such as another engineer, a bookkeeper, or a sales representative. Most studios, however, consolidate jobs to cut costs. The owner might direct, produce, and act as engineer, too. The head musician might write the lyrics and melody, arrange the music, and copy the charts, *besides* performing on the session.

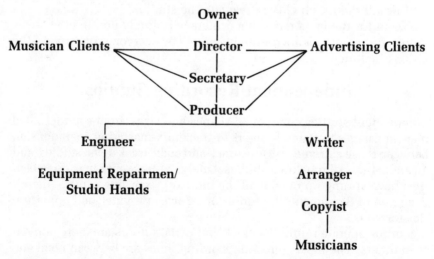

Here's a breakdown of job duties:

Owner

Most studio owners I've known are retired or active musicians or sound technicians who rent out PA equipment, mix sound for bands, and eventually fulfill their dream of owning a small studio. If the studio is small, the owner may directly oversee everything. He'll also promote his studio to musical and advertising clients.

Director

In larger studios, say 16 to 24-track, a director may be employed more or less as a manager. This is especially true in cases of absentee ownership. The director makes sure everything gets done, from carpentry to client bookings. His responsibilities are not creative, unless he is doubling as a producer.

Secretary

The secretary's main job is to juggle time slots so that the studio is in use continuously, and not book time at 6:30 a.m., 10:45 a.m., 3:30 p.m., and midnight with nothing in between those hours. If the studio is small, the owner will handle this, but in a busy studio, the director can't be bothered with booking times, answering phones, and billing clients, so a secretary is hired.

Producer

Whereas the director and secretary work on a salary basis, the producer works as an independent contractor. He recruits clients, secures a budget, hires the musicians, pays for studio time, and if he hasn't spent the entire budget, gets to keep what's left. A few studios hire a producer full-time, but many musical clients act as their own producers. Thus, instead of employing one in-house producer, studios keep a list of them just as they keep a list of musicians.

The producer's job is bilingual. Not only must he be able to express himself in technical terms to the engineer, he must also be creative with musicians. This has led to a predictable overlap in duties. Sometimes the producer (who may also be the director, remember) acts as engineer, or sometimes it's the other way around.

A good producer assumes responsibility for pre-production work, the recording session itself, and post-production work. The knowledge needed to organize and coordinate is usually acquired with experience.

Engineer

The engineer's job is basically a technical one. In the absence of a competent producer, however, the engineer may be required to make creative judgments such as how much bottom the bass needs, or how loud the background vocals should be. Engineers are usually schooled in electronics, and understand how to use sophisticated recording equipment and effects units. Larger studios may employ a couple of part-time engineers ("mixers") to help with complicated or hectic sessions. The fulltimer then becomes the "chief engineer."

Equipment Repairmen/Studio Hands

A studio may employ one full-time "handyman" to check equipment and do miscellaneous tasks such as positioning microphones, carrying instruments, and soundproofing booths. Part-time repairmen and studio hands are more common.

Writers

Rarely does a studio employ songwriters on a 9:00 to 5:00 basis. Instead, songwriters are usually hired by the producer on a freelance basis. "It's not necessary for a writer to be able to write lyrics and melody," said a local director. "Actually it's rare to find a musician who can do both well. Most will try to do both parts and come up with a crummy product. I prefer to pair a good lyricist with a good melody writer."

A typical writing job is a jingle. Melody writers must understand commercial format and length, and lyricists must be able to write the kind of witty, brand-plugging lyrics advertisers expect.

Producers want melody writers and lyricists who can arrange the music for instrumentation and vocals, copy the parts onto charts if needed, and play on the session. This saves time and reduces hassles for the producer while putting more cash in the songwriter's pocket.

Arranger

After the music is written, someone has to score the parts for each session musician and vocalist. This job falls to the arranger, who, more often than not, wrote the material and will act as copyist. An arranger should have a good understanding of music theory.

Copyist

A copyist is usually an arranger who's doing the tedious task of copying charts for each performer. Charts are needed for wind and brass instruments, but typically ignored for keyboards, piano, guitar, bass, and drums. For these instruments, chord changes and the number of measures is sufficient. In many studios, the arranger doubles as copyist for a small fee.

Musicians

Studio musicians are hired on a freelance basis exclusively. Producers reach for their little black books—alphabetized by instrument—grab the telephone and go down the list of players until they complete a roster for the session. The musicians at the top of the list are "in-house" or "on-call." They make it a point to be around when the phone rings (which, of course, can be any time day or night). How do you get your name in that book, and eventually at the top of that list? Read on!

It's Dog Eat Dog

Studios tend to be cliquish. Each place has its own tight circle of musicians, writers, arrangers, and copyists. Through experience together, these people become close friends. When there's a job open, friends call friends. Even in small studios in small communities, the atmosphere is highly competitive. Why? Because the money is great. Part-time studio work coupled with teaching or live performances makes for a tidy income.

You'll encounter strong favoritism. A superior keyboardist might continually be passed over in favor of a lesser player. Why does the less talented keyboardist get the gigs? She's easy to work with (or maybe she's the producer's girlfriend). Producers also prefer to hire *proven* musicians over new talent. Why should they take a chance on an unknown when they've got a sure thing a phone call away?

A lot of secrecy surrounds studio hiring procedures. A producer doesn't have time to discuss it, and working studio musicians hesitate to explain for fear of losing work to you. It's the competitive spirit—or maybe just insecurity.

The pressure is always on to be perfect. There's little room for errors. One of the simplest qualities producers want is the ability to play a part the same way over and over again, no experimenting. They want mechanically accurate players, yet the finished product has to sound lively.

To assist you in studio survival, you should be a good reader. In most studios you won't have to read much, but a reputation is built on dependability. If the first nine jobs don't require any reading, but the tenth does, you might not get called for the eleventh. Producers want consistency. Before tackling studio work (now, perhaps?) learn to read music.

That Winning Personality

Phil is a hot saxophonist, but he has trouble getting into any one studio's regular "on call" rotation. He's always at the bottom of the list—not the top. "Look, the guy can play well, read, and even arrange charts, but I won't recommend him unless I have to," confided a producer. How come? "I just don't like the guy."

If Phil knew why he was being passed over—his insistence on playing parts *his* way—he might change. In the studio, though, decisions are seldom explained. Once you're cut, it's good-bye.

"Temperament is *the* most important—just a little more so than talent," said a director. "Studio work can be tedious when you've got a client who's a real jerk. A musician can't act discouraged or disgusted with a client."

"You're walking a fine line," advised an in-house studio guitarist. "You've got to know when to contribute and when to shut up. You should *suggest* changes, like, 'How would this sound?' Or 'Maybe this is what you want,' but you can never *tell* a client what he wants, even if he doesn't know anything about music."

"You have to please the client 'cause he's paying you," offered a pianist. "Sometimes the musician is the buffer between the engineer and the client. You have to be willing to mediate differences, because it can be a power trip in there."

Discipline is another desired personality trait. "I've seen many fine musicians who just didn't understand discipline," said a director. "For some reason, drummers come to mind. They can't seem to play the exact same part twice in a row! It'll sound fine one time and then be different the next. I'll ask, 'What happened to that fill?' and they'll say, 'Oh, yeah. Where did that go again?'"

Nobody likes complainers. Everyone wants the cut to sound as clean as the latest Steely Dan release, but most studios can't touch that clarity or production quality. Let the client do the complaining. After all, she's the one paying for it.

Studio personnel appreciate promptness, but it can be overdone. Read what this secretary had to say: "Musicians hang around here all day! They might record from 10:00 to noon, but they'll show up at 9:00 and sit around for 50 minutes in the lobby. This place isn't very big. It makes me mad when they do that!" You'd be surprised how much influence a secretary can have on a producer (in many cases, she's the one who calls the sessionists). Show up ten minutes early, or just in time to set up your instrument. When the session's over at noon, don't hang around until 6:00 watching other people tape. "In-house" doesn't mean you hang out day and night; it means you're available when they call, and you get in and out fast when you're supposed to.

Make an effort to be friendly and helpful to everyone in the studio, be they engineer or part-time copyist. Give the secretary a hand filling the copy machine with paper. Compliment the owner on the acoustics, and tell him you recommended his studio to a friend. Listen attentively to other musicians when they talk to you. Friendship makes a tremendous difference in the number of calls you'll receive. If the people there enjoy your company, you'll get called just because they haven't seen you in a while.

Be grateful for any studio work you receive. A stuck-up musician is the last person a producer will call. "It's that prima donna syndrome," said one. "You know the guy. He's never quite made it, but he's got a $7,000 guitar custom made by Mr. Les Paul, and he wants to play every note he's ever learned. Luckily, these people are few and far between. Musicians are very likable as a group. The clients are much more difficult."

Breaking In

Formal approaches are no good for getting studio gigs. Stan, a string player, learned the hard way. "I didn't think I'd have any problem with the local recording studios. I had played in two major philharmonic orchestras, and this is a relatively small city compared to Philadelphia and Los Angeles. I sent personal biographies to four studios three months ago and never have gotten one call."

Producers won't bat an eye at a letter or even listen to your demo tape. They're too busy. Besides, why should they? They already have a list of musicians they *know* are dependable. Your letter and tape won't work, no matter how impressive the credentials or crystal clear the music. Their most important questions—can you get along with others? Do you know when to contribute and when not to? Will you work in as a steady session player?—go unanswered. Like Stan, you may not even get a letter of rejection.

There are two common ways to break into your local studio scene. A working studio musician can recommend you to the producer, or you can work on a friend's project while she rents studio time. Producers often check out who's recording, and if they like your sound, they might ask if you'd be interested in session work. If you don't have any friends presently working in studios or paying for a project, rent an hour yourself. It's likely the producer, director or engineer will hear you, and if you're hot, they may ask you to do work for them.

"Word-of-mouth is the traditional way of finding out about someone," said Martin, a director. "I'll ask the drummer, 'Do you know any good bass players?' and if he's good, we'll put him in the list. Then he'll either work out as a professional studio musician and be called frequently, or work out as a sideman, and only get called once every four months."

By developing your live act into a popular local attraction, you'll improve your chances of getting a studio offer. "I had a reputation for playing around town. One day Mike (the studio owner) just called me," said John, who eventually was working on three to four sessions per week.

To prepare yourself before venturing into local recording, it helps to know what producers and directors want in musicians, and the relative importance of each trait. A survey of these people listed the following six traits in this order of importance:
1. Personality
2. Adaptability
3. Talent
4. Instrument Quality
5. Availability
6. Reading Ability

I've already explained the reason personality is so important. Adaptability also rated high. A pianist explains: "You must quickly adjust to different styles of music—I might go from country to blues to punk to Lawrence Welk. Each has to be played uniquely, without influence from the others. You need to know the standard, obvious cliches of each style."

Producers also look to your instrument as an indication of your value. Some styles, for instance, only sound "right" on a certain kind of guitar. If you've got a guitar for every style, you'll endear yourself to the producer and engineer. "If he has a Barney Kessel, that's super, but if he's got a $19.95 Sears Silvertone, what good is that? The sound potential has to be there," said a director.

Though producers rated availability fifth, they were quick to point out that musicians who don't return calls or are never at home fall down the list. Once you say "Yes!" you can't say "No," too many times.

Reading ability, as I mentioned earlier, isn't a foremost consideration for most local studios. "Usually someone says, 'Do some lead part here,' " said Martin. Their experience puts the notes together. Its all *feel*. You can't chart that for a musician."

You Know Those Corny Late-Night Commericals?

I think every town has their own peculiar late-night TV advertisers. When traveling with bands you see them every night on the tube—homespun ads for waterbeds, carpeting, sewer service, and mobile homes. Despite the amateurism of the owners-turned-announcers, the soundtracks for these and other TV and radio spots represent a fair amount of studio work available to musicians.

The quality of these commercial "jingles" isn't as important as the efficiency with which they're made. "You're not under any great pressure to play something artistic," said a bassist. "If he wants 'country,' you just play a simple, recognizable country lick."

The clients paying for the spots are not musicians. They're antique dealers or car salesmen. Instead of judging the finished product by musical merit, as you would, her bottom line is money. How many studio hours did it take? What's the total bill for the completed commercial? An advertiser always has her eye on the budget.

The client may know what effect she wants, but since she's not a musician she can't specify beyond "country," "jazz," "slow," or "fast." "Can you get the L.A. sound?" is the kind of ambiguous request producers receive all the time.

But clients in your community who want to advertise on radio or TV rarely go to an independent recording studio themselves. Instead, they go to an advertising agency with their budget. The agent finds out what the client wants to get across in the ad, and then decides how the budget should be spent to achieve the desired result.

Ad agencies cut lots of corners to increase profits. Small agencies buy cheap studio time at radio stations, and slightly larger agencies have their own in-house four-track studios. But although they avoid the expense of an independent recording studio, the finished commercial is usually inferior to a good independent production.

And the independent studio isn't the only loser from ad agency business methods. Musicians get the shaft, too. Hiring studio musicians is a major expense out of $500 (and often exceeds that amount). Radio station studios are set up as broadcast facilities—without quality recording equipment—so bringing in musicians isn't feasible. In-house agency studios are also poor excuses for live recording studios. The ads are made by using prerecorded, "canned" music instead of you. Here's how one ad agent explains this logic: "If my client will only spend $300 for a spot, I can't afford to rent studio time, pay musicians, *and* pay myself. This way I can just rip some music off an album and overdub the announcement. If I only need a guitar or piano part, I can hire one musician and still make enough money."

The majority of locally produced advertisements use canned music. Both radio stations and ad agencies maintain libraries of canned music. The savings to an agency can reach 300 percent. With this kind of incentive, there's no way agencies will hire musicians or go to an independent recording studio unless the client demands it. Thus, the best way for you—the studio musician—to get this kind of work is to actively recruit clients for independent studios, and bypass agencies altogether (see "Drum Up Your Own Business" in Chapter 15).

Album and Demo Sessions

The other way to make money as a session musician is to assist musicians on their own album, single, or demo tape recording. Many 8 to 24-track studios depend on musicians for a major portion of their business, as opposed to courting advertising clients.

Many artists, before recording, plan on using the free services of musicians in their band or some players they know. This can cause problems, because what sounds good live can sound pitiful on tape. Acoustics, settings, relative volumes and tones all differ markedly between live performance and studio. This means your guitarist might take too long trying to find the sound he wants, not understand standard studio techniques, freeze up, or just sound bad on tape. This creates business for studio musicians. They can smooth out your cut and give it a "produced" sound.

Another thing a studio taping might reveal about your band is sloppy timekeeping. The tape doesn't lie! If the drummer isn't solid as a metronome, you'll hear it when the tape's played back. Maybe you never noticed it before, but now, you need a studio drummer.

I played with one bassist who unconsciously slapped the bass between every beat. Unfortunately, when it came time to record in a studio, he couldn't kick the habit. Call in a studio bassist!

Maybe the most common fault a taping session can reveal about a group is sour vocal harmonies. It goes completely unnoticed in a loud live rock show, but you'll grimace when the studio monitors play back the tape. Vocals are overdubbed onto the basic tracks, so you'll need studio background vocalists, unless you redub the parts yourself.

All of this means a great deal of work for studio musicians as session players on other musicians' projects. Rates vary, but are in accordance with jingle recording.

It's even more fun to work on album or demo projects than on jingle tracks. More time is usually spent on these projects, and the quality standards are higher. After all, the judge of your job is no longer a tone deaf car salesman, but another musician. Thus your job is harder, but much more satisfying. And you'll be able to get a copy of the album or cassette you worked on for your portfolio.

Studios that cater to musicians instead of advertising clients are feeling the uncertain effects of policy changes within the record industry. Musicians are slowly learning the ineffectiveness of sending demo tapes to record companies, so demo taping business is falling off. "We don't tell musicians it's worthless, because that's like cutting our own throat," said a 16-track studio director, "but we encourage them to use the tapes in other, more productive ways." These other ways include submitting to music publishers, independent producers, audiovisual firms, and booking agents. Demos are also used in promo packages and are a good way for local groups to hear how they actually sound on tape.

While the demo business is slackening off, regional printing of albums and 45 singles is increasing rapidly. Selling your album from the stage and in local record stores (Chapter 20) is a proven way to make money. Smaller four to eight-track studios, however, aren't benefitting from this boom in local vinyl. For a permanent recording, musicians tend to go with 16 or 24-track studios, so while smaller studios are losing demo taping business, they're not regaining this loss. Expect more and more small studios to either upgrade equipment, go broke, or concentrate on advertising clients.

Why Not Produce or Write Charts Yourself?

By itself, session work isn't a full-time job. Smaller studios don't have enough business to support you full-time. Playing piano for studio gigs is a great way to *augment* your live music income.

Once you become an established studio musician, and are on call with producers, you'll probably top out in salary soon. After five years, you'll get the same $50 per session that you received after five gigs. Seniority in local studios doesn't result in better pay; it just means you'll be asked to work more often.

This presents a problem. The goal is to increase your hourly wage, but working as a studio musician doesn't allow it. How can you lift the roof off that premature price ceiling? By getting more involved in other duties associated with studio work: producing, arranging, copying charts, and writing. This is an easy way to double your session fee!

Don't be scared to try. Usually, these jobs are done by musicians just like you. Since you *are* a musician these jobs are easier. You'll have an instinctive ear for what's right.

In the last twelve years, musicians have assumed much greater production control over their album projects. A few are becoming recognized as legitimate producers, and are in demand by other artists to help on their albums. For you to be "in demand" by advertising clients and fellow musicians is much simpler. You don't need Todd Rundgren's production track record; a sensitive musical ear and a willingness to hustle up clients is enough.

A studio owner won't hand over a job to an unproven producer. To be recognized, you'll have to bring a project or client into the studio and produce the sound. If the owner likes the final product, he'll call you when he needs a producer.

"I use my reputation from playing in the band and working here at the store to find clients," said a guitarist. "Sometimes they'll approach me, but most of the time I talk to businessmen I know, asking about how they advertise. Then I tell them I'm a producer. If they're interested, I'll prepare a budget, say for $1,000. The client will give me the $1,000, I'll put a down payment on the studio time, write the thing, hire a few musicians, and record it. I can make $400 if I've hired only four or five players. If I do all the instruments myself, and just hire an announcer or singer, I can make $600 or $700."

Local producers usually work for a "package deal." They agree on a budget beforehand with the client, and must keep expenses low enough to make a profit. When you submit a written proposal to a potential client, have expenses—including musicians, studio time and tape—carefully itemized.

One organist/producer suggested a good way to get a director to hire you, rather than finding your own clients. "Agree to produce for studio time instead of money," she said. This is a good trade that can benefit both parties, since most musicians need studio time sooner or later.

If you want to write lyrics and/or melodies for studio clients, first the producer must see you as an accomplished songwriter. Contact businesses and ask if you could write an advertising jingle for them, on speculation. As your charts are being recorded, make sure the producer knows *who* wrote the material. Writing music for a band or singer to record will get your foot in the door, too, but there aren't as many local jobs available. An ad writer is a hot commodity!

Once studios are familiar with your writing, expect to be called on for practically anything. "I give writers three kinds of assignments," said a studio director. "With the first, I'll hand the writer a paper and say, 'This is a piano thing some guy wrote at home. You need to spiff it up, because it really sucks.' That's a rewrite. With the second assignment, I'll say, 'Okay, this is a car dealer, this is his address, and he wants to sing about his mother.' The third kind is when a singer walks in and says, 'I want to sing a song, but I haven't got any original material,' so I'll assign a writer to come up with something."

Make Your Own Breaks!

The best assurance that a local producer will scratch your back is to scratch his back. Encourage your musician friends to record at his studio. Talk to business owners and suggest they spend some of their advertising money at independent studios, with professional announcers, singers, and musicians. Advertising agencies might charge $500 to create an ad costing them only $60! By dropping the agent, the client could spend the same amount of money on recording time and musicians, and end up with a unique, refreshing jingle that listeners will associate with their business. Make sure the studio producer realizes the effort you went to. If you're cordial and a good musician, you'll stand a very good chance of being called for further work.

If you can't steal business from ad agencies, get to know the agency personnel and get on their list of session musicians. Small agencies don't use musicians as a rule, but occasionally they do when something out of the ordinary is needed.

Audiovisual Projects

In the local audiovisual field, musicians are in a rough battle with companies selling elaborate canned music for sound filmstrips. Canned music used to be obvious because it was bland and unimaginative. Now a few national music suppliers, such as the Network Music Library, offer high quality contemporary music, though the rental cost can be as expensive as a live session.

Educational filmstrips are a large part of the AV field, but unfortunately, poor quality canned music enjoys wide use here. "I sold educational films to school districts throughout the U.S.," said a four-track studio owner, "and used musicians exclusively. Most educational productions, though, unless you just had a writer narrating with acoustic guitar and flute, use canned music."

Some independent recording studios do audio production work on films or slide shows for local businesses and political candidates. Politics are particularly promising because of large campaign budgets and the constant striving to promo candidates as "fresh" and "in tune with the times." Just make sure you get paid up front.

A friend of mine, Donna, has written commericals and made slide shows for assemblymen and other local candidates. "You have to know when the elections are coming up," she said, "and just start calling PR agencies. I watch for those little notices right at the beginning of a campaign, that say, 'Paid for the the So-and-So Campaign Committee.' If you call them early enough in the campaign, they'll still have plenty of money." You should call the campaign manager or public relations firm and ask for an appointment to show some things you've written, and explain your ideas for audiovisual presentations. Writing for candidates is very similar to writing jingles: You plug away on a definite image, and sell it hard.

Contacts in the AV field can be made the same way as you get into any studio: word-of-mouth, being seen in the studio working on another project, or contacting the business and public relations firms yourself.

Approach local businesses and organizations just as you would if you wanted to produce a commercial for them—with some definite ideas, and an itemized budget. Make sure you include rental costs for slide projectors, screens, and P.A. equipment, unless you already have these. Multi-image projections will probably be expected, so you'll need from two to four projectors, depending on what kind of show you plan to stage, and how much money the client can afford.

Create Your Own Music TV Program

Jerry Campbell had an unusual television experience. His rock band was playing in a L.A. club when a producer approached them and asked if they'd be interested in performing on a children's TV show. Eight shows, eight songs, and about $12,000 for each of the six musicians.

"We recorded 15 tunes at Sound City Studio, and submitted them to the CBS censors for lyric scrutiny. They approved eight. The pre-production and recording took three and a half weeks; then we lip-synced all eight video sessions in one day. We made $8,800 apiece *that day!*" Unfortunately, Jerry's group got stuck with a bad production company, so this incredible opportunity—though it made them a lot of money—didn't lead anywhere.

Television is a wild business, and TV people make a lot of money. The jobs for musicians, however, are rare. Television soundtrack recording, based in New York and Los Angeles, is a hard nut to crack. For you, chances are much better at home.

Local TV stations rarely employ musicians to make soundtracks. Canned sound is faster, cheaper, and that's what their production rooms are equipped to handle. But your local cable or public TV station might be interested in a music instructional program. If you have taught music previously, you may be qualified to host a show.

The key to interesting a TV producer is to have a well-thought-out plan. Stations are flooded with ideas for new shows, but few individuals take the time to package their proposals so they're attractive to the producer. She's busy with her own programs; she isn't interested in anything that she'll have to pamper and develop. That's where you come in!

First, you need an idea. What kind of a show could you host? How about "Guitar Playing Made Easy," "Reading by Notes," "Musical Games for Children," or "Rock Vocal Techniques?" Educational programs like these are what public TV—and especially cable—are searching for.

"Producers look for several things," said Jack Frost, production manager for the "Music Is" series made in 1977 at WETA, Washington, D.C. "Describe on paper what each show covers, one through ten, listing educational objectives, content, and the visual aspects—props, talent, guests, setting, and who the host is."

"Give an itemized estimated budget. Without that, a producer may not be on your same level of thinking. Explain who the target audience is, and how the show will help them."

Where can you find guidelines for putting together your proposal? The best place to look is at the station you're planning on presenting the proposal to. Ask for a copy of their preliminary program proposal guidelines. Most cable and public stations find it advantageous to hand these out to interested people.

"It's important that you mention how the show will help the station," said Frost. "Will it receive promotion? Maybe new viewers and subscribers? Tell them how they'll benefit."

Probably the best preparation you could provide is a completed half-hour script. A videotape of a pilot show will achieve the same thing, as long as the program is visually exciting. Otherwise, stick with a written script.

Back up the proposal with a personal biography, detailing musical qualifications. Any education credentials would also help. "Have a list of educators who will be willng to work on the project in an advisory capacity, to give it that stamp of authority," said Frost. "On the 'Music Is' program we had vast panels of experts who said, 'Here are the things this show must include to make it educationally valid.' "

You won't become an independently wealthy star by appearing on a local daytime public TV show once a week, but it can lead to bigger financial rewards. If the show is good enough and the station's behind you, try syndicating the program to other markets. This will yield a syndication re-use fee. Also, you'll become an acknowledged music expert in your own community, and receive offers for teaching, giving performances, sessions, and seminars, or helping out with other productions.

For Further Information . . .

If you're interested in maximizing studio income, you'll need to understand copying and arranging skills, and be able to write music clearly. Gerald Warfield's *How to Write Music Manuscript (in Pencil)*, David McKay Co., Inc., 2 Park Ave., New York NY, 10016, shows how to print neat copy and explains copyist rules. The book's understandable style makes it perfect for beginners to intermediates.

If you know the basics, you can expand your knowledge with *New Music Composition*, by David Cope, Schirmer Books, Macmillan Publishing Co., Inc., 866 Third Ave., New York NY 10022. Written as a college text, the book contains definitions, techniques, instrumentation, examples and lists additional works for study. Another good advanced book is *Music Notation: A Manual of Modern Practice*, by Gardner Read, Crescendo Publishing, 132 W. 22nd St., New York NY 10011.

If you'd like more information than your local TV stations can provide you with concerning forming your own music instructional program, write the Music Educators National Conference (MENC), 1902 Association Dr., Reston VA 22091, for a copy of Thomas H. Carpenter's *Televised Music Instruction*. Although it is written for TV in a classroom setting, it provides good tips on studio visual technique, program format, and details some interesting case studies of televised instruction.

• CHAPTER FIFTEEN •

How to Organize a Home Recording Studio

Why not record for free? Many musicians do. Recording in your own small studio is a lot of fun—vocalists and instrumentalists alike are infatuated with the idea of studio recording, of testing talent against tape. One clear taping can tell you more about your style, technique, and commercial potential than months of live performances. Having the facilities to record any time, without time reservations or rental fees, is a dream come true.

A private studio can cement your position as a local money-making musician, but naturally the idea deserves serious thought. Setting up your own studio is expensive, and furthermore, the benefits of having a studio in your garage might not coincide with your career direction. It's too big an investment in time and money to consider lightly.

The Studio as a Career Base

There may be no better place to base your musical interests than in a home studio. A studio has the potential to interrelate all of your different musical means of making money, thereby unifying your various career directions. The result is a very efficient use of your time, space, and investment capital. Look at these seven ways your studio can be put to use:

1. *You can rent time to musicians working on their own projects.* This is the most common source of income for small four and eight-track studios.

2. *You can produce soundtracks for local businesses, organizations, and associations.* This work is quite lucrative. Most studio owners don't actively pursue it because advertising agencies have superior sales tactics, and because the business doesn't come to the studio—you have to go out and find it.

This new tape deck by Fostex is typical of the growing commitment of audio manufacturers to developing new equipment specifically for home recording. The deck is the first of its kind to record 8 tracks on ¼-inch tape. This allows you many more recording options in an inexpensive tape format.

3. *You can use the studio as a rehearsal room for your live act.* This isn't a direct income source unless that the group pays you a rental fee, but it can save money. For example, rehearsing in a soundproofed studio assures that the group won't be forced by nagging neighbors to rent an expensive rehearsal house or industrial area warehouse.

4. *You'll record promo package cut tapes for free.* This is especially attractive for Top 40 acts since you've always got to have the latest hits on your cut tape.

5. *You'll record demo tapes to be mailed to music publishers, record producers, advertising agencies, audiovisual companies, managers, booking agents, play producers, and songwriter contests—for free.* Studio access is a must for songwriters, and with a home studio you can casually hone your songs to perfection—and the price is right!

6. *You can use the studio as a teaching room for students.* Some teachers working out of music stores do so because personal conflicts prevent them from bringing 50 students a week into their homes. A studio solves this, plus provides a soundproof barrier so that lessons aren't heard throughout the home. Innovative teachers also teach groups of students in all phases of studio operation, from how to mix down tapes to how to feel comfortable performing.

7. *You can record, mix, and master your own single or album.* This involves substantial amounts of time, so recording for free is increasingly important. Even if you don't consider your four-track studio capable of producing master quality material, the techniques you'll learn will reduce the time you need to rent when you go to a 16 or 24-track studio.

Managing your own studio will not be a matter of using the studio in each of these ways at different times. You'll be busier than that! Most small studios are used in four, five, or six of these ways *simultaneously*. It's not unheard of for the owner of a small studio to be rehearsing with his band from 11:00 a.m. to 2:00 p.m., copy someone else's finished tapes till 3:00 p.m., mix and produce a cut tape for a group until 6:00 p.m., eat dinner, teach a couple lessons, and just make it to the club by 9:00 p.m. A small home studio is a hub of activity.

Is It a Sound Investment for You?

Before answering this question, you need an idea of *how much* of an investment we're talking about. Remember, also, that most studios are not financed instantly with the wave of a wand. They're added to, component by component, panel by panel, until they're usable. Even then, the patchwork buying and construction continues.

I've seen four-track home studios in functional condition for under $1,500. No sweat. A limited investment like this is made possible by building some of your own electronic equipment and buying what you can't build used. More common is a four-track set-up for under $5,000, including equipment, construction materials, and maybe an old acoustic piano.

Next up is the "permanently modified" garage, either four or eight-track, with a few in-studio instruments besides the piano. This can cost $5,000 for construction, $5,000 for instruments, and $10,000 for electronic equipment. When musicians invest more than $20,000 or $30,000 in a studio, they usually move to a commercial location and concentrate full-time on studio operation in order to recoup their investment.

Question: Will investing in a studio help your career? You certainly don't want to spend $5,000 or $10,000 and let the place go unused. For such a large commitment to pay off, it's got to work for you. Do you play in a live act? If so, the studio will get plenty of use, but you won't make much—if any—money from it. You'll just save from doling out rental fees to other studios. Are you interested in mixing and producing cut tapes and demo tapes for *other* musicians? This requires learning some technical skills, but it'll pay the bills. Are you willing to record jingles "on spec" for local businesses? This requires songwriting ability and a feel for commercialism. Self-produced jingles can fill in dead studio time.

In short, do you plan a diversified career? *The more diversified, the more sense it makes to build a home studio.* Then the studio will be busting with business and earn you back your investment many times over.

If a studio sounds interesting, you'll have to set up a schedule for buying equipment, and begin saving money. You'll also need to consider where you're living. Do you plan to move in four months? Are you renting a house or apartment? A studio can easily be built in a rented residence, but it may not be as soundproof or as aesthetically pleasing as a permanent studio.

Don't Know AC from DC? No Problem!

The first time I stepped into a studio I was bewildered. Where did all those cords go? What were all those knobs for? As I was repeatedly exposed to studios, however, and learned the function of each electronic component, I became comfortable in the control room. Now I can tape at home and accurately predict the effects of direct mixing and noise control, and understand how to pinpoint a problem in a control room "logic chain."

You can, too. If you're willing to learn about electronics, you'll pick up concepts and theory without realizing it. It just comes with practice, by trial and error. Here are some quick definitions of studio components:

Semi-Professional Equipment

Virtually all home studios are outfitted with recording equipment specifically designed for musicians. This equipment combines the most desirable features of professional units, but sacrifices some durability and sound quality. Still, this is the newest market in audio equipment, so companies are rushing to introduce new units, while dropping list prices to just above what audiophile home stereo equipment costs.

Tape Recorders

When you begin planning your studio, your first decision will be what "track format" the studio will be capable of producing. Usually, more tracks = better sound = higher cost.

A cassette deck is usually a 2 channel (stereo), 4 track deck that plays $1/8$ inch wide tape. Two magnetic tracks run one direction; when the tape's done, you flip the cartridge over and the other two tracks play, record, or erase. The two main variables affecting sound quality are tape width and the speed at which the tape moves. The more space magnetic signals have to be recorded on the tape—created either by moving the tape faster or recording on a wider surface—the better the sound will be. Semi-professional recorders use the following formats: $1/4$ inch tape, 4 channel, 4 track; $1/4$ inch tape, 8 channel, 8 track; $1/2$ inch tape, 8 channel, 8 track; or 1 inch tape, 16 channel, 16 track. The most common tape speeds for semi-pro decks are 15 ips (inches per second, moving over the tape heads) or $7 1/2$ ips. Most home studios are based around 4 track or 8 track recorders, referred to as "multi-track" machines.

Mixing Console

The console, or "board," is the heart of any control room. Even a modest 8 track board may look imposing, but once you understand the controls for any one channel, you'll see that the multitude of knobs are just *repeated* for each channel, so it's really not that hard. Basically, the signal caught by the microphone is routed through the mixer, where, at your discretion, you can adjust volume, tone, position of the signal between right and left channels, and send the signal to the tape deck for recording, or back through monitors or headphones.

All these decisions—and more—affect the outcome of "the mix," or final mixdown, when you transfer what you've recorded on an 8 track or 4 track machine onto a 2 track stereo tape deck.

Microphones

A microphone has either a diaphragm or small ribbon, which is stimulated by a sound wave (like your voice or a piano). The sound wave is converted into an electrical signal, which is then transferred via cord to the mixer. A "pick-up" can be substituted for a mike by attaching it to an acoustic instrument, such as a guitar, flute, or drum shell. A "direct box" can be plugged into an electronic instrument and then into the mixer; thus eliminating the need for a microphone. A direct box won't pick up any "bleed through," or noise from other instruments being played simultaneously, so the job of mixing the instruments together will be easier.

Noise Reduction Units

Dolby, and especially DBX noise reduction systems, are commonly used in home studios to diminish high frequency "hiss," which can be easily heard when inexpensive tape or an inexpensive tape deck is used. Noise reduction is routed through the mixing board.

Signal Processing Units

Equalizers, compressors, limiters, expanders, reverb units, filters, and digital delays either add desirable effects or subtract undesirable frequencies during mixing. Because of cost, the home enthusiast may not own any of these, or have a small rack housing an equalizer, compressor, and digital delay, for example. Ideally, the initial recording is clean so hardly any signal processing is required.

Playback Monitors

In your control room, you'll need one pair of good speakers acoustically matched to the control room to insure a flat response. Then all frequencies can be heard equally while mixing. You should have an inexpensive pair, too, so you can hear what the final mix will sound like on an "average" stereo. Headphones for the musicians will also be needed so that they can conveniently monitor their instrument or voice as it sounds in relation to the other musicians or previously recorded tracks.

Art Versus Technology

When you record, you're blending artistry with technology. You're an artist when you perform the music, you're a technician when you capture the performance on tape. But often, the line dividing artistry and technology is not so clear. For instance, when a musician assumes control over the recording process, are his decisions based solely on technological aspects of recording? No. A great many of his decisions are musical considerations.

To record in your own studio, you need both skills. A technical genius with little or no "feel" for music won't get any business because he won't understand how to relate to the musicians, though he may be very efficient. A musician who can't operate the equipment to its maximum potential won't get customers, either. Even though he'll know what he wants to achieve, he won't know how to go about getting it. Since you're already a musician, you just need to acquire the technical know-how.

"The way you find out if you'll like it is to start fooling around with a stereo machine. Then you'll go on to four-track and so on," said a home studio owner. "You learn on your way up."

"You're constantly learning," said a drummer/studio owner. "Every once in a while I'm surprised that something works or sounds good."

If you've patched together P.A. systems and mixed your group's sound at live gigs, you'll be surprised by how much you already know. The rules are different—at live shows the surrounding acoustics dictate what you do—but much of the equipment is the same as that used in studio work.

Though "hands-on" experience is the usual method of learning how to record in your own studio, equipment manufacturers like TEAC, Altec, and Fostex sponsor seminars on home recording, and they also publish booklets of recording tips. Many local studios host in-house weekly recording classes, and a growing number of colleges offer courses on recording. Magazines like *Modern Recording & Music* and *Recording Engineer/Producer* carry articles on new equipment, new techniques, and explain how professional engineers and producers achieve their finished sound.

If you want to get going on building a studio immediately, but don't feel you have enough knowledge, consider teaming up with a friend who has the technical expertise you lack. He can be an investment partner, but this isn't necessary. Electronics people are usually delighted to help organize a home studio. They learn a lot, too!

One guitarist friend of mine has had considerable experience operating sound systems for live shows, but when he decided to set up a studio, he went in with a friend of his who had formal schooling in electronics and works for Hewlett-Packard Company. By jointly building and organizing, they have the artistic and technological skills needed to successfully run a home studio. (See photos on page 247.)

Baffling the Garage Studio

After you dcide to set up a studio, you'll have one major question to answer: Is it going to be temporary or permanent? Your answer will determine the extent of your investment, time and probably the quality of your studio environment and recorded sound.

The cost difference between a permanently modified room and a temporarily deadened room is substantial. "I went to an old building that was being torn down, and gave them $50 for as much carpet as they could pull up in two hours," said a guitarist who set up a temporary studio in his garage, carpeting the floor and each wall three times. He estimates his entire studio could be dismantled in a day.

If you are renting or living at home with your parents, you probably have no choice but to set up a temporary studio. A garage, because of size and relative isolation from the rest of the house, is the favorite choice. A large bedroom or den can also work. Common soundproofing materials are egg cartons, foam rubber, fiberglass insulation, blankets, and carpeting.

The main drawback of temporary studios is the lack of an adjoining control room. Properly mixing tracks is very difficult if you're in the same room with the live music instead of listening through monitors in a control room—hearing the instruments firsthand can really confuse your judgment. But a soundproof control room is difficult to build in a temporary studio, so either you sacrifice quality, or run lines to another room of the house. That's what a singer did: "I hung blankets all over the garage and ran a snake through the garage door, across the lawn, and into a bedroom. We had the monitors, amp, e.q., and board there. It turned out real good." To communicate, you'll either need telephones in each room, an intercom set-up, or a messenger running back and forth.

If you plan to build a permanent studio, your options increase. Books (listed at the end of this chapter) describe materials, diagram building procedures, and rate soundproofing effectiveness.

You should carefully consider studio arrangement before beginning construction. "I hate running in and out to answer the phone," said a guitarist/studio owner. "By having our band office here in the control room, I don't have to leave the room. We're totally self-contained."

If you can build a permanent studio, you'll want to construct a small but comfortable control room to house electronics. This can be a booth built right inside the garage or room, or a room immediately next to your studio, in which case you'll need to have a door connecting the two rooms and a glass window overlooking the studio from the control console. A laundry room next to the garage or basement is a favorite.

All doors will have to be soundproofed. Sometimes doors are simply "doubled"—two doors hinged in one doorway and opening independently of each other block sound very well.

Some studio owners try to get around installing a window between the two rooms, relying instead on buzzers, lights, or intercoms. They help, but a great deal of communication is nonverbal—expressions of positiveness, satisfaction, and rejection. Not having eye contact in a studio wastes time.

Some permanent designs are really a "room within a room," where you build new walls and a ceiling flush up against the existing basement or garage. Not only does this superbly baffle sound, it also looks clean and attractive. "I had a basic garage," said a drummer/studio owner, "so I added six inches of insulation and covered that with plasterboard. Then I added more insulation and another layer of plasterboard."

Most home studios are built without aesthetic considerations. Figure up how much time you'll spend in your studio between recording, rehearsals, and office work. Do you want to be cramped in a cold, dark dungeon? Make the rooms attractive. Rough-cut wood paneling absorbs sound well and looks great. Hang plants in the studio—they create a relaxing atmosphere and look beautiful. Lighting is usually overlooked, too. "Studios all have florescent or incandescent lighting. I'm sick of that! I'm putting two big skylights in this studio," said a bandleader.

Building portable, stand-up baffles made of wood, foam, and cloth is an easy way to help isolate instruments from each other and eliminate recording bleed-through. They are useful in both temporary or permanent studios.

After installing the majority of your insulation but before adding the final touches, have your band rehearse inside while you roam around outside the house with a dBa meter to test whether the sound penetrating your studio will make neighbors complain. Check with county or city officials for allowable levels (even though your neighbor's lawnmower exceeds it every Sunday morning) and add insulation if necessary.

Low Overhead, Quick Profits

To outfit your studio, follow the same buying philosophy recommended for outfitting your live act: the less initial investment, the quicker you'll be reaping profits. How much should you spend on equipment? The cost will easily exceed the amount of construction, though by how much is up to you.

First, decide what track format the studio will use, and what basic equipment you need, then give yourself plenty of time to buy selectively. Used studio components can generally be bought safely, including preamps, equalizers, noise reduction boxes, and compressors. Mixing boards, the center of any control room, should be carefully checked if bought used. The major component you are better off buying new is the tape recorder, since even machines that appear immaculate can hide a great deal of wear inside. But the buys are out there. People who buy semi-professional audio equipment don't go out and play ice hockey with it.

You'll need plenty of accessories, such as microphones, headphones, monitors, cords, patchcords, tapes, rolls of duct tape, some pillows, and padding cloth.

It's okay to get caught up in wanting the latest state-of-the-art equipment as long as you don't buy it. Next year's innovations will make this year's model obsolete, and a bargain for you.

The Service-Oriented Studio

"I really involve myself with whoever comes through, unlike studios I've recorded in," says a guitarist/studio owner. "Most studios are just like a big machine, cold and impersonal. You go in, watch the clock, get up-tight, and you can't play because you can't relax."

I've heard this echoed by many musicians who've bought time in larger 16 and 24-track studios. If you can provide better, more personal service, your small four or eight-track facility will prosper. Word-of-mouth is the advertising lifeline for a studio.

"I do more for them," says Bruce, the guitarist/studio owner. "If they want me involved in production, I'll dive right into it. I don't want anything going out of here that might reflect badly on the studio's capabilities. When they rent my studio, they're getting the facilities, an engineer, a producer, and any expertise or suggestions I can give—if they want them."

Musicians appreciate it if you show a sincere interest in their music. Help them with it. Seldom will a musician disregard your opinion unless he's had considerable studio experience himself. Most are eager for any advice you can offer.

Your biggest job, besides the actual taping, is making the musicians comfortable. They've got to feel good in order to perform well. Mood is easily transferred through tape: Some sessions sound dead while others sound alive. The best way I've found for relieving their anxiety is to set up a meeting several days before taping to introduce them to the studio, equipment, and procedures. This also gives you a chance to find out about their style—and learn what they'll expect from you.

"You've got to treat them special," says Kirt. "Otherwise, you lose return business."

Trading services for studio time is becoming increasingly popular. With money in short supply, it's no wonder! You'll receive offers for everything from plumbing or yard work to swapping amplifiers to art work for a band backdrop. One enterprising home studio owner I know made enough contacts with musicians to have the insulation, carpeting, and air conditioning work on his *new* studio completed before he moved into it!

Drum Up Your Own Business

For the musician with a home studio, writing, arranging, and recording advertising jingles to sell to local businesses takes on a whole new light. Suddenly your budget isn't determined by studio recording fees! This is a lucrative part-time job for many musicians.

You can enter the jingle field on your own or with your whole band.

Spend a couple of days intently watching TV or listening to radio to analyze the commercials. Make a list of the local businesses that advertise, and answer these questions for each business:

1. What is the style of background music in the ad?
2. Do the song lyrics directly mention the product's name, and if so, how many times?
3. Is the singer or announcer male or female?
4. What is the theme of the ad?
5. Was it a "hard-sell" or a "soft-sell" approach?
6. Does the ad use comedy or startling statements to capture attention?
7. What was the length of the ad?
8. Would you consider the music heavily produced?
9. Did you like the ad?

After you've analyzed the ads, try to come up with lyrics and a melody you think the advertiser would like to have his product associated with.

Record a nearly finished tape, with both lyrics and melody, and approach the owner with the tape. Would he be interested in listening to it? This is called working on speculation, since you are speculating that he *might* want to buy the advertisement. This is risky and will prove a poor use of your time if he says no, but this is the way you'll have to break into jingle recording. Eventually, if you analyze commercials carefully and sell a couple of recordings, these owners will call you whan they want a new ad. They might even have ideas for you. This is called working on assignment, since you are assigned (and paid in advance or guaranteed payment) to make a commercial.

It is important *not* to present a finished master tape on speculation, since advertisers will frequently want something altered. Just as important, if they reject the tape, you can go back in the studio and simply lay another vocal track over the same musical bed—then move on to the next advertiser!

When the jingle you worked day and night on for a week is rejected, it's not a rejection of you or your talent. It's just mismarketed, given to the wrong business. Someone in the community will love your work— you've just got to go out and find him!

Business owners who appear on their own advertisements (frequently the least professional ads) require special care when trying to sell them a commercial. They often have a large ego wrapped up in those ads, and are opposed to any suggestion that they quit, even though it would probably help the store. If you're writing an ad for a business whose commercials feature the owner, write the lyrics for him to read over your musical bed. He'll appreciate your recognition of him as *the* company spokesperson (just don't laugh until you're out of the office!).

As a final enticement for trying your ear at making jingles, they pay very well. Five hundred dollars is low, and for a local business to pay $1,500 to $3,000 for a finished 60-second spot is commonplace.

For Further Information . . .

You might try looking in the local library for a copy of Jeff Cooper's *Building a Recording Studio*, Recording Institute of America Press, that is now out of print. Of particular value is Cooper's listing of dB reduction for various types of insulating materials.

Another worthwhile book that is more recent is *Home Recording for Musicians*, by Craig Anderton, Guitar Player Books, available from Music Sales Corp., 33 W. 60th St., New York NY 10023. Besides showing you how to squeeze a recording studio into your closet, Anderton specifies how to build several components you'll need in the control room.

Home Recording Studio

Most home studios are outfitted with recording equipment that includes the most desirable features of professional units and costs just a little more than top-of-the-line home stereo equipment. (all photographs by Jim Dearing.)

Soundproofing around cracks and doors is tough but important. One way to solve this is to double up all doors leading into the studio.

In this permanently modified garage studio (Trullion Studio, Sacramento, California), the sound control booth was built *inside* the garage since an adjoining room wasn't available for conversion.

A nice way to block out a noisy hot water heater. Vents above and below the entry hatch allow the pilot light to remain lit.

A ceiling was constructed to soundproof the top of this garage. Things previously stored here are now kept up above.

• CHAPTER SIXTEEN •

WHY LET ALL THAT EQUIPMENT SIT AROUND?

Musicians are notorious for accumulating considerable inventories of instruments and electronic equipment. When you go to buy a new amplifier and are shocked to learn your old amp will only bring $100 in trade, you tend to buy the new amp and keep the old one. It's the same with keyboards, P.A. mains, mixers, and guitars.

I've met some musicians who put the old equipment to work for them by renting it out. Then after several rental fees they've made back what the store offered them as a trade-in, and they still own the equipment.

Renting out equipment is also an option for musicians whose home studios aren't yet fully operational. Once their facilities are complete they usually find it's more convenient to keep their studio equipment "in-house," but often will continue renting out extra P.A.s or spare amps to help pay the bills.

Defining Your Rental Market

Many people are involved with sound rentals on a full-time basis, but they're not working musicians. Since you're an active musician, renting equipment will only be a part-time job.

When I ask musicians if they've considered renting equipment, most scoff at the idea, replying they don't own enough to rent. But how much do you really need? You won't be miking Shea Stadium! A group of high school musicians may consider your old Shure Vocal Master P.A. the answer to their dreams. More experienced bands won't need your old P.A. but they'd rent your home studio's digital delay for $30 a night. No matter how limited your inventory of sound equipment, someone is willing to rent it. You've just got to advertise to the right people. Tell your musician friends, place cards on music store bulletin boards, buy inexpensive classified ads in local musician, college, or weekly newspapers, and consider running an ad in the Yellow Pages.

Working with a limited amount of equipment means you'll have to turn down a lot of offers. Your Vocal Masters won't cover Shea, let alone an average bar. "That's been important to my success," says Dave, a guitarist who runs his own sound company. "I ask a lot of questions, and if necessary, go out to the place to see if it's beyond the capability of my equipment or my ability as a soundman. Accepting a job you can't handle is the worst thing you can do for your reputation."

For rentals, your reliability and integrity are paramount. "Bad news travels fast" warns one renter. He's right. Among musicians, word-of-mouth is the primary means of getting business.

There is also a great demand for sound rentals from nonmusicians. The people staging business conventions, banquets, audiovisual presentations, large parties (remember mobile discos?), and political rallies always need a sound system, but rarely ever have their own. They do the most convenient, logical thing: Flip to the Yellow Pages in a hurry and call a sound rental company.

There are two ways you can rent equipment. You can either rent the equipment by itself, or you can rent the equipment *and* your professional services.

Renting Equipment Without You

If you're in a full-time group, you won't have time for much—if any—sound engineering. Some jobs are scheduled during daytime hours, but most events are held at night, when you'll be performing with your group. So any rental business you'll pursue probably won't include your services as a sound technician. There are a few problems with this approach.

First of all, most people who rent sound systems also want a sound technician to set it up, operate it, and tear it down. This limits your potential clients to musicians who feel comfortable running the sound themselves.

Second, since you're performing full-time, you'll be using your best equipment at the gigs, so you'll need a backlog of equipment available for rent.

Perhaps the most important disadvantage is advertising. If a band rents your equipment and doesn't get a good sound, those musicians, as well as others in the audience, will make a mental note not to rent from you, despite the fact it was their inability to operate the equipment that caused the problem. This severely damages your reputation.

To have confidence in your equipment's performance ability, it must be well-maintained. You won't be on the scene where it's being used, so you won't be available to repair or replace a part. Every five to six jobs, sit down with the equipment and hook it all up. Are there any trouble spots, any shorts or blown fuses? The most common trouble area is the yards and yards of cable used to connect the system together. Sight-check every solder and screw-down connection, and every terminal point. Look for wires that might be broken, loose, or disconnected. Another common trouble area is the diaphragms in horns and speakers, which can be damaged when the system is overdriven. Listen for a crackling sound, which indicates a bad diaphragm.

As an owner, your business objective is to place the risk of damaged equipment on the renter. Ideally, you'll know the people you'll be renting to, or trust them, but even this is no guarantee that something won't be broken, blown out, lost, or stolen.

"I got some legal advice and drew up a contract that specifically holds the renter responsible for any unusual wear and tear, and for any damage," says John, a bandleader who rents gear (see Figure 16.1). If you'll be renting out equipment often, you should also consider buying insurance, that will cover both liability and full dollar replacement value.

Insist on full payment *in advance*. When the gig's over, all your leverage is gone. "Hey," says Dave, "if they can't come up with the rental fee in advance, what reason do you have to believe they'll be able to pay you afterwards?" You can speculate on a gig with promoters or a band, but realistically appraise your chances by examining advance ticket sales and checking to make sure the promoters are committed to aggressive advertising. Many small concerts or nightclub jobs flop miserably in ticket sales.

To further protect your investment, you should require that renters fill out a comprehensive credit report listing land, house, auto ownership, and references. It's common for people to question the necessity of this, but if they refuse, you should likewise question whether they're going to skip town with your equipment. Call their former employers and ask about their trustworthiness. Check the Yellow Pages for credit associations that will provide you with a credit check if you can't get in touch with employers or you have other reasons to be suspicious. The renter should pay for the credit check.

COMPANY NAME
ADDRESS
PHONE

RENTAL AGREEMENT

Please Print

Date _____ Previous Application   Yes ☐   No ☐
Phone _____ Authorized by _____
Rate _____ Month ___ day ___ week (circle 1)

Name _____

Address _____ Apt. No. _____

City _____ How Long At This Address _____

MAKE	INSTRUMENTS (including all accessories and cords)	SERIAL	MODEL	STOCK NO.	VALUE	RENTAL RATE EA.

The undersigned hereinafter known as Rentor hereby rents from [Company Name] the above described instrument(s), the agreed upon value of which is $_____. Rentor agrees to pay rent in the sum of $_____ in advance of the 1st day of each and every month commencing _____, 19____ and continuing until said instrument(s) is/are returned to [Company Name]. Receipt of the first and last month's rent in the amount of $_____ is hereby acknowledged by [Company Name]. The further sum of $_____ (10% of agreed upon value of instrument(s) is hereby deposited with [Company Name] which amount shall be refunded to Rentor in the event that said instrument(s) is/are returned in good working condition. [Company Name] shall have the right to inspect said instrument(s) upon its/their return and shall, in its sole discretion, determine whether or not said deposits shall be refunded. Rentor shall bear the entire risk of loss, theft, destruction or damage of said instrument(s) from any cause whatsoever. No loss or damage shall relieve Rentor of the obligation to pay rent. In the event of loss or damage, Rentor shall, at the option of [Company Name] (a) Replace same with like instrument(s) in good condition and repair (b) pay to [Company Name] the agreed upon value of the instrument(s) plus the total rent due and owing at the time of said payment. Without the prior written approval of [Company Name] Rentor shall not assign, transfer, pledge or otherwise dispose of said instrument(s) or rental agreement. Neither shall Rentor permit said instrument(s) to be used by anyone other than Rentor. Rentor shall not remove said instrument(s) from this county. If Rentor fails to pay rent or any other amount when required or if Rentor fails to perform any other condition of this agreement, [Company Name] shall have the right to any or all of the following remedies: (1) Take possession of said instrument(s) wherever same may be located, without any court order or other process of law and occasioned by such taking of possession. (2) Recover the sum of all rent due plus any other sums due by the terms of this agreement. (3) In the event of repossession, [Company Name] may sell said instrument(s) and apply the net proceeds to any sums owing by Rentor. (4) Lessor shall pay [Company Name] all costs and expenses, including attorney's fees, collection agency fees, and other expenses incurred in enforcement of this agreement. (5) [Company Name] may pursue any other remedy available by law or in equity. All payments 10 days past due or more are subject to a service charge of 5% per month, not to exceed $5.00 on any individual payment. Rentor acknowledges having read all the above provisions and agrees to be bound by said terms and conditions.

_____ Sign _____

Cosigner _____ Our Previous Address _____ How Long _____
Spouse's Name _____ Position _____ Salary _____ How Long _____
Spouse's Place of Employment _____ Driver's License No. _____ Car License No. _____ Signer's Age _____
Signer's Social Security No. _____ Address _____ Bus. Phone _____ How Long _____
Signer Employed by _____ Earnings _____ Other Income _____ Badge No. _____
Position _____ Year _____ If buying who is legal owner _____
Make of Car _____ Branch _____ Check _____ Savings _____
Bank _____ Relationship _____ Address _____ Phone _____
Nearest Relative _____   Active Credit Cards _____

Monthly Payment
Plan Accounts (1) _____ (2) _____ (3) _____
Landlord _____ Address _____ If Buying List Mortgage Co. _____
Personal References: IS THIS APPLICATION COMPLETE?
1.   Please double check . . . .
2.

Adding Your Services to the Package

If you're only performing part-time, you might have enough nights open to rent yourself with your equipment. Most renters want you to provide a sound technician, and by handling the equipment yourself, you avoid the complications of equipment-damage contracts and credit reports.

What skills will you need to mix sound for events? You've got a head start on most people because you're a musician. You understand the subtleties of music. You're sensitive to mood and dynamic changes. Sound technicians with a strictly electrical background lack this musical sense. On the other hand, musicians often lack the technological skills needed to run a sound system. A sound technician must be able to quickly and routinely patch together a system. By repetitive on-the-job experience, the task becomes faster and easier. Nevertheless, it's the nature of a complex electric system set up hurriedly to have problems.

"It's always something," says a 17-year veteran of live sound engineering. I never expect the system to sound perfect when I turn it on. Lots of times it won't even click on. I try to anticipate problems because something always needs to be fixed."

The best way to become proficient at operating your equipment is to think of the electronic interaction as a "logic chain." In the simplest chain, your signal originates at the microphone, is transmitted to the mixer, then to the power amp, where it may go through processing devices (such as a graphic equalizer), and then from the power amp it's transmitted to the speakers.

"After doing it for awhile," says Dave, "you begin to recognize where in your logic chain something has gone wrong." You'll then have to repair it, replace it, or reroute your chain to circumvent the trouble area. Though you don't need a comprehensive knowledge of circuitry, knowing the basics of positive and negative cables and being able to use a soldering iron and replace fuses is necessary. Hauling along a spare amp is recommended if you have one.

Manufacturers such as Fostex, Altec, and TEAC sponsor touring recording seminars that are a good investment. These deal mostly with studio operations, but the studio mixing concepts apply directly to live stage mixing. *Modern Recording Magazine,* The *Sound Engineering Magazine,* and *Modern Recording & Music* are consistently good sources for new products, recording and mixing information, and do-it-yourself projects.

Because so many things can go wrong in setting up a P.A. system, the job can be very frustrating. This means sound technicians should keep their cool on the job. Someone with a bad temper can put an icy freeze on the performers.

"Don't let a blown speaker faze you," advises John. "I try to lay down a groundwork of confidence, assuredness, and goodwill. Then even when that speaker blows, the guy who's hired me will give me a little encouragement and stay out of my way."

The most important question is: "Will this meet my hourly wage?" Since you're renting a limited amount of equipment, rates won't be very high. If you're only renting the gear, most clients will be able to afford the rates, but when you have to work six to nine hours yourself, the majority of the fee will be going towards paying for your time—not the equipment. Seventy-five dollars isn't bad, but your hourly wage will suffer. You'd do better making jingles or teaching students.

"It's a long day," said Dave. "We're the first people there, most of the pressure is on us to make things happen, we rarely hear a 'thank you,' and we're the last people to leave."

What, then, should you charge? I know musicians who'll do a job for $40 and others who need $150 to come out. Certainly, you can ask a lot less if the client has his own sound person.

A good rule is to be very selective of the jobs you take. Estimate how much work they'll entail—not just how much equipment will be needed. A sound gig for a local rock band may pay $200, but if they've got eight musicians and five vocalists, you're going to be pulling your hair out. A small banquet may only pay $60, but all you need to do is set up one mike, kick back, and relax.

• CHAPTER SEVENTEEN •

THE AGENT-MUSICIAN

We've looked at ways of getting more money for your band (negotiating), adding to band income (equipment rentals, studio work), and even supplanting band income with other primary job opportunities (private and public teaching). Now comes a way to vastly increase your wage: Book yourself into casual gigs, and *then* throw a group together for the performances.

After operating as an agent, some musicians I know can't decide if they are a "musician-agent" or an "agent-musician." If they stick with it, most agree on "agent-musician," since the agent work dictates when and where they'll work as musicians. Eventually, this career trend may carry them into more ambitious booking, management, and promotional ventures, though away from performance.

Turn $50 into $300—In One Hour!

"Well, Andy, all we can afford is $400."

Andy didn't even shrug. "No problem. I'll get you a great dance band for that," he said.

It was December, and the Bank of America wanted a band for a Christmas party. Bank of America! Why didn't Andy negotiate up to $750 or $1,000? Because he's not that greedy. He knows when *not* to push a good thing too far.

Andy is more than the agent. He's also the band leader, so he calculated what his expenses would be—a guitarist and drummer at $50 apiece—while on the phone, and agreed. He made $300 that night.

"That's the best thing about casuals," said Robbie, a guitarist. "All they want to hear are rock standards. I played a senior ball last month for

$1,500. I hired three other guys, $150 apiece, and rented a smoke machine and tuxedos. I cleared over $800 *myself*."

The concept of the limited agent—a musician who operates an agency to find himself gigs—is an old one. It's been going on for years. You act as an agent without disclosing that you're *also* the musician (because, as mentioned in Chapter 9, many employers think music and business are mutually exclusive). With more casual jobs available than ever before, it's surprising more musicians don't jump on the bandwagon.

Seventeen states currently regulate booking agents. New York, California, and Michigan have the toughest standards. These are imposed to limit "fly by night" characters who skip town without paying you your money. In California, for instance, agents not only are licensed and bonded, but are also required to operate out of a separate business office. For a musician5than ever before,
it's surprising more musicians don't jump on the bandwagon.

Seventeen states currently regulate booking agents. New York, California, and Michigan have the toughest standards. These are imposed to limit "fly by night" characters who skip town without paying you your money. In California, for instance, agents not only are licensed and bonded, but are also required to operate out of a separate business office. For a musician who wants to work as an agent-musician, this is uneconomical, since he can't work out of his house. Paying rent will wipe out his profit! If your state regulates agent activity, you'll probably do better to *only* book bands you play in. Then you can't be considered an agent, since you are not representing other acts. If your state doesn't restrict agents, you're free to book yourself and other acts.

The main condition of working as an agent-musician is you can't be in a full-time or even a part-time band. The other members will tell you where to go if you net six times as much money as they do. On your own you can freely contract musicians to play. Since you'll usually be able to offer them better than average wages (casuals pay well), they'll be glad you called, and you'll earn the bulk of the money with no obligations to be "fair".

Many musical jobs complement this lifestyle. Careers in private teaching and studio recording both allow you to play casuals at night, as do renting out studio time, renting P.A. equipment, or performing as a church musician.

Your goals as an agent-musician differ significantly from those of a standard agent. She's trying to book bigger and better rooms, corner exclusive representation of artists, and hopes to make it big by one of her clients becoming a star. You want to use your agency to line up casual bookings as a very profitable way of performing. The musicians you hire just back you up.

What Background Will You Need?

Tuesday morning was unusually busy for Liana. A young man called at 10:00 a.m. sharp. Do you know of any ukulele players, he asked. Why yes, she replied, she just happened to know of an excellent musician who sang, played ukulele, and would even arrive in Hawaiian apparel.

The second call came 20 minutes later. An older woman was looking for a flamenco guitarist for her daughter's wedding reception. Did Liana happen to know of any? Well, as a matter of fact, yes, she did.

Liana answered her third call at 11:15. A committee staging a rally for a freeze on the nuclear arms build-up needed a band. They could afford $300. Could she recommend anyone? I book a great blues band, she answered, and sewed up her third job by 11:30—just in time for a lunch break.

"The blues group is so easy to throw together," she said, "but I'd better learn some new material. If I sing "House of the Rising Sun" or "Born in Chicago" one more time, I'll go crazy."

To be a successful agent-musician, like Liana, you need to play several instruments in many different styles. If you aren't versatile, you'll end up turning down three-fourths of the calls you receive. You should be a lead singer, since many requests are for solo acts. Singing all the leads yourself also puts the responsibility for the act squarely on your shoulders. That's good. As long as you know all the vocals, the instrumentalists you hire can concentrate on following you—something an experienced player won't have any trouble doing.

An agent-musician needs an incredibly extensive repertoire. The number of songs you know lyrics and music to is the major factor for accepting or rejecting jobs, or finding another act to play the engagement. Liana's flamenco guitar job was two hours long, so she had to know *at least* two hours' worth of flamenco-style material. Frequently a performer is asked to stay longer for a quickly renegotiated price. With some styles of music (flamenco among them) you can stretch pieces much longer than they were intended by improvising. These styles—usually older material—suit agent-musicians well, since they can't rehearse this material much. They need many more songs on instant recall than can possibly be rehearsed at one time.

You should read music and have charts to pass out to the musicians you hire. If the people you hire can read music, and you've got the charts, the sound will be much tighter at the performance.

Do you get the impression you're not capable of working as an agent-musician? Remember, you can't be in a band. And not only must you be a very good and versatile musician, you must also have enough experience performing to have accumulated a large mental library of material. It doesn't happen overnight. But that's why you should be aware of this technique for getting jobs. In a few years, you might have enough experience to make it work.

You'll need some agent personality traits. You're selling the other party on an act, so you have to be a good salesperson. Sounding dull and uninterested in your worst monotone voice will turn customers off. They'll call another agency.

Always sound perfectly confident of whatever act you're recommending. You won't have any trouble making other acts sound professional, but be especially careful of downgrading yourself. Referring to the act you're secretly going to put together as "part-time," "almost professional," or "a little rusty," assures you won't get their business. *Sell* that image!

But on the other hand, be careful not to accept jobs you can't handle. As with equipment rentals and private teaching, word gets around, and that's the fastest way to ruin your reputation.

Any agent-musician needs a full personal phone book of other musicians. After Liana received the call for a band, she systematically phoned bassists, pianists, and drummers until she reserved the players she needed to round out her blues band. You'll need the names of musicians who—like yourself—are long-time pros and know most every song that ever came out. Musicians who need rehearsals won't cut it for this kind of work; they've got to be able to pick it up *immediately*. As you play, you'll meet the experienced musicians who can do this. When you do, get their phone numbers!

The Bandleader Extraordinaire

Besides projecting confidence and actively selling your act while dealing as an agent, you'll have to be a forceful leader on and off stage. Here's the onstage personality you'll have to assume:

1. *Be dynamic.* You're the whole show. If some of the musicians you've hired are good entertainers, all the better, but you can't count on them. They'll have their attention riveted to beginnings, chord changes, and endings since the show hasn't been rehearsed. Plan on being the audience's focal point.

Be energetic—act lively! Move around onstage. In no other situation do you have to be more of an entertainer, since the music won't sound as tight as a steadily working band.

2. *Be talkative.* Keep your face in the microphone. Say *everything*. Witty monologue is crucial to satisfying customers.

3. *Be assertive.* You set up the gig and organized the band. You're the link keeping the chain together. The other musicians may never even

have met before. Direct everything onstage—no one else is going to do it! You make all the decisions.

While off-stage, before the show, on breaks, or talking to employers, you must be the sole band representative (since this isn't really a band, none of the other musicians will even know what to say). You're the band leader now, not the agent. The only person—besides you and the band—who will know you're also the agent will be the employer. As long as you sound good and put on a good show, he won't care. Ask the musicians not to mention that this is just a collection of musicians and not a steady band. It's their gig, too.

Target Your Employers

Flip through your marketing research sheets and pull out all the organizations, associations, and businesses that hire musicians for casuals. Include caterers and any other services that might get entertainment requests for weddings or parties.

Now analyze your musical strong points. What instruments can you play? What styles of music do you prefer? This should narrow your list, although the more instruments you can play in different styles the better.

Let's say you're a keyboardist. You've got an electric Yamaha grand piano, a Crumar synthesizer, and a tape deck. Your mother made you take piano lessons, so you played lots of classical compositions. Then in high school you learned jazz piano, joined a rock band, and played Top 40 material for two years.

As an agent-musician, you've got several ways of billing yourself:
1. Classical pianist (with strings from the Crumar prerecorded on the deck).
2. Jazz pianist.
3. Easy listening music soloist.
4. Pop pianist (with or without a drummer; you play bass lines on the Crumar).

If you sing well, opportunities *triple*. This combination is perfect for wedding ceremonies and receptions and countless social gatherings.

After you figure out your own strong points, ask yourself *who* is likely to buy this kind of entertainment. Most agent-musicians find it easier to cater to an older crowd, since they already know the songs this age group enjoys. Other musicians will know them, too. A crowd of 21-year-olds will want the latest hits, and these are impossible to play without rehearsing. Pick audiences who will enjoy the music you learned a long time ago.

The single best place to advertise is the Yellow Pages. Think about it. If your mother had to organize a wedding reception, she'd probably look first for a caterer, and then call a talent agency for entertainment. Our pianist would ideally pay for a small ad reading, "Midwest Talent Agency: classical, jazz, easy listening, pop music for weddings, parties." Listing yourself as an agency along with the full-time agents provides you with a year-long ad in every home in the county.

Playing the Agency Game

If you are talented and experienced enough to work as an agent-musician, you'll still have to decide whether you will advertise as an agent but only book yourself, thus not become an actual agent, or if you will advertise as an agent and represent other acts besides youself, thus becoming a legitimate agent. If you decide to become a real agent, be prepared to spend an incredible amount of time with the agency to make it pay for itself (especially if you're planning on renting an office and employing a secretary). You'll need to keep up on all the current band information in town and maintain lists of groups who are willing to play casuals. Agenting is easily a full-time job, and chances are it will steal a considerable amount of time away from musical jobs. It's a different lifestyle. If this is what you choose, be sure to inquire about a license from your state labor commission. Your musician's union will also be interested in the business, asking for a regular "agency operating fee." As with most musician employers outside of the three recording industry centers, however, small agencies generally pay little heed to the AFM.

If you decide to only book yourself, acting as an agent-musician, you'll probably want to set up shop in your home. An agent lives by the phone, so the first thing you'll need is a business line. Trying to juggle business and personal calls is ridiculous. Potential employers are bound to be greeted by your eight-year-old son, who doesn't quite sound convincing as a professional secretary. Get a separate business phone so that everyone knows when it's a client on the line, and little Mikey won't slobber all over the receiver. Answering machines are inexpensive and a professional addition to your business.

When you're talking on the phone with a client, the house should sound like an office. You don't need to play a tape of prerecorded typewriter clatter in the background, but a nice, calm atmosphere will give the impression that you're in an office. If you're married, maybe you can talk your spouse into answering the business phone in a pleasant secretarial voice. Believe it or not, it all helps, and people expect to pay more for professionalism.

One of the reasons experienced musicians can make very good money as agent-musicians is that they already have contacts built up over the years with employers. If an employer unfamiliar with you calls seeking a band, she's not going to want to hire the act before she's heard it. She can't "come out to the club," since you're not playing any clubs. Because of this, you need a demo tape ready to mail for each style of act you book yourself in. When sending band tapes, explain that there have been some personnel changes since the tape was made, but the group sounds as good as ever. Our hypothetical keyboardist would have four tapes displaying his classical, jazz, easy listening, and pop styles.

• CHAPTER EIGHTEEN •

CHECKING OUT CHURCHES

Here is a musician employer you might have overlooked. Churches offer many full-time and part-time job openings for musicians. And before you pass up this opportunity, get two things straight: not all churches require that you be a church member or profess the church's beliefs; and the role of the church musician is evolving faster than ever before, expanding into nontraditional instrumentation and music styles.

Come All Ye Faithful!

Two types of people get involved in church music programs. The first joins the program out of duty to the church; the second joins the church out of duty to the music program. For the former, the situation is especially pleasant. "There's more involved than money," said a church pianist. Indeed, if you are a regular church-goer, getting involved in the music program is your contribution to the church. Any money earned is a fringe benefit.

For the other person, involvement in a church music program is a matter of economics. It's either worth your time investment or it isn't. Fortunately, most ministers realize the importance of music in their churches, so music budgets can be quite large.

Virtually all churches of all denominations rely on music to inspire their congregations and breathe life into their services. Best of all, this is a growing field. Many books have been written on church choir directing and liturgical music, and several informative periodicals for the church musician are available (see "For Further Information").

The paying positions available in churches aren't easily definable; yet "choir director" and "organist" are probably the two most common job

You should be good at inspiring people if you want to direct a church choir, since most choirs are volunteer. Section leaders, organists, and other instrumentalists may be paid a salary, however, along with the director.

(photograph by Ellen Forsyth)

titles. The choir director is primarily responsible for rehearsing and presenting the church choir. Her duties—in a church that doesn't employ a "minister of music" or "music director"—include picking selections to teach the choir, rehearsing an instrumental ensemble, and maybe even composing music herself. The organist is traditionally the main accompanyist for the choir, performing selections picked by the choir director. Larger churches may hire a music director or minister of music to coordinate the overall music program with the church's activities. Music directors are also in charge of arranging special concert series for the congregation, and developing new performance formats.

Less time-consuming jobs are available as "singer/choir section leader," who is in charge of arranging parts for the singers within his section and delegating solos, and "instrument accompanyist," who must be able to read sheet music given to her by the choir director.

Ministers are always on the lookout for multi-talented people who combine musical talent with business or youth leadership skills. "It's very popular to go through a theological seminary specializing in both music and youth," said a music director. Frequently in smaller churches or churches with limited budgets, an organist will direct the choir and pick musical selections. A larger, well-established church may employ a full-time minister of music, full-time choir director, and pay organist, pianist, flautist, and several singers part-time salaries.

Performing as a church musician acts as subliminal advertising for many singers and instrumentalists alike. The offers they receive to perform at banquets, weddings, or funerals often outearn their church income. "My congregation is so large that offers to play at private gatherings never really slacken. They've seen me play every Sunday, so I'm the first one they think to ask," said an organist.

Approaching the Altar

There's more than one way to get hired by a church. Compare the following examples:

John was a substitute grammar school teacher. He played piano, organ, and guitar at home as a hobby. Even though he had never performed in public as a musician, a friend recommended that he audition for a recently vacated music director position at a nearby church. "I wasn't that nervous because I never believed I'd get the job. I wasn't even sure I wanted it," John said. He was immediately offered the dual position of music director and youth coordinator, which he accepted. "I'm sure my teaching experience had as much to do with it as my musical ability," he said.

Dottie volunteered to play organ for her church as a way of being religiously involved while keeping her keyboard technique sharp. Eventually, dissatisfaction with the unimaginative selections the director handed her prompted action. "I'll play at evening mass" (which was unpopular with the congregation) "if I can choose my own selections," Dottie offered the pastor. Soon Dottie's evening mass was more popular then the music director's morning mass! "I was named head liturgy coordinator," she said, "and that paved the way for me to move on to other churches."

These examples illustrate the two most common methods of getting a job as church music director, choir director, or organist: Either someone in the church recommends you to the minister (word of mouth), or you join the music program as a volunteer and climb up within the program. There are other ways, too. If a minister isn't able to fill a vacancy from within his congregation, he'll advertise and audition applicants. Many choir directors and organists are hired just before the Christmas and Easter seasons, as desperate ministers rush to throw together a special music presentation. "I got my first job by walking up to the minister and saying, 'Hey, you could use a folk choir. May I help?" said a music director.

The qualifications for becoming a church music director are divided between musical ability, knowledge of vocal harmony, liturgy, and hymnody, and communicative skills. Perhaps the most important of these is how well you communicate, and whether you can keep a whole choir happily singing. "The right education helps," said a music minister, "but I've seen a lot of people make it without it, and the ones with the schooling occasionally blow it because they were locked into the rules and forgot about the people they were working with."

Since most directors have a volunteer choir, you're actually working with them more than directing them. Will you be able to handle the obstinate 70-year-old who's been in the choir since the church first opened, along with the 18-year-old newcomer to the area? Quipped a preacher, "You need enthusiasm and a good night's sleep!"

Whether directing, singing, or playing an instrument, musical ability—especially on keyboards—is required. Get as much performance time as you can. Can you play several instruments and sing too? If so, you're worth more money to a church. Grab any opportunities to lead school choirs or bands. Probably the best musical preparation is to perform in a church choir yourself. Then you can judge firsthand how much this style of music appeals to you.

Check church music magazines for lists of workshops and seminars you can attend to learn more about religious music education. Colleges offer classes in harmony, hymnody, music history, choral and instrumental conducting, and music theory. A degree in music looks fantastic on a job application.

Learn a variety of skills—communication, education, business, and creative arts experience or degrees all increase your value to churches. If you can handle many different jobs, you'll save the church money—because they won't have to hire additional staff.

All churches strive to interest young people in their programs. Youth is a church's future. If you are qualified as singer, instrumentalist, or director, and also young, you are valuable to the church because ministers know that just one young choir member—or better yet, a young director—can quickly lead to several more young members as the others sense that it's "okay" to be in the choir.

Organizing Your Weekly Program

Techniques for picking music, rehearsing your choir and/or instrumentalists, and presenting the show vary according to whether you're working with four singers or 1,200 (or any number in between). It's a good idea to be hospitable at rehearsals, but hors d'oeuvres for 1,200 is beyond the call of duty. With that in mind, let's look at how choir directors of 12 to 60 singers, along with instrumental accompaniment, arrange their weekly presentations.

One of the challenges of directing is to blend traditional church music with contemporary classical music. "The young members especially get bored with the same old sounds," said a director/organist. "But they're just awestruck by Bach."

The amount of church music available is overwhelming. How do you narrow down your choices for each week? Here are some simple rules to follow:
  1. Check the liturgical calendar. Does the selection match the season you're in?
  2. Ask the minister what the scripture reading will be about. Does the selection match or complement his homily theme?
  3. Will the selection wake up the congregation? Are there elements of rejoicing present (if the season is one of rejoicing)?
  4. Is the selection musically worthy?
  5. Can the choir and/or instrumentalists pull it off?
  6. Will they be able to learn it in time to perform it?

After deciding which selections you want, you'll learn one of the frustrating aspects of directing a church music program: Unless your church can afford to pay the entire choir, you'll have to compromise between what you want to do musically and what your volunteer choir is willing to do. You'll be able to sense how far you can push your group after you've spent some time together, and you know their personalities. "You need a lot of patience when working with volunteer choirs," said Lynn, a university music instructor who conducts a church choir. "You need to feel the right pacing, when to push or slack off, and use a little psychology and common sense." You may be the only professional in the whole bunch!

You'll probably have to forgo any homework assignments, vocal drills, or individual rehearsal. They'll do it if they want to! If a selection is unusually difficult, introduce it to the group long before you want to perform it so they'll have several rehearsals to learn it. Asking them to cram the week of the Christmas Eve service is probably futile.

Most church choirs rehearse once a week for one and a half to three hours. Try to keep it light. A volunteer won't put up with drudgery for long. "Keep them happy," says Dottie. "I always feed my choir. It's the little things—common courtesies—that count. You can get so caught up in what the good book says as well as the rules of music that you'll forget the individuals who are making your music possible."

A good—albeit sneaky—way to squeeze in another rehearsal is to request that everyone show up 45 minutes early Sunday morning. This will give you a 30-minute review before the service.

Try placing the choir and instrumentalists in various spots in the church; their impact on the congregation can be heightened by thoughtful positioning. In some small churches with very "live" acoustics, a 30 to 40-person choir can be too loud if they stand too close to the congregation. On the other hand, expansive churches with the choir positioned above in a loft can cause problems. "We can't make the people feel like a part of the music," complained a choir director. "We're 200 feet away! Even though we know what's happening down there, we still feel like we're looking through a pair of binoculars." Ideally, the singers and musicians should feel like part of a circle that includes the minister and the congregation.

Staffing Your Choir

Much of your time will be spent encouraging church members to join the choir. You have to make it sound fun and exciting! Post signs and make announcements of special activities the choir is planning, such as softball games or picnics. Schedule field trips to religious workshops or college religious music recitals. Younger church members need more than a sense of fulfilling their duty to the church—they need to be enticed. Recruitment is an ongoing part of all church music programs.

Occasionally, however, you'll run into the opposite problem. How do you get rid of someone, say, a tone-deaf fledgling singer? Luckily, churches can always use volunteers in some capacity, so in a tactful, diplomatic way, ask them to provide some other service. Suggest something specific so they won't feel too rejected. You can only go as fast as the slowest person in the group.

There's plenty of room for musical growth in most church programs. In your haste to "modernize" your church, think about how little church music has changed over hundreds of years; there's a strong, firmly rooted resistance to change. Even Bach is a little adventurous for some churches, and guitars and flutes may be downright prohibited.

The way to win over the minister and his congregation is to make very subtle changes. The changes can be in the selections you pick or the way you choose to execute the music. "We've added gradually for two years," said a music minister. "I'm now rehearsing a choir with strings, brass, reeds, and percussion. We're going to have fun!"

One music director I know has chosen to combine her Sunday night folk mass with her regular Sunday service choir. The result is a folk mass, but it's taken over a year of accustoming the Sunday congregation to the folk instruments, one by one. Now they enjoy hearing the folk mass, which is really quite different from what they were listening to only a year ago.

There's a very important bonus to moderning church music programs: It attracts young singers and musicians. "Instrumentation seems like a big thing to high schoolers," said a director. "The standard choir and organist just doesn't excite them."

Popular Music in Religion

Church music directors voice concern over the dwindling number of young musicians involved in church music. Many young religious singers and musicians find church music dull. Even in its more contemporary forms, church music sounds dated compared to the rock, pop, country, and jazz heard on the radio. But some young musicians are rapidly bridging the gap between the church and popular music by singing about God in a modern context. "Christian rock" or "Christian folk music" can be mistaken for normal popular music unless you listen closely to the lyrics.

A religious band can find it hard to locate work. There's always an offer to play for free, but good money is rare. The places religious bands perform typically don't sell alcoholic beverages, so the employer's primary income source is dry. If you want to play religious music, conduct market research (Chapter 4) first to realistically appraise your job opportunities. Most will come from churches. Search for clubs with religious owners, and inquire at church clubs or ask ministers about any church picnics, celebrations, or similar informal gatherings. Colleges will occasinally hire religious groups, and some areas have ministries specifically organized to showcase religious music to young people.

To attract young members, churches have greatly expanded the times of services. In an effort to combat bar rooms, many now offer Thursday,

Friday, and Saturday night functions with Christian rock bands.

Advance planning (or warning) and careful booking are required to play at churches. You can't greet the Sunday morning congregation sounding like Pat Benatar even if you are spreading the gospel. "It's always the beat that bothers them!" said Ralph, guitarist for a Christian pop band. "These people are easily offended. We're very careful to find out what age our audience will be and then cater to them. You've got to be very understanding playing churches."

"Never bill yourself as 'contemporary' to a minister," cautioned Rebecca, a singer. "Be very frank and label yourself an electric guitar band if that's what you are."

Some groups can make a good living touring churches as a full-time ministry group. If you're working through an agent, be certain she represents you accurately.

Just as with more traditional church music, the money isn't necessarily the deciding factor. "We don't like to turn down offers because they can't pay us," said Ralph. "We'd rather play it for free, because we get something out of it anyway. We're serving the Lord."

For Further Information . . .

Church music periodicals are especially good sources of new music, how-to articles, and information on choir management and leadership. Here are four: *The Choral Journal*, P.O. Box 17736, Tampa FL 33682; *The Church Musician*, 127 Ninth Ave., Nashville TN 37234; *Journal of Church Music*, 2900 Queen Lane, Philadelphia PA 19129; and *The Organist*, P.O. Box 4399, 8432 Telegraph, Downey CA 90241.

• CHAPTER NINETEEN •

SELLING LYRICS AND MUSIC— BY MAIL!

After you've written some original songs and test-marketed them with your live band, you're ready to generate some excitement about yourself through the mail. Similarly, if you've been writing jingles for local businesses, those soundtracks serve as a ready portfolio for advertising agencies searching for creative writers.

If your presentation is attractive enough to grab their attention and your tape fresh enough to startle them, you'll earn money—and possibly *the best* money—right in your own home.

Should You Enter the Music-by-Mail Business?

If you've written any material, or plan to, the answer is yes! It's well worth a try. Here's why:

1. *The time investment is small.* I don't mean that writing music is a cinch. It requires discipline, concentration, an awareness of feelings, the ability to put those feelings into words, and a thorough study and understanding of melody, rhythm, phrasing, and rhyme. But you're already learning about music through your other musical jobs. If you're now a full-time performer, for instance, the extra time devoted to music because of songwriting will be minimal. Performing fosters songwriting.

2. *The money investment is small.* The only overhead you'll have are office supplies, postage, copyright costs, and studio fees. With a home studio, you've got it made.

3. *The potential pay-off is big.* Certainly, interesting a publisher, who in turn interests a recording artist, who in turn makes your song into a hit, is a long shot. But the industry has been flooded with mediocre songs for years, so the odds are in your favor if you're an exceptional songwriter. If you write from the heart in a unique "voice," you'll attract attention.

The art of songwriting is painstakingly
choosing the best words and matching them
to the melody.

That attention can translate into big bucks. If your publisher places one of your songs on an album that sells platinum, the publisher will receive $40,000 (standard mechanical royalty rate of 4 cents x 1,000,000 records sold) half of which, $20,000, will be sent to you, provided you're the only writer. If your song is chosen to back the album's hit on a single, and the single sells 500,000 copies, you and the publisher will receive an additional $10,000 apiece. If your song is the hit, income from record royalties, airplay, canned music, sheet music, movie rights, foreign and domestic rights can range from $50,000 to $250,000 and up. *That's for one song, written in your home.*

Since you're already involved in music, publishing isn't a market to dismiss. You can write at home in your spare time, whenever you please (or feel the need to). The band that recorded your song and made it a hit might have struggled together ten years for their big break. You penned the song in ten minutes, with a couple days of editing and rewriting. They poured all their life savings into their group. You spent 84 cents for postage. Yet the record royalties they'll receive won't match your publishing receipts. Inequitable? Yes. What should you do? Stay where you are, pick up a pencil, and begin writing.

The Writing Life

To become good at anything, you have to work at it. For a songwriter this begins with constant exposure to music. Listen to everything, all the various styles that are music. Broaden your musical appreciation to all extremes, from classical to tribal. Explore music from different cultures around the world. What do they sing about? How are their songs structured? Then investigate the heritages of the music you prefer, studying how it has evolved into the music you now enjoy.

Your writing will benefit from the steady performing you do as a working musician. All kinds of writers, from poets to publicists, know that it's much easier to write about subjects you understand and which are familiar. As a performer you'll be in touch with other songwriters and/or their music. Also, publishers prefer to sign songwriters who perform, since concerts sell albums, which increase royalties.

To place songs in the commercial market, you need to be up on what's happening. Reading *Billboard* every week, for instance, will help you understand popular tastes and predict industry trends. You'll also get a feel for the way record companies promote and ride trends.

Your writing should be based on your own feelings—that's the main ingredient of successful songwriting. You don't have to guess at how others feel, because most people share the same basic emotions. Actions may differ, but true emotion rarely does. If you felt so miserable that you broke down and cried when she left, it's probable that 100 million AM radio listeners have felt the same way. Your songwriting success depends on your ability to get those emotions down on paper forcefully, succinctly, and *not* the same way a million other writers would say it. You've got to be different!

People also fantasize much the same. They'll listen if you write about love, romance, sex, or leaving it all behind. Again, rely on your own feelings.

Most bestselling songs tell a story. One songwriter describes it as taking a feature-length movie and compacting the story into thirty lines. The characters, the background, the encounter, the complication, and the resolution all have to be there. Near the end, listeners should sense that the song is completed.

"Professional Songwriter" is a title that doesn't come easily. You have to place songs with a publisher before you become professional. There's really no middle ground—you've either sold a song or you haven't, and until you have, you'll be treated like a beginner. But you can *act* like a professional, and in the process improve your chances of selling. How? By devoting your time to writing. Initially, don't worry *too* much about quality—that'll come later after studying successful songs and going through reams of binder paper. Nor do you have to write songs, per se. For now, just *write*. Try a regimented schedule, where you write so many words at a certain time, every day. Expressing yourself, even if it takes you four pages to say "I love you," has to become second nature.

Sometimes when you lock yourself in your room, you won't be inspired to write anything. But tomorrow morning you might be. Or on the way home from work. Inspiration strikes freely. I get many of my best ideas lying in bed. I either jump up and begin writing, or I'll scribble a note to bring my mind back to that point of inspiration later. You, too, should always be prepared for a burst of inspiration. Carry a notepad or small tape recorder with you to catch your thoughts.

Great lyrics have been carefully honed to perfection. It's no accident that they sound simple and natural together. The real art of songwriting is painstakingly choosing the exact "right" word. It might more accurately be called "song editing" or "song tightening." You take that stack of thoughts and feelings you've written and narrow, condense, and economize every line. This strengthens the song. Everyone who hears the song should know what you mean.

And then there's the melody. Writing music is different from writing lyrics—it's another language, with its own rules and peculiarities. If you're adept at both, that's great. But there's no sense in recording your dynamite lyrics with a poor melody. A publisher might not listen to your words or read your lyric sheets if the music is lousy. If you can't set your lyrics to a good arrangement, look for a partner.

You can find a collaborator through songwriter associations and workshops, among your musician friends, or by advertising as you would for a band member. Collaboration works comfortably when the two of you agree previously *in writing* to what percentage of each song you own. Is this one your song or her song? Most collaborators work on a 50/50 basis, but whatever you decide, get it down on paper.

If You Try for a Hit, You'll Miss

Top 40. What does that mean to you? If you'd describe it as frivolous, unskilled, and rather insulting to your intelligence, you're not going to make it as a popular songwriter. You don't have to like the majority of hits, but you certainly have to respect them.

A hit is usually a simple song. For the song to be well received and gain hit status, it has to appeal to a broader group of listeners than musicians. People who don't know electric from acoustic have to enjoy it, though they might not know why. That's popular taste. If you've sold several symphonic pieces and you plan on writing a few commercial tunes just for the money, don't buy a new house on the expectation of imminent success. You'd do better to wait for the reality of form rejection slips from publishers. Even though the songs may seem simple, the style and the sound are an art. It's easy to sense when someone is "writing down" to an audience. Those songs never make it because they lack sincerity and emotion.

There is no magic formula for writing a hit song. How many interviews with hit composers have you read where they say the equivalent of "This was the last cut on the album I expected would make it"? All the torturous hours of editing a song down to exactly 2:30 and sticking to a rigid verse-chorus format won't pay off. You've either captured a special feeling or you haven't.

You can learn a lot of things about writing popular songs by studying and dissecting former hits. About each song ask, "What makes this song work? What kind of feeling does it leave the listener with? Does this song make me think of something similar that happened to me? How do the lyrics and music complement each other?" In particular, identify each of the following for every song:

1. *The lyrical hook.* This is the "catchy" part of the song that is most remembered—people walk around singing or humming it. It may be a single line (often the title) or several lines in the chorus.
2. *The lyrical theme.* What is the song about? What emotions are played on? Look for the reason the writer wrote these lyrics.
3. *The melody.* Write down the chord progression for each song. Note any unusual patterns.
4. *The rhythm.* How do the accents fall? What's the beat? Is it $2/4$, $4/4$,

salsa, or swing? What's the tempo? Is the song a ballad or is it played at breakneck speed?

5. The *rhyme*. Study to what extent each song uses lyrical rhyming, and how closely the melody and rhythm accentuate the rhyme.

Analyze as many hits as possible; then put your own compositions to the test. Could your songs be mistaken for hits, judging by these criteria? Are your hooks strong enough? Are your rhythms within the limits set by past hits?

After critiquing your songs, test-market their effectiveness in your band. Pay attention to audience reaction. Do your songs hold audience interest? Then look for way to improve audience response, such as speeding up the tempo, using a broader dynamic range, or letting someone else sing the lead. Your main concern should be to discover how each of your songs is best displayed. Once each song finds its own "niche," you're ready to record.

Multiplying Your Efforts

Nearly every book written for songwriters details exactly how to submit your tape to potential buyers. Two of the most comprehensive are the annual *Songwriter's Market*, edited by Barbara Norton Kuroff, and the *Music Business Handbook and Career Guide*, 3rd Edition, by David Baskerville. Some of the more obvious tips include: The demo should be recorded well enough to maximumly illustrate your strong points; vocals must be clear and audible; you needn't go to elaborate production measures unless the song truly needs it; all songs should be copyrighted before being mailed; a query letter should be mailed first to ascertain whether the buyer is interested in listening to your material, and a self-addressed, stamped postcard should be enclosed for her reply; when you receive notice that a buyer is interested, arrange the tape, lyric sheets, lead sheets (if requested), and SASE in a package, with everything clearly labeled and impeccably typed.

Often overlooked is the sheer quantity of packages you should send out to increase your chances of acceptance. Every letter sent is a long shot. The odds are that you'll receive a polite, impersonal "No thanks." So why not better your odds? Songwriters who sell from their homes do it by aggressive salesmanship.

Your first move should be another market analysis, similar to how you researched live music employers in Chapter 4 (don't worry; this one isn't so tough!). Your goal is to narrow down the fields of music publishers, record producers, artists, artist managers, advertising agencies, audiovisual companies, and play producers and publishers to those who are most likely interested in your material.

Can you narrow this list already? Probably. If you're only interested in writing advertising jingles your field is immediately narrowed to ad agencies. If theatrical productions are what really turn you on, you'll concentrate on play producers and publishers. If you're writing what you hope is popular music, you'll start with music publishers, record producers, artists, and artist managers.

The resources you need are the annual *Songwriter's Market* (for precise information on what each of many music publishers, record companies, record producers, ad agencies, audiovisual companies, managers and booking agencies, and play producers and publishers want), the *Musical American International Directory of the Performing Arts* (for listings of classical music publishers and artist managers), the *Billboard International Buyer's Guide* (for a more complete but less in-depth listing of music publishers than the *Songwriter's Market*), and the *Billboard International Talent Directory* (for listings of U.S. artists, their personal managers and booking agents).

Once you have access to the resources you need, begin studying the weekly trade journals *Billboard* and *Cashbox* to find what kind of songs each publisher is currently featuring. The advertisements will provide just as much information as the copy (if you'll be trying to sell to ad agencies, audiovisual companies, or play producers and publishers, skip this research and go straight to the *Songwriter's Market*).

Music publishers are by far the best channel for selling your unheralded songs. If you have any personal contacts within the industry, use them. If you know any recording artists, contact them. Most musicians don't have reliable contacts, though. If you've written material that you're sure is perfect for a certain artist, send it to them, their personal manager, or their booking agency. Chances are, however, that an active publisher has better contacts than you and also knows other artists besides your favorite who might be interested in your writing. Everyone, record companies included, turns to publishers first when they need material, because the publisher functions as a "gatekeeper," or a first line of defense against poor material. If it's in a publisher's catalog, reasons an artist, manager, producer, or record company A&R person, it at least has some merit.

Scanning album jackets will sometimes turn up the names of publishers and producers whose material is on the record. Check out artists you think would like your music and note their publishers.

Songwriter's Market lists what each publisher wants, and how they want material presented. Go right through the book, earmarking pages with possibly receptive publishers listed. Here's a sample entry:

MAD EAGLE MUSIC, Box 8621, Anaheim CA 92802. (714)636-1208. President: Alice Maenza. Music publisher. Estab. 1980. BMI. Member BMI and Southern California Songwriters Guild. Pays standard royalty.

How to Contact: Submit demo tape and lyric sheet. Prefers cassette with 2-10 songs on demo. SASE. "We ask that all material be protected before mailing." *Music:* Blues, C&W, easy listening, gospel, MOR, novelty, punk, R&B, rock, and top 40. Recently published "Things I Should've Said," recorded by Eddie Dare/ Love Records.
Tips: "We are a new company building a catalog. *All* our writers are new and unknown. We are interested in all writers that show potential. Demo tapes must have lyrics clearly audible. The song should be interesting enough to grab the listener after he's heard a couple of lines. Long intros are a waste of time for a publisher. Good quality tape is a must."

Now that you've got a list (the longer the better!) of potential buyers, you've got to send query letters to as many companies as possible. Always query a company first, even if their listing in *Songwriter's Market* says it's not necessary. Why? Their catalog may have changed drastically since the latest *Songwriter's Market* went to press, and demo tapes are sufficiently expensive not to throw away. It's preferable to spend a few cents on two-way postage for a query letter and postcard.

Three or four songs per tape is an acceptable amount for most companies. Don't save the best for last. Put the best song first, and arrange it so that it catches listener attention immediately—at least within the first eight bars. Pick three of your songs that sound good together, not necessarily cut from the same mold, but at least in the same style. Have the master tape duplicated onto cassette and reel-to-reel tapes. You'll need at least thirty all together. You won't know which format tape each publisher will want until they respond affirmatively to your query.

They'll also tell you whether they want "lyric sheets" or "lead sheets," or both. Lyric sheets are simply typewritten pages with the words to your songs on them. Each song's lyrics should be on a separate page, with a copyright notice. Type each page once; then have them photocopied. Lead sheets contain the notes, rhythm, and lyrics written out in musical form. They should be professionally prepared. If you haven't written charts yourself, call your local musician's union, a college music department, or some music stores and ask about a professional copyist.

Each letter of introduction must be neatly typed and carefully addressed to a specific person. If you can't find individuals to contact for one company, call and ask to whom the letter should be sent (and get the name spelled right!). Simple courtesies stand out when you're sitting behind a cramped desk overflowing with letters and packages vaguely addressed: "A&R Department," or "To Whom It May Concern."

Send out ten individually typed letters *briefly* describing your music. Be very businesslike (refer to "How to Organize All Those Notes, Names, and Numbers," Chapter 4). You should recommend artists that this company has previously sold to if you think your material might interest them.

(Your name and address)

Date

Mr. Alan Brackett
One for the Road Music Company
3317 Ledgewood Drive
Los Angeles, CA 90068

Dear Mr. Brackett:

I've been writing songs and performing them locally for several years. After hearing Randy Meisner's latest album, I think I have several pop/rock songs that might interest you.

Please fill out the enclosed self-addressed postcard and return it to me at your convenience.

Thank you for your time. I look forward to hearing from you.

Cordially,

(Your name)

The enclosed addressed stamped postcard should be preprinted in a form similar to this:

```
Date _____

(  ) Yes!  I would like to hear your material.
      Please send the following:

      _____ cassette
      _____ reel-to-reel
      _____ lyric sheet
      _____ lead sheet

(  ) Query me again in _____ months.
(  ) No, I'm not interested.

Name: _____    Title: _____
```

As soon as you begin receiving cards marked, "No, I am not interested," send out a new query to another company. Try to keep ten queries for your three songs out at all times.

Hopefully, you have more than three songs that you consider salable. To really boost your chances of acceptance, have three different tapes made, each featuring three songs. Keep ten queries in circulation for each tape.

You needn't put the same style of music on each tape. In fact, diversifying into various fields by recording one progressive sounding tape, one country tape, and one pop tape, for instance, will further increase your chance of sales. And if you can write for different audiences, your value to a publisher will triple since you are a potential "cross-over artist."

All this requires a lot of paperwork, but none of it's very hard. The biggest problem is remembering what material you've sent to whom, and when it was mailed. Here's what I've done to organize the hassle:

1. I typed a master list of all the companies I thought might be receptive to my songs.
2. I purchased a 2'x3' cork peg board and some 3"x5" cards.
3. I labeled the board, from left to right, with slots for "Song Ideas," "Queries Sent," "Preparation," "Tapes Sent," and "Accepted and/or Published."

The title of each original song I work on is written on a card and tacked onto the board under "Song Ideas." When I've tested its appeal with my local group, I record it with two other songs on a demo. I have copies made, and then list the ten companies who are being sent queries on a card, and tack it under "Queries Sent." When a publisher sends back a "No thanks," I cross him off the card, write another company in on a second card, and send that company a query. When a company asks me to send them my tape, I write their name on a new card, and tack it under "Preparation," until it's in the mail; then that card is moved to "Tape Sent." If they write back and say, "No thanks," or return my tape, that card is taken down. If they want to negotiate for publishing rights, the card is permanently and victoriously moved into the "Accepted and/or Published" column.

If you've had experience producing jingles for local businesses, I strongly suggest you send queries to advertising agencies. Music publishers and record companies receive the bulk of letters from songwriters; ad agencies and audiovisual companies don't receive nearly as many submissions. Musicians tend to be afraid of them (that's your cue—dive in!).

Always remember the odds. Even though they're against you, by sending out more queries, you multiply your chances. Above all, don't feel that a rejection is a reflection on your songwriting. Rather, your letter just wound up in the wrong hands.

Before your letter winds up in the *right* hands, you should have some guidelines on songwriter/publisher contractual agreements. The organization most representative of songwriters is the American Guild of Authors and Composers (AGAC), 40 W. 57 St., New York NY 10019. Write AGAC for a copy of their "Popular Songwriters Contract." The provisions in the contract are decidedly pro-songwriter, so it will provide you with a sense of fairness when you're confronted with a pro-publisher contract. Also write Broadcast Music, Inc. (BMI), 320 W. 57 St., New York NY 10019, and the American Society of Composers, Authors and Publishers (ASCAP), 1 Lincoln Plaza, New York NY 10023, and SESAC, 10 Columbus Circle, New York NY 10019, for pamphlets outlining fair songwriter/publisher agreements.

When a music publisher is interested in your material, it's time to negotiate. The publisher may want to meet you in person (you'll probably want to meet him, too!). The only problem is that you're in New Jersey and he's in L.A. Who's going to pay your air fare? Use your best judgment on the phone, making sure he's *really* interested. If he is, offer to split the ticket 50/50, or pay the entire fare yourself, on the condition that he reimburse you if you come to terms. Often deals are made over the phone when person to person meetings are impossible or expensive.

The publisher may only be interested in one of your songs. Personally, I like this arrangement, since it leaves me free to market other songs to other publishers. If he wants to sign you to an "exclusive representation" contract, which entitles him to any song you write, however, be a little more cautious. What is he really saying? It's the equivalent of, "Gee, this guy's really hot! I'd better get a big piece of the action!" If he wants exclusive representation, you've just climbed up a few rungs on the negotiating ladder. With either kind of representation, demand a reversion clause—a time limit of six to twelve months on the contract. If he really thinks you've got potential, he'll place some of your material with recording artists within that time. If he doesn't place your songs, you still have a chance to sell them elsewhere.

One of the most important issues of your negotiation will be the amount—if any—of your advance money. Bargain for the biggest advance you can get! (See Chapter 10, "Wheeling and Dealing with Customers for Cash!") Publishers place the most selling emphasis on songs in which they have some money tied up. A common publisher ploy is to trade your $500 advance for "high-quality" demo tapes and lead sheets that they'll have made. Don't let them do it! Accept the $500 and rerecord yourself in a good studio. That way you'll still have some of the advance left over.

Remember: You have absolutely no guarantee of receiving one penny from royalties, so get some cash up front! Another option is to try to persuade BMI or ASCAP to give you an advance. If the publisher does want exclusive representation for all your songs, tell him you're going to need a "subsistence advance," consisting of monthly payments mailed to you for the duration of the representation. In exchange, he'll probably want you to submit a designated number of new songs every few months.

Be wary of signing a contract which gives the publisher all the rights to your songs for the perpetuity of the copyright. Publishers often ask for this when they fork over an advance. If you're given a choice between an advance and a reversion clause, keep your rights. Otherwise your song could languish in his catalog forever and there's nothing you can do about it—you'd never get any royalties or the pleasure of hearing it recorded.

If you've looked over advice from AGAC, BMI, ASCAP, and SESAC, you'll have a good idea of what's fair (single-song contracts are usually only one page long). If you don't understand something, don't sign. Negotiate for your advance, then take the unsigned contract home with you to scrutinize it more carefully with the help of a local songwriter's organization or a music attorney.

Your finished songs are technically your property as soon as you've marked them with a copyright symbol (Copyright © 1982 by James W. Dearing), but to insure receipt of licensing fees, they must be registered. Write to the Register of Copyrights, Library of Congress, Washington, D.C. 20559, for the forms needed to copyright your songs as a collection. Alternately, you could send your songs to a bonded song registration service like Songwriters Resources and Services, 6381 Hollywood Blvd., Suite 503, Los Angeles CA 90028, until you're sure the songs are going to be recorded. Then you should apply for individual song copyrights from the Register of Copyrights. The current fee is $10 per song.

For Further Information . . .

To get a feel for where songwriting is headed, subscribe to either *Billboard*, Billboard Publications, Inc., 9000 Sunset Blvd., 12th Floor, Los Angeles CA 90069 or *Cashbox Magazine*, Cashbox Publishing Co., Inc., 6363 Sunset Blvd., Suite 930, Hollywood CA 90028. You may be able to bargain to read *both* magazines with the manager of a local record store.

You should be armed with a copy of the latest *Songwriter's Market*, Writer's Digest Books, 9933 Alliance Rd., Cincinnati OH 45242 to help pinpoint your selling efforts. A comprehensive list of music publishers is found in the *Billboard International Buyer's Guide*, 2160 Patterson St., Cincinnati OH 45214, though no marketing information is included.

• CHAPTER TWENTY •

REGIONAL, THEN NATIONAL GROWTH

Don't look to make money on records, singles or albums, until you've had several major sellers back-to-back.
—Kenny Rogers and Len Epand,
Making It With Music

In a sense, this book ended with the last chapter. The book's purpose is to help you make as much money as you can with music, "no matter where you live." That means considering educational opportunities, live bands, studio recording, private teaching, church music, advertising as an agency, setting up a home studio, equipment rentals, and selling lyrics and music through the mail.

So what's next? What do you do after achieving your immediate local goals? Most musicians are eager to expand their careers. The rewards are greater esteem, a feeling of accomplishment, and—maybe—more money. The vehicle for this growth is the record album.

This chapter isn't—nor could it be—a complete guide to getting your sound down on an album and out to the buying public; rather, it's a first step toward geographic expansion. It outlines how you can tempt a record company to offer a contract, and, if that fails (or if you want total control over the project), how you can make and sell the record yourself. Excellent books covering the recording industry and independent recording are listed at the end of this chapter, if you want more specific information.

The Dismantled Recording Industry

Ten to twenty years ago, a musician could mail demo tapes to record companies with realistic hope of landing a recording contract. If the mails failed, he could take his act to L.A., book gigs in a well-known nightclub, and stand a decent chance of being heard by record company executives. Both methods became obsolete in the early '70s. Now, besides making great music, a band must satisfy a complex set of business and economic criteria in order to get a recording contract.

Once your band has decided to reinvest profits in sound equipment, instruments, and lighting, you can start working original material into your shows, release a single locally, and use your following to vault you into the local hit charts. Steel Breeze, pictured here, did this, found an independent producer, and signed a contract with RCA Records.

(photograph by Greg Savalin)

Why have conditions changed so drastically? One reason, though not a primary cause, is intensified competition among musicians battling for recording contracts. Before the Los Angeles pool of musicians flooded over, talent scouts would hunt for quality performers at nightclubs in and around the L.A. area. Then demo tapes began to replace live scouting. It was easier for the A&R departments; now the talent was coming to them. As more and more people were lured by the possibility of becoming recording stars (one out of five Americans plays a musical instrument), the recording centers—and L.A. in particular—swelled with tens of thousands of talented, hungry musicians.

But the supply of contracts was being shut off. As successful artists bargained for more and more production control, recording work was almost exclusively limited to an "inner circle" of musicians who knew and recommended each other for work. An unknown could no longer break in. Instead of hiring capable, unknown back-ups, bandleaders opted for sure winners: Elton John helped John Lennon on an album, so Lennon sang on John's album. Michael McDonald sang on a Kenny Loggins album, as did Stevie Nicks. Carly Simon hired Steve Gadd, Steely Dan hired Gadd, Paul Simon hired Gadd, and so did everyone else. Soon guest stars and studio musicians were the rule rather than the exception. Record companies no longer had to search for fresh, new groups. Instead they just dipped into their proven clique of musicians and "formed" a group.

While this has obviously been devastating for musicians trying to break in, it has also proven artistically stifling for the entire industry. The majority of popular, mass-selling albums sound similar; the music sounds homogenized. Rock is in a rut.

But what has become quite clear—as evidenced by the proliferation of small record companies—is that despite their attempts, the industry cannot force-feed the listening public music it does not want. There are still plenty of double-platinum selling albums, but the large companies are not willing to gamble on anything but a style of music with proven sales potential. They can't afford to. A small record company can show a profit on sales of 20,000 copies, but a major label might need to sell 100,000 copies to break even due to bigger production budgets, hundreds of employees, and extensive promotion. Thus in these hard times, the big companies are perhaps no better off than the little companies.

What does this mean to you? It means that you should be cautious about aiming for a recording contract with a major label. You'll get a bare subsistence advance, and in order to make decent money you'll need a gold album (500,000 copies).

If, on the other hand, you sign with a small company, selling 500,000 copies will make you wealthy (as it did for George Thorogood on Rounder Records, based in Somerville, Maine). After proving your sales potential with a small label or by making and selling the album yourself, the major labels will line up, contracts in hand, eager to negotiate concessions, advances, and promotional budgets with you. You'll have the bull by the horns!

Small record companies and recording studios have proliferated for several reasons. According to Diane Sward Rapaport, in her book, *How to Make and Sell Your Own Record*, Quick Fox Publications, this growth occurred because influential bands convinced record companies to advance them money to build their own studios, successful producers began to contract independently of the major companies, and the home recording revolution of the '70s made recording equipment inexpensive and readily available.

All of this has resulted in a diffusion of recording techniques and specialists nationwide. Sixteen-track studios exist matter-of-factly. Twenty-four tracks are not uncommon in cities of 100,000 people.

This means you can sign a recording deal in your own area, in perfect keeping with the philosophy of this book: There's good money available right where you live.

A Plan for Recognition

The Career Flow Chart in Chapter 5 shows how to go straight from your own locality to signing with a major label. This approach (detailed below) works as long as your music is really hot. If the industry reception to your sound is cool (no matter how good you actually are), you'll be better off signing with a small, regional label.

All the members in a band pursuing a recording contract need to be in agreement on direction. Ultimate goals should be clearly defined, and short-term goals must be discussed at band business meetings and brought to a consensus.

That your band needs songwriters seems obvious; yet many groups start out with a recording contract in mind but concentrate solely on copy material. You've got to have very catchy original songs. Test your more commercial material on dancing bar audiences.

Everyone must always remember that the band *has not* been formed to return a short-term profit. When one or two musicians bring pressure on the group to pay larger weekly dividends, the band's goal will be in jeopardy. Much of the profit must be reinvested in equipment, lighting, clothes, staging, roadies, transportation, and publicity in order to be an attractive "take over" candidate for a large recording company. All of this points to the necessity of working at a non-band-related job to support yourself.

Whereas the impact of demo tapes has faded, the value of recording two songs on a single has escalated. A local band heading for the top has to build excitement within its locality. You need a local hit! Peddling singles to live audiences and record stores is a good enthusiasm builder.

"Every phenomenon in rock 'n' roll has come from a regional area," says independent producer Kim Fowley, who has worked on 56 gold and 15 platinum records. "It's very hard to develop yourself as a musician in New York, Nashville, or L.A., because the minute the band is formed, you have the distractions of attorneys, groupies, dope dealers, jerks, and everyone knows the top brass at Warner across the street. Consequently, all the bands from these centers are recorded prematurely. Their sound isn't allowed to age.

"We have bands here (in Los Angeles) that can sell 2,000 tickets to a local performance, yet they can't persuade an A & R person to sign them to a contract. The A & R people would rather fly to Kansas to check out some locally matured talent. Smaller cities have their own circuits, and those bands can really polish their style. They have to play copy songs, sure, but they get to stick in an original once in a while. That's what the Beatles did in Hamburg, which was certainly a "regional" area. Isolation breeds art. Producers realize this now."

Another strike against New York and Los Angeles is the incredibly high cost of living. Even five or six band members living together can hardly afford to rent a house so that they can live and practice.

"Don't come here to learn how to compete," advises Fowley. "If you can write 'radio' songs, the local airplay plan will work. *Real* talent is so scarce, that if you get enough positive feedback locally, and you're convinced you've got the talent, go for it. *Everyone* down here stops and listens when an artist is truly original."

The importance of local radio stations to a band's access to major record companies can't be overemphasized. Radio is a very crucial link in a band's progress or failure, but don't expect a station to play your single because they feel sorry for you. Annual Arbitron ratings (conducted by an independent market research firm to determine station popularity) make airplay selections a business consideration. The more listeners a station attracts, the more money the station can charge for advertisements. This is why you must take a business approach to getting airplay.

In your community, small business help each other so each may survive. Cooperation is imperative. If you help the station now, when your single comes out, they'll help you.

What can you do to help your local radio stations? Negotiate radio advertisements when you book club gigs, and specify which station the ad will run on. Make luncheon appointments with station managers and show them that you're responsible for bringing them consistent revenue. Emphasize the point that you've settled for less money in order to give the station business. They'll be indebted to you. "How can we return the favor?" they'll ask. You won't be at a loss for words. "When our single comes out, just spin it twenty-five times a week."

Spread the advertising to as many influential stations as you can, without diluting the plan's effectiveness. For stations to justify playing your single, they need to feel a demand for the song. Ask your following, the people who come to support the group night after night, to continually phone in requests to stations.

The release of your single must be well-timed. Summer months are slow for industry hits (the big rush is November-December because of Christmas), so it's a good time for your single to be released. You probably won't have to battle new hits by McCartney or the Police for airplay.

The single will have to be stocked in local stores a few days before you start selling from the stage or giving the single to disc jockeys. When a listener hears your local hit in her car, she should be able to go to the record store and buy it.

Sales from the single can offset your investment in the recording and pressing of the disc, but sales are not the aim of your premeditated release and airplay. The idea is to stir up enough demand from listeners to jam the radio stations and record stores with requests for the song, thereby vaulting your "hit" into the local "Top 40." These lists are assembled by record stores and radio stations. Once your band is on their list (with a bullet, maybe?) ask them to mail copies of the list to the national trade journals. Do it yourself if necessary. Industry magazines make a point of mentioning local airplay sensations, and record companies watch for those news flashes like hawks. They also closely monitor local charts. This is now a standard mechnanism for companies to find out about hot unsigned acts.

"We're not looking for new acts. Why should we, when we've got Frank Sinatra, Gordon Lightfoot, Neil Young, Randy Newman, and Leo Sayer?" says Bill Perasso, West Coast Sales Manager for Warner/Electra/Asylum (WEA). "New acts don't interest us, but I'll tell you what we are looking for: Hits! We're looking for hits. Absolutely. If you can create a local hit in your area, it means everything to a record company.

"If someone comes into my office and says, 'Wow! I've got this great band that you've just got to see,' I won't go. Why should I? But, if he comes in and says, 'I've sold 18,000 records in Northern California,' all of a sudden I've got something that's really important. We signed Greg Kihn a while ago, not because he was new, but because he had proven himself. A small label, Beserkley, did a great job selling his albums. That's what record companies are looking for, and it's not that difficult. Once you manufacture your album, get it distributed, and start banging those local radio stations, we'll notice. We can't ignore it! If you say, 'We're a solid band, with proven sales, and a local hit,' we'll listen. We have to, or some other company will. Local airplay makes all the difference."

Because of the economic crunch gripping the record industry, large companies are extraordinarily selective when investing hundreds of thousands of dollars in a band. They want to be sure you justify their support. Record company executives are just as likely to look at your balance sheets as your song sheets.

The magical words are "self-contained." If the group is independent and secure, you'll be welcomed as a rose in their catalog of thorns. Here are nine points they'll consider when looking you over:

1. *Does this act have any large, outstanding debts that must be paid off?* The company already has many expenses involved in getting your album on the market. They can't afford a $50,000 payment to an investor who wants the company to buy him out.

2. *Does the group own quality instruments, amplifiers, staging equipment, and lighting already?* "Already" is the key word here. Companies used to spring for all the touring and performance necessities, but now you'll pay for it out of your advance (which might not be budgeted for it).

3. *Does the band have a large enough P.A., and a truck to carry it in?* Same point. This can save the company $40,000.

4. *Does the group have a support system?* Companies prefer it if you've found people to work for you, such as a small road crew, road manager, business manager or personal manager, and an accountant. This spares them the problem of finding compatible, honest people for your team—something you've already suffered through.

5. *Is the group fiscally responsible?* It's easy to overextend your credit with the record company when on the road. They want a band which has learned by necessity to spend meagerly.

6. *Is the group easy to work with?* Many bands lack interpersonal skills. You're a musician, but they want you to act courteous, maintain a good attitude, and be responsible for your actions when they're dealing wih you (translation: Businessperson).

7. *Are they experienced live performers?* They know you can play well, but has the group learned how to entertain an audience? They'll also want to know about the band's stamina. A band is worthless unless it can tour consistently. Can you stage a stellar performance night after night after night?

8. *Is this band a solid relational entity?* Companies will give you the cold shoulder if you reveal that the keyboardist and lead singer hate each other. They are not willing to invest $200,000 only to watch the group dissolve three months later.

9. *Are the individuals emotionally stable?* Companies have had to deal with too many musicians who either act like little kids or prima donnas. They want you crazy onstage, but cool, calm and collected while phoning from a tour or in the studio recording.

Once major labels are interested in your act, you'll be confronted with their contracts. These will be written to heavily favor the company. (Remember: Their lawyers wrote the things.) No matter how hot an item you are, you'll still be in a weak negotiating position for increasing royalties or expanding your control over the recording project since they are going to pay for your entire album. The negotiator will tempt you with a $75,000 advance, but this will be spent on recording costs such as studio rental, musician fees, tape, and producer fees. If there's anything left, it'll go for new instruments and feeding the band. And *all* these necessities that the company is "paying" for will later be charged against your royalty earnings, if you have any. Even though you'll be offered a lump advance, the company still holds all the aces by signing you to a "standard" industry contract. If you reject the offer, will life pass you by?

Fortunately, you have a choice. You can politely turn down the offer, but—and this is very important—tell them you're still interested. Explain that you will relieve the company of any financial commitment by contacting your own investors, hiring an independent producer, and recording the album master tape (the final studio recording used to make the record) yourself. The boldface words in the chart below show what you'll be responsible for. Stay on good, close terms with the company executives, and ask their advice on producers. They'll appreciate your approach and interpret it as a sign of your commitment.

GETTING A BETTER DEAL

Record Company Interest
↓
Find Financiers
↓
Contact & Hire Independent Producer
↓
Book Studio Time
↓
Transport Band & Instruments
↓
Record Album Tape
↓
"Master" the Final Mix
↓
Send Finished Tape to Various Companies
↓
Sign Record Company Contract
(essentially pressing, distribution, and promotion rights)
↓
Album Jacket Graphics are Designed and Printed
↓
Records are Pressed and Packaged
↓
Promotion Strategy is Planned
↓
Album is Released for Sale

The real value of shopping around record companies with a finished master is that with a well-known independent producer, you should be able to stimulate a bidding contest between two or more companies. The *Billboard International Recording Equipment and Studio Directory* lists record producers you can query with a letter of explanation and your single.

Two "name bands" who've used this method successfully are Quarterflash and the Police. Both groups had record company offers as a result of local hits. They turned down the offers, and opted instead to hire independent producers. The producers presented the tapes to various labels, and *voila*—bidding contests!

Getting good legal advice about recording contracts isn't easy. Most music lawyers are based in the industry centers, and are quite expensive. An excellent alternative would be to use nonprofit groups like Volunteer Lawyers for the Arts (36 W. 44th St., Suite 1110, New York NY 10036); Bay Area Lawyers for the Arts (Fort Mason Center, Building 310, San Francisco 94123); and Songwriters' Resources and Services (6772 Hollywood Boulevard, Hollywood CA 90028). *Songwriter's Market* lists over 65 songwriter organizatons, clubs, and workshops thoughout North America devoted in part to providing legal advice.

The Smaller Labels

There are several reasons why you might not sign with a major record company:
1. They don't like your music enough to offer a contract.
2. They like your music, but don't consider it salable enough to recoup their investment.
3. You may not be willing to sign one of their "standard" contracts.
4. You don't want to be a little fish in a pond of piranhas.

The best reason to turn down a major label in favor of a smaller label, I've saved for last. Having never released a bona fide album, your bargaining position is weak. By first signing with a small company and selling a lot of albums, you set yourself up for a very juicy offer from the majors once your first contract expires (or you choose to buy it out since Warner is dangling a $100,000 advance in front of you). Many, many popular artists have used smaller labels as stepping stones to the majors once they felt their track record would justify a better than average contract.

"Groups are having to make it more on their own, with a smaller label at first," says Mariam Abrams, of Olivia Records. "It used to be that a major company would take an unknown artist and really groom her, putting a lot of money into making her a big star. You don't see that now. An artist will do one album by herself or with a small label, and then try to move up to a big label."

You won't be paid royalties any quicker by a small record company, but it is quite possible to make more money overall. If you were not able to secure a large advance from a major company, for instance, and production costs were still high, you might not make any money besides the meager advance if the record sells under 100,000 copies (and that's a lot of vinyl). If you get a larger advance, you'll be better off, even though four out of five artists on major labels in 1981 never received *any* royalties from record sales! A small label won't offer as big an advance, but because of their reduced overhead and smaller investment they can cover their costs by selling fewer albums, so they'll pay you royalties almost assuredly.

If you feel that a definite market exists for your music, but it doesn't number over 50,000, pursue the small labels for a deal. Having an album that sells 50,000 copies is a flop to a major label, but a best-seller to a small label! Most small labels specialize in distinctive styles of music, and thus can market their records with greater precision than a mass-market-oriented major company.

A common worry among musicians is that by signing with a small label, the record will never be distributed to its full potential. While this is possible, it's not necessarily true. Most small labels are affiliated with major labels, and can get a hot regional album into national distribution by using the large company's distribution network.

A small label will usually offer better contractual conditions, too. Though you might only get a $15,000 advance (from which the album will have to be made), you should be able to bargain successfully for either publishing rights, a couple extra royalty percentage points, or a specific, minimum amount to be spent on promotion.

Here's one worthwhile scheme: Bargain for the biggest advance possible, say $20,000, and then offer to divert $10,000 of your advance into a promotional tour budget *if* the company will also kick in $10,000. Since promotion sells records, and sales benefit you *and* the company, they'll like this idea. At the same time, it increases their investment in you, so their commitment to selling your record is greater.

Making the Album Yourself

As you develop a local following, stock stores with your single, and follow it up with local airplay, things will be moving fast. If you get on your local charts and have copies sent to the industry magazines, you'll be expecting some attention from record companies.

What happens if the phone doesn't ring? You've got all this local excitement going, but all you hear from national companies is overwhelming silence. Nothing. Your fingernails are the shortest they've been in years.

If nothing happens, you'll realize the plan failed. What should you do now? You could write me nasty letters, but, even after the big labels *and* the little labels have snubbed you, there's still another choice. You can make the album yourself, and to hell with the record companies (for now)! It'll take longer and involve more work, but you can do it. And dare I say it? Yes! You can even make *better* money than if a label was putting out your record!

The plan for recognition already detailed works fine if you put out an album instead of a single, too. Making your own record takes more time and costs more money than a single does, but you can make a respectable profit off album sales, whereas you'll be forced to sell singles at a price only slightly higher than what you pay for them. This means that if you're constantly booked and selling albums at your performances, you can gain record company attention without working at a 9-to-5 job to support yourself! Thousands of artists have realized this and have invested in their own labels.

"These artist-owned labels often sell a major portion of the records directly to their audiences," writes Diane Sward Rapaport, in *How to Make and Sell Your Own Record*. "As a result, they often show profits with sales of less than 3,000 records, depending on their recording costs. Those artists who are able to keep expenses low and sell more than 10,000 records (and there are many who have) can make small fortunes. For them, small is indeed beautiful."

The lure of independently releasing your record is the money. Instead of receiving 8-percent album royalties, you receive all the royalties. Instead of signing away publishing rights and income, you receive *double* the amount for writing the songs. You take the chances, but you reap the profits.

"Musicians come up on break and ask what label we put our album on, and I tell them we did it ourselves," said a lead singer whose band crisscrosses California. "You can see them snicker, like, 'Oh, I thought it was a *real* album.' What they don't understand is that by selling 40,000 copies at gigs, we've made a helluva lot more money than most recording bands ever make."

The work involved in making your own record shouldn't be underestimated. You've got to do the best job you're capable of in order to sincerely promote and sell it. You'll have to plan and research the album's potential sales according to the performance schedule you'll play (the busier, the better). Are there several local radio stations you can key advertising into? Are there record stores nearby? You'll have to establish your business, write the songs, develop the album concept according to song selection, rehearse the material, record and master the tape, have the records pressed, decide on the jacket design, have them printed, and complete and seal the albums.

When the album is finished, you'll have to place it in record stores, with distributors, in catalogs, and explore mail-order sales. This will have to coincide closely with promotional activities, such as live shows, newspaper reviews, radio airplay, mailing lists, and advertisements. Making your own album will prove time-consuming, frustrating, educational, and, finally, satisfying. You'll have a right to be proud.

Nor is making your own album a dead-end street. It serves the same purpose as signing with a small label: that of proving your salability to a large label. This is the long road to a major recording contract. It might also be the best, since you'll hone your songwriting and performing abilities, build a track record, learn a great deal about album production and promotion, and make some money along the way. You'll know the in's and out's of the recording world firsthand.

Investors: Friend or Foe?

Have you dreamed of being saved from the drudgery of everyday musician life by a rich saviour who sees the great potential of your music? Investors offering to back unknown bands with $50,000 or $100,000 are not unheard of.

But, of course, no one just "gives" away $100,000, now, do they? No. They get something in return. Unless you refuse or amend the agreement, that something is your soul.

It's not easy to say no to a huge chunk of money, but your most careful consideration is urged. You might sell four million albums and not be entitled to any royalties whatever.

Ideally, you've got the money yourself. Then you can finance the project and direct your own destiny, with the help of people you hire. But how much will you need? If you're going to make and produce your own record using studio facilities in your own area, a budget of $10,000 is realistic. If you've succeeded in getting a major record company interested, but now want to sell them a finished master tape, you might need $75,000 to $100,000 to pay an independent producer, buy studio time, and support your band while in Nashville or Los Angeles. That's not spare change (or even life savings!) most musicians have to spend.

You may be able to borrow the money from family or friends who are sufficiently interested in the project, believe in your fortitude, and don't need to be paid back within the near future. Combining Dad's money, a neighbor's money, and your savings account is a common way of financing an album.

To raise large sums of capital, you'll probably need to draw up a detailed financial report, itemize expenses, and offer the prospectus to friends or businesspeople as an investment opportunity. Instead of giving up decision-making power, you'll need to offer a good return on their investment. Here's how a friend of mine raised $100,000 to finance a three-week move to L.A. and a finished master tape:

"Investors are easy to find. They were people who regularly came to see the band. These people *believe* in us, so we didn't have to 'sell' them on anything.

"We said, 'Hey, you put up your money, and we'll return every penny from the first income we generate, until you get paid off. Then, as a group, you'll get 20 percent of our profit off the record. $5,000 buys one point' (a "point" is a one percent ownership of a recording). If the record hits, that's a very good return."

The important thing is to retain all your business and artistic direction. This is the reward for finding your own investors, rather than having them proposition you with a large amount of money that might be hard to resist.

Other methods of financing your project are limited partnerships, general partnerships, joint ventures, and corporations. Write to the Volunteer Lawyers for the Arts, the Bay Area Lawyers for the Arts, or the songwriter services listed in *Songwriter's Market* for more information. If you describe your particular situation, they'll be able to recommend the method of fund raising best for you, and assist in drawing up financing agreements.

"Everyone has a hometown, a place where they can start," adds WEA Sales Manager Bill Perasso. "That's the only way to do it. You can make a living while you fine tune your act. Why pack up and move to a big city? The hometown approach is not easy, but the artists that are willing to take this road and work at it are going to make it."

For Further Information . . .

If you are going to pursue a recording contract, there's one book you must have: David Baskerville's *Music Business Handbook and Career Guide*, 3rd edition, The Sherwood Co., P.O. Box 21645, Denver CO 80221. This is the most complete text available on the big-time music business. Though the book is not written exclusively for musicians, it provides information about opportunities in all phases of the industry.

There is also one best book covering independent recording: *How to Make and Sell Your Own Record*, by Diane Sward Rapaport, Quick Fox, 33 W. 60th St., New York NY 10023, provides planning worksheets for all stages of the album process. The book details recording, manufacturing, printing, and promotion—and more.

An interesting book on local musicians is *On Becoming a Rock Musician*, by H. Stith Bennett, The University of Massachusetts Press, Amherst MA. The writing is stiff, but the anecdotes are humorous in this revealing sociological study of how people learn to become rock musicians.

• **AFTERWORD** •

I believe in the concepts and premises of this book, and I invite you to write me with questions you may have concerning the information contained herein. I'll give you what advice I can. Send your letter, along with a self-addressed stamped envelope, to me, care of Writer's Digest Books, 9933 Alliance Road, Cincinnati, Ohio 45242.

• INDEX •

Accounting Procedures, 143-46
Acoustics, 45
Adventure of music, 6
Advertising: for musicians, 62-63; agencies, 227
AFM (American Federation of Musicians), 76, 178, 262
AFTRA (American Federation of Television and Radio Artists), 76
AGAC (American Guild of Authors and Composers), 285, 286
Agents, 49, 54-55, 138; musician-agents, 256-63; promo packages for, 125-26
Agreements, written: for equipment rental, 252-53; for performances, 142
AGVA (American Guild of Variety Artists), 195
American Association for Music Therapy, 214
Amphetamines, 190
Appointment calendar, 75, 79
Arrangers, in studios, 222
ASCAP (American Society of Composers, Authors, and Publishers), 285, 286
Audience conflicts, 180
Audio-visual projects, 230-31
Audio wireless systems, 128
Auditioning: arranging for, 126; for church positions, 267-68; information by telephone, 68; setting up, 69

Backdrops, 115-18
Bands, see Groups. Religious bands, 271-72
Billboard, 26, 281, 286
Billboard International Buyer's Guide, 281, 286
Billboard International Talent Directory, 195, 197, 281
BMI (Broadcast Music, Inc.), 285, 286
Bookings for groups, 139-40
Breaking into studio operations, 225-26
Business meetings, 147-50
Business side of band, 134-51

Cashbox Magazine, 26, 281, 286
Cash disbursement records, 146
Choirs, church, 270

Choosing music, 95-97
Choral Journal, The, 272
Churches, as employers, 264-72; auditioning, 276-79; choir staffing, 270-71; music resources, 272; organizing the program, 269-70; religious band, the, 271-72; satisfactions of work, 265-67
Church Musician, The, 272
Classic Guitar Contruction, 91
Commitment of band members, 70
Composition of new music, 233
Confidence of musicians, 33
Conflicts, situational, 17-18
Contemporary Keyboard, 89
Contracts, performance agreements, 141-42
Copygroup vs. original music band, 27-28
Copyright, 286
Country Instruments, Makin' Your Own, 91
Creativeness of music, 5
Cut tapes, 123-24. See also Tapes

Diversification, 30-34; anticipating trends, 25-26; mixing old and new, 26; rock vs. other styles, 21-23; using different names, 24
Dress, outfits, 113-14
Drinking: effects on playing, 188; by minors, 178-79; during performance, 105; during rehearsal, 100-01

Earnings, 6-7, 152-73; Bottom Pay Scale, 153; for business leadership, 137; from equipment rental, 248-55; holiday rates, 171; from home studio operations, 244-46; for musician-agent, 257-58; rating jobs, 154-57; from recordings, 296, 298, 300; from selling lyrics and music, 275-77, 286
Electronics information, 88-89
Employers: Alcohol Beverage Control board lists, 42; negotiating with, 160-64; promo package to, 125-26; rating them, 53-56; restaurant owner's list, 42; targeting for musician-agents, 261-62; what they want, 175-76

Employment: church opportunities, 264-72; create your own TV program, 231; educational A-V's, 230-31; session work, 227-30; in studio operations, 217-33
Engineer, studio, 221
Equipment: building your own, 88-89; checklist of, 86-87; choosing it, 81-85; for home studios, 238-40; instruments, 86; ownership of, 90-91
Excitement of music, 5
Expenses: of being a star, 6-8; of business leadership, 137; cutting, 84-85, 172; of equipment, 29, 83-84; of home studio construction, 241-43; of running a group, 53-56; of taping, 123-24; for travel agency, 195-96

Fees, see Earnings and Expenses
Finances, building a base, 157-98
Frequency intensity, 184-85
Friendliness, 180-81
Full-time vs. part-time, 12-19
Full-timing, making the move, 14
Fun of music, 5

Goals for bands, 72-74
Gratification of music, 6
Groups, 57-79; auditions, 68-69; how to start, 61-62; making timetables, 75-79; mixing sexes? 65-65; selecting members, 72; unit strength, 63
Group teaching of music, 208

Handbook of Stage Lighting Graphics, 131
Health of musicians, 182-97; alcohol, 188-89; amphetamines, 190; happiness without drugs, 191-92; hearing loss, 183-85; marijuana, 189-90; physical conditioning, 188; smoke-filled rooms, 185-87; touring rules, 193-94
Home music teaching, 203
Home recording, 246, 298-300
How to Make and Sell Your Own Records, 292, 299

Image, defining it, 111-12
Income taxes, 147
Instruction of Music Theory, 213
Insulation of rehearsal sites, 99
International Musician, 77
Inventory, 86

Investors, 300-301

Job opportunities, see Employment, Employers
Journal of Church Music, 272

Keyboardist, 66-67

Labels, see Recordings, Record albums
Legal advice, 297
Lighting, 127
Local base, building one, 9
Logos, 114-18

Male-female band members, 64-66
Management disputes, 177-78
Marijuana, 189
Market research sheets, 46-53
Markets for music, 36-56; for equipment rental, 249; lists of markets, 42; for lyrics and music publishing, 280-83; rating markets, 53-56; telephoning for, 43-44; word of mouth advice, 45-46; yellow pages, 37-41
Microphones, 239-40
Mixing console, 239
Modern Recording and Music, 89, 254
Music Librarian, 212
Music manuscripts, how to write, 233
Music Notation: A Manual of Modern Practice, 233
Music pupils: dropping, 206; recruiting, 204
Music stores: shopping in, 87; teaching in, 203; working in, 88
Music therapist, 212
Myths of music, 6-8

National Association for Music Therapy, Inc., 214
Negotiations: Social-Psychological Perspectives, 173
Negotiating: with employers, 160-64; pay scale, 158
Nightclub information, 49-50
Noise, unnecessary, 179

On Becoming a Rock Musician, 301
Organist, The, 272
OSHA (Occupational Safety and Health Administration) noise guidelines, 184-85; smoke-level guidelines, 186
Ownership of equipment, 90-91

Index

Part-timing music, 15-16
Pay scale, 53; bottom rates, 153-54; at casuals, 172; finding best-paying gigs, 44-45; for local musicians, 13; job rates, 154-57
Personality of musicians, 32, 64, 71-72, 223-24, 260-61
Photographs, 119-22
Playback monitors, 240
Popular Electronics, 89
Power of Positive Thinking, The, 196
Practice, 101-02
Printed material, 115, 118
Producer, in a studio, 221
Professionalism of musicians, 175-81; avoiding conflicts, 180; drugs, 178-79; friendliness, 180-81; management disputes, 177-78; punctuality, 176-77; unnecessary noise, 179-80
Promo package, 118-119; getting it out, 125

Query letters to publishers, 282-84

Record albums, making them, 289-301; getting a better deal, 296; getting a contract, 292-96; making your own albums, 298-300; recording industry today, 289-92; smaller labels, 297-98
Recording in a home studio, 234-47
Records, of expenses and earnings, 143-46
Rehearsals, 94-108; efficiency test for, 108; eliminating the headaches, 100-01; minimizing time for, 99-100; sites for, 98-99; vs. practice, 101
Representative for business, 138, 178
Rock vs. other styles, 21-23

Selection: of band members, 72; of music, 95-97
Selling lyrics and music, 274-86; agreements for publishing, 285-86; finding markets, 280-82; formulas for writing, 279-80
SESAC, 286
Session work in studios, 227-30
Showmanship, 104-06, 127-29
Small acts, 31-34. *See also* Soloing
Smoke levels, 185-87
Smoke machines, 128
Soloing: in a band, 103-04; performers, 31, 34

Songwriter's Market, 195, 197, 281, 282, 286, 297
Songwriter's Resources and Services, 286, 297
Sonic Design: The Nature of Sound and Music, 214
Sound control, 129-31
Sound Engineering Magazine, 254
Sound technicians, 130
Stage fright, 192
Starting a group, 61-63
Stationery, 115
Steel-string Guitar Construction, 92
Studio musicians, 222
Studio operations, 54, 217-33; independent studios, 219-20; personnel for, 220-223; rehearsal, 124
Studios, home, 234-47; arrangement, 241-43; as a career base, 235-38; equipment needed, 238-40; getting business, 244-45; service orientation, 244
Style of music, 55-56
Submitting music to publishers, 281-86

Talent, 9, 33-34
Tapes: cut-tape of band, 123-24; tape recorders, 239; videotapes, 125
Teaching music, 200-214
Technicians for sound, 130-31
Telephoning employers, 43-44
Televised Music Instruction, 233
Television: creating your own programs, 231-32
Tempo, 97, 103
Theater, playing for, 171
Timetables for bands, 75-76, 78-79
Trends, anticipating them, 25-26

Unions, 76-77. *See also* AFTRA, AFM

Vans, 90
Videotaped promotion, 125
Visual effects, 128-29
Visual rehearsing, 106-07
Volunteer Lawyers for the Arts, 297

Writers/writing: of lyrics and music, 277-80; as studio employee, 222

Yellow pages for markets, 37-41
You Can If You Think You Can, 196
You Can Negotiate Anything, 173

Other Writer's Digest Books

Music Books
Songwriter's Market, $13.95
Making Money Making Music, by James Dearing (paper) $12.95

Art/Craft Books
Artist's Market, $13.95
National Directory of Shops/Galleries, Shows/Fairs (paper) $12.95

Photography Books
British Journal of Photography Annual, $24.95
How to Create and Sell Photo Products, by Mike & Carol Werner (paper) $13.95
How You Can Make $25,000 a Year with Your Camera, by Larry Cribb (paper) $9.95
Photographer's Market, $14.95
Sell & Re-Sell Your Photos, by Rohn Engh $14.95

General Writing Books
Writer's Market, $18.95
Beginning Writer's Answer Book, edited by Polking, et al $9.95
How to Get Started in Writing, by Peggy Teeters $10.95
Law and the Writer, edited by Polking and Meranus (paper) $7.95
Make Every Word Count, by Gary Provost (paper) $6.95
Teach Yourself to Write, by Evelyn Stenbock $12.95
Treasury of Tips for Writers, edited by Marvin Weisbord (paper) $6.95

Fiction Writing
Fiction Writer's Help Book, by Maxine Rock $12.95
Fiction Writer's Market, edited by Fredette and Brady $16.95
How to Write Best-Selling Fiction, by Dean R. Koontz $13.95
How to Write Short Stories that Sell, by Louise Boggess $9.95
Writing the Novel: From Plot to Print, by Lawrence Block $10.95

Special Interest Writing Books
Children's Picture Book: How to Write It, How to Sell It, by Ellen E.M. Roberts $17.95
Complete Book of Scriptwriting, by J. Michael Straczynski $14.95
Guide to Greeting Card Writing, edited by Larry Sandman $10.95
How to Write and Sell Your Personal Experiences, by Lois Duncan $10.95
How to Write & Sell (Your Sense of) Humor, by Gene Perret $12.95
How to Write "How-To" Books and Articles, by Raymond Hull (paper) $8.95
The Poet and the Poem, Revised edition by Judson Jerome $13.95
Poet's Handbook, by Judson Jerome $11.95
Writing for Children & Teenagers, by Wyndham/Madison $10.95
Writing to Inspire, by Gentz, Roddy, et al $14.95

The Writing Business
Complete Handbook for Freelance Writers, by Kay Cassill $14.95
How to Be a Successful Housewife/Writer, by Elaine Fantle Shimberg $10.95
How You Can Make $20,000 a Year Writing, by Nancy Edmonds Hanson (paper) $6.95
Jobs for Writers, edited by Kirk Polking $11.95
Writer's Survival Guide: How to Cope with Rejection, Success, and 99 Other Hang-Ups of the Writing Life, by Jean and Veryl Rosenbaum $12.95

To order directly from the publisher, include $1.50 postage and handling for 1 book and 50¢ for each additional book. Allow 30 days for delivery.

Writer's Digest Books, Department B
9933 Alliance Road, Cincinnati OH 45242
Prices subject to change without notice.